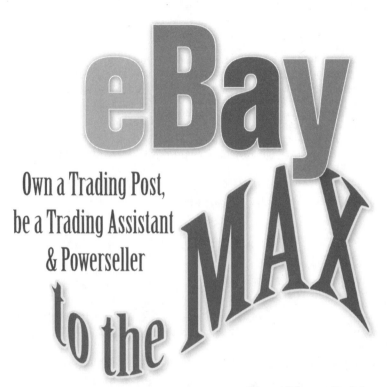

eBay

Own a Trading Post,
be a Trading Assistant
& Powerseller

to the MAX

Ron Mansfield

800 East 96th Street
Indianapolis, Indiana 46240 USA

eBay to the Max: Be a Trading Post Owner, Trading Assistant, and PowerSeller

Copyright© 2006 by Que Publishing

International Standard Book Number: 0-7897-3468-0

Library of Congress Catalog Card Number: 2005930261

Printed in the United States of America

First Printing: November 2005

08   07   06   05   4   3   2   1

Trademarks

All terms mentioned in this book that are known to be trademarks or service marks have been appropriately capitalized. Que Publishing cannot attest to the accuracy of this information. Use of a term in this book should not be regarded as affecting the validity of any trademark or service mark.

Warning and Disclaimer

Every effort has been made to make this book as complete and as accurate as possible, but no warranty or fitness is implied. The information provided is on an "as is" basis. The author and the publisher shall have neither liability nor responsibility to any person or entity with respect to any loss or damages arising from the information contained in this book.

Bulk Sales

Que Publishing offers excellent discounts on this book when ordered in quantity for bulk purchases or special sales. For more information, please contact

U.S. Corporate and Government Sales
1-800-382-3419
corpsales@pearsontechgroup.com

For sales outside the United States, please contact

International Sales
international@pearsoned.com

Associate Publisher
Greg Wiegand

Acquisitions Editor
Stephanie J. McComb

Development Editor
Laura Norman

Managing Editor
Charlotte Clapp

Project Editor
Tonya Simpson

Copy Editor
Kate Givens

Indexer
Ken Johnson

Proofreader
Heather Waye Arle

Technical Editor
Michele Brantner

Publishing Coordinator
Sharry Lee Gregory

Interior Designer
Susan Geiselman

Cover Designer
Anne Jones

CONTENTS AT A GLANCE

TABLE OF CONTENTS

III Fine Tuning Your Operation

ABOUT THE AUTHOR

Ron Mansfield is an eBay sellers' consultant, instructor, and freelance writer. He recently spent more than a year helping the team at www.i-soldit.com roll out the country's largest eBay drop store franchise network.

In his spare time he enjoys collecting, restoring, buying, and selling collectible electronics from the '50s and '60s. He has achieved PowerSeller status, runs an eBay Store, and maintains an active online community for enthusiasts of mid-century electronics.

His bestselling, award-winning books have been published by Que and others in 18 countries, in more than a dozen languages.

DEDICATION

To hard-working PowerSellers everywhere.

ACKNOWLEDGMENTS

Books are always team efforts, and because so many people help, writing the Acknowledgements page always seems a little daunting to me.

I could not have written this book without the help of my life partner An. Her encouragement, love, and patience are constant sources of fuel and inspiration.

My trusty agent Carole McClendon, and the rest of the gang at Waterside Productions, get the job done right, as always. Thanks, everybody!

The folks at eBay are amazing. Countless employees stopped dead in their tracks at eBay Live! 2005 to cheerfully answer my endless questions or point me in the direction of someone who could. Special thanks to Michael Dearing, Walt Duflock, and Elizabeth Ferguson.

Then there are the PowerSellers. Once again, there are way too many to list, so I will just single out a sampling. Over the years I have gotten to hang out with dozens of successful sellers at each of the eBay Live! events I have attended, and have learned from them all.

There are perhaps a hundred iSold It employees and franchisees I should thank. There wouldn't be an iSold It without the hard work and dedication of Elise and Rick Wetzel and the headquarters team they built from the ground up.

Or without the amazing franchisees like Bruce Richardson, whose analytical eye, and "go get 'em" style should inspire any new business owner. Richard and Helene Chemel, whom I think of as great friends, are examples of just how far two people can take a dream when they work together. Michelle Naranjo, another franchisee and savvy eBay PowerSeller spends what seems like half of her life helping other sellers. She makes that old eBay slogan "people are basically good" seem true.

It's only a book if you can read it and without the hard work of the amazing team at Que, this would be nothing more than 30-some Microsoft Word files on my laptop. This is not my first book with Que, but it has been one of the most pleasurable to work on thanks to a cheerful, helpful, and competent team.

Senior acquisitions editor Stephanie McComb got the concept right away, and kept me on track without nagging. Laura Norman, my development editor or "DE," is slaving away on the details as I write this. Maybe "D" really stands for Delightful, or "Diligent." Thanks for all the hard work and kind words! Michel Brantner, the project's technical editor (and Ebay seller, by the way), came through with some great tips and observations that found their way onto these pages.

Well, this could go on for pages, so, instead, let me just say thanks to all of you, and know that I wish you all the best, and please let's keep in touch!

WE WANT TO HEAR FROM YOU!

As the reader of this book, *you* are our most important critic and commentator. We value your opinion and want to know what we're doing right, what we could do better, what areas you'd like to see us publish in, and any other words of wisdom you're willing to pass our way.

As an associate publisher for Que Publishing, I welcome your comments. You can email or write me directly to let me know what you did or didn't like about this book[md]as well as what we can do to make our books better.

Please note that I cannot help you with technical problems related to the topic of this book. We do have a User Services group, however, where I will forward specific technical questions related to the book.

When you write, please be sure to include this book's title and author as well as your name, email address, and phone number. I will carefully review your comments and share them with the author and editors who worked on the book.

Email: feedback@quepublishing.com

Mail: Greg Wiegand
            Associate Publisher
            Que Publishing
            800 East 96th Street
            Indianapolis, IN 46240 USA

For more information about this book or another Que Publishing title, visit our website at www.quepublishing.com. Type the ISBN (excluding hyphens) or the title of a book in the Search field to find the page you're looking for.

Look for this burner—it's the only genuine Oil-Air Burner, the most economical and efficient burner in the world. See trade-mark on top.

"GOODYEAR 1851"

Hard Rubber Combs

are unequalled for
satisfaction
and service

**SMOOTH
STRONG
SANITARY**

Look for
the Trade Mark
on Every Comb You Buy

Introduction

What was it, I wondered, that made these two otherwise similar PowerSellers so different? One loved his business; the other was nearly in tears. The idea for this book came to me on a redeye flight home after a long, exhausting week on the road.

I'd been helping folks open new eBay Trading Posts—drop stores where customers bring in their items for the store's employees to sell on eBay. I had overseen the opening of one new store that week, and visited another that had been running for a couple of months. They were both in similar, mid-sized, upper-middle class neighborhoods, both owned by bright, successful people, and one was already off to a great start.

The worrisome store had been open more than 60 days, and should have been doing much better than it was. There weren't many customers, much of what folks brought in was not valuable enough to sell on eBay, and the items this store was listing had a pretty dreadful sell-through rate and relatively low average selling prices.

By contrast, the brand new store had a line of people waiting outside with great stuff to sell when I arrived on opening day. The store owner and employees had listed some of their own belongings two weeks earlier (before the doors opened) to get some practice and work out the store's kinks. These items had almost all sold successfully at respectable prices.

The busy store had been generously covered on multiple local television stations and in local and regional newspapers. Their biggest problem was likely to be coping with their almost instant success.

In the course of my work over the past 18 months I have worked with more than 100 PowerSellers, sometimes digging into their P/L statements with them, other times sifting through their inventory bins or celebrating their victories over a beer. I even managed a Trading Post briefly. It has been eye opening and rewarding.

This book, I believe, contains many of the tips, techniques, resources, and best practices that successful eBay PowerSellers use to excel. I've tried to point out some of the pitfalls and challenges you are likely to encounter along the way. It will also help you set realistic goals that are complimentary to your own lifestyle and work expectations. What are the keys to success when selling on eBay? What does it take to earn a living as a PowerSeller or Trading Assistant, and how does one run a successful Trading Post?

Because e-commerce is such a moving target, and because there are so many online resources available to us these days, I have added some related materials and links to my web site, www.RonMansfield.com. Besides updates to the book, you will find links to resources, discounts, many of the examples mentioned in this book, and much more. And as always, I am interested in your reaction to my writing, so please feel free to drop me a note. The address is ron@RonMansfield.com.

WHAT'S INSIDE?

This is not a beginners' book. My approach assumes that you have sold at least something on eBay and are hungry for the tips, techniques, best practices, and resources necessary to run a high-volume online auction business.

If you are a casual eBay seller, you will see how to how to take your selling to the next level. PowerSellers will learn how, why, and when to become Trading Assistants and see what it takes to open and run a retail Trading Post (also known as an eBay drop store).

You will read about eBay's latest PowerSeller tools including Selling Manager Pro, custom listing headers, new eBay store features, buying keywords, and eBay's new Resellers' Marketplace, a wholesale source exclusively for PowerSellers.

I've tried to include information about the technical, management, and marketing skills necessary to grow your business to the level you desire, be it a profitable kitchen table operation, a mom-and-pop retail presence, or a regional chain of eBay drop stores.

In addition to the obvious eBay selling tasks—taking great photographs, writing compelling descriptions, picking the best listing categories and starting times—you need to understand customer service, fee setting, and marketing. To truly excel, you must know how to hire, train, and manage employees. Setting up a retail storefront requires an understanding of real estate, local regulations, insurance, and other issues. That's what this book is all about.

Along the way you'll encounter Notes, Tips, and Cautions that provide helpful tidbits that you don't want to miss. Most chapters end with a checklist or other information that takes what you've learned in the chapter and boils it down to a useful guide that you can flip to any time along your journey to PowerSeller status and beyond. And, be sure to visit my site, www.RonMansfield.com, for additional information and tools to help you along the way.

TAKING EBAY SELLING TO THE NEXT LEVEL

in this Part

In this Chapter

TEN KEYS TO SUCCESS

As I mentioned in the introduction to this book, I have been privileged to hang out with a lot of eBay sellers, many successful, some struggling. In the process I've drawn a few conclusions. There are, I believe, 10 key ingredients required to run a successful eBay selling business, regardless of its size.

1. COMMITMENT

Any enterprise requires dedication, and your eBay selling business is no exception. There are going to be days filled with elation when a little $5 statue you found in a yard sale sells for $1,000. And I still get a kick out of seeing customers return, or receiving especially flattering feedback, or learning that buyers have added me to their favorite sellers list. It's easy to go to work on those days.

But once in a while you'll discover that a $1,000 statue was lost or damaged in transit and, as a result, you have received your first negative feedback even though you packed and shipped it carefully.

Halfway through listing 500 vintage phonograph records you might look out the window one beautiful summer morning and say to yourself, "Is this really worth it?"

Yes, you might rather be at the beach (and the cool thing is, as an eBay seller you might be able to sneak off for an afternoon now and then), but generally you are going to need to summon a great deal of willpower, focus, and *commitment* to make your business flourish.

You will get knocked down. You will get bored. You might feel underpaid for a while. If you work alone you might feel isolated at times. For your business to work you will need to get right back up and come out swinging. So, "dogged commitment" is the first and probably foremost key to success.

2. SUFFICIENT START-UP FUNDING, WELL SPENT

What happened? Ask anyone who has started a business that subsequently failed. The common answer? "We ran out of money. It was a great idea, everybody loved us, but we just couldn't hang on long enough."

This is what I call "Mansfield's Law" at work. Things generally take four times as long to accomplish, and cost at least twice as much as you'd expect.

You need money in the bank to not only feed yourself and your spawn, but also to acquire inventory, to advertise, and to purchase the tools of your trade—hardware, software, services, and much more.

How much is enough? It depends. We will look at some budgeting and "guesstimating" tools in Chapter 4, "Budgeting, Forecasting, and Cash Flow," and you can find spreadsheet templates to explore on my web site (www.RonMansfield.com/downloads.htm); but as a rule of thumb, if you are starting from scratch, a garage-scale operation might squeak by with a nest egg of $5,000 to $15,000. A professionally staffed and equipped Trading Post could require $50,000 to $100,000 or more.

How long will it take to get your business into the black? Garage operations with low overhead and a small hard-working crew can probably inch out of the red in a few months. Larger operations—particularly Trading Posts—might take six months to a year or more to become profitable in any satisfying, consistent way. The bigger and more expensive the operation, the longer the haul and the larger the long-term potential.

Having enough money to start your business is one thing. Spending it wisely is another. Yes, it would be cool to drive up to customers' houses in a tricked-out Cadillac Escalade to pick up things to sell, but I would avoid the temptation. Think "lean and mean" instead.

When eBay got started new employees worked on folding tables, and when it was time for eBay to purchase real desks employees were required to assemble them themselves. At Enron, on the other hand...you get the idea. Which model sounds better to you?

3. EFFECTIVE, PERSISTENT MARKETING AND PR

Since that first caveman drew a picture of his awesome hunting accomplishments on the wall of his cave folks have been bragging graphically about their ability to get things done. Everybody wants to be known as the "go-to guy." Today we are bombarded with "hey look at me" messages. And for your business to even get noticed (never mind chosen), you are going to need to make a lot of noise in many different places.

For example, I recently moved to a new town. Without knowing it I drove by a local Trading Post probably 100 times. Drove right past it, and never saw it! Do you know how I finally found it? First someone told me about it, but she couldn't tell me exactly where it was located or what it was called. So the next few times I drove around the neighborhood I looked for it. I drove slowly and looked, and looked.

Then I did a Zip code search of eBay's Trading Assistant Directory (which requires a little searching to find as well). There was a Trading Post listed in my Zip code, and the address sounded right. I promised myself I'd go there and check it out one day soon.

A month passed. Then two months. One day I opened the local paper and spotted a small display ad for the store. I ripped it out, walked to the garage, and put the ad on the seat of my car as a reminder. "Monday," I promised myself. Another week passed. The weekly paper came out again, I saw the ad a second time, smacked my forehead, but did not move from the couch.

Does this sound familiar? We all do it. Advertising very rarely pays for itself on day one. It has a cumulative effect on consumers, and for this to happen advertising needs to be noticed over and over and over again, ideally in different places.

In fact, the thing that finally got me off the couch wasn't the ad at all. It was a little public relations piece in a local real estate magazine—"Moving?" The title wondered. "Let eBay Help Clean Out Your Garage." I had made more than 100 drive-bys, experienced multiple exposures to that Trading Post's print ads, but the pivotal moment for me was a short fluff piece that likely cost the Trading Post little or nothing to get placed.

In Chapters 13–15 you will look at specific advertising and public relations strategies and tricks. For now, take away this: Effective advertising and PR are key ingredients to your success.

Oh, and by the way, even if you are not a Trading Assistant and only sell your own things on eBay you should advertise and promote your items to the eBay community. You'll learn more about this in Chapter 25, " Listing Items."

4. FIND GREAT STUFF TO SELL

It takes time to properly photograph, list, baby-sit, collect money for, pack, and ship auction items. Wouldn't you rather spend your time and energy on $100 items than on $10 items? Chapter 16, "What to Sell," and Chapter 17, "Getting Great Stuff to Sell," will show you how to decide which products make the most sense for you to sell, and help you track them down.

For some of you this will mean clever, aggressive shopping at garage sales, estate sales, and flea markets. For others it will mean making arrangements with manufacturers, distributors, or local retailers for a reliable supply of items you can resell at an acceptable profit. For Trading Assistants and Trading Post operators it means finding folks in the neighborhood willing to trust you with their "good stuff."

Other sellers have found that they can make the most money by manufacturing their own products for sale on eBay, or by adding value to items they acquire cheaply. For example, I manufacture a line of restoration kits and tools for collectors of vintage transistor radios. I also buy old radios on eBay, restore them, and resell them at a profit.

The message here: Finding and then reselling interesting, profitable stuff is another crucial key to success.

5. NEVER SELL JUNK

This is more than just restating success key four in the negative. Avoiding junk is important for many reasons. Obviously, junk won't sell for much, so you will have gone through the motions for little financial gain. But something else happens. When potential buyers get interested in you, they will often click on your "View seller's other items" link. If they find a lot of junk there they will think less of you as a seller. And all that junk will make it harder for interested bidders to see the good stuff you are also offering.

Moreover, selling junk consumes eBay and PayPal fees that could be better spent. Many savvy sellers set a minimum dollar value. If they don't think an item can sell profitably for $30 or $50 or whatever, they won't list it.

Now, obviously, if you sell a whole lot of junk and gouge folks on shipping you can make money this way, but it will be a tenuous and, for many, an unrewarding existence.

Here's a special note to Trading Post owners. It will be very, very tempting to take junk from customers who walk into your stores, especially during the first weeks and months after you open. You and your employees will rationalize junk selling 10 different ways. "Hey, we need the practice." Or, "After they see what a great job we do on this old Timex, they'll come back with their Rolex." Or, "She's my neighbor. I don't want to tell her that handbag's junk!" And most of us have a hard time saying "No" under any circumstances. It's human nature.

The problem is, when that Timex watch sells for $5 and the owner gets a check for six cents, she won't be back with her "good stuff." She will be saying to her friends and neighbors "What a waste of time that was! I stood in line. I waited weeks for the check, and look at this...*six cents*. I should have donated it instead."

6. GIVE GREAT CUSTOMER SERVICE

I just read a fantastic article written by Fresno, CA author Autumn Bell. She maintains that every new contact a seller has with a customer results in a "moment of truth." Each encounter shapes customers' opinions and determines the likelihood of their maintaining ongoing relationships with us.

You've had those moments. Did the dry cleaner lose one of your shirts? Did a Starbucks team member run around the counter to hold the door open for you when you had your arms full? Sometimes even a smile on the right day can be a moment of truth.

eBay buyers have expectations. Was their email handled promptly? Did the item arrive quickly and was it carefully packed? Take a look at Figure 1.1. Do you think customers would buy another collectible radio from this guy? Talk about a moment of truth!

FIGURE 1.1

Every customer encounter makes an impression. Would you buy from this seller again?

Think about your favorite commercial encounters—a visit to the local Apple Computer store, a Sharper Image purchase, maybe your FedEx delivery person's demeanor. What about these encounters pleases you? How can you bring similar attributes to your own business? What brings *you* back? What drives you away? Think like a customer. (By the way, Chapter 18 looks at the finer points of customer service.)

7. CREATE AN EFFICIENT, PLEASANT FACILITY

Okay, you have made the commitment, you've squirreled away some startup funds, you are willing to market the heck out of your new business, you have rounded up some great items to sell, and you are thinking like a customer. *Where* you work can be as important as *how* you work.

Your space need not be huge, but it should be efficient and complete. Just as there are great kitchens to cook in and others that are downright annoying, I've seen wonderful PowerSeller workspaces and some that are dreadful. We'll get into more detail throughout the book, but for now realize that you will need to put some time and money into creating a comfortable, efficient workspace regardless of whether yours will be a kitchen table, a garage, a warehouse, or a retail storefront. At a minimum you will need

★ An area to safely store items you plan to sell

★ A reliable digital camera and lighting

★ A backdrop, or area suitable for staging photos

★ A reliable broadband Internet connection

★ A reliable, contemporary computer

★ An ergonomic workspace (desk, chair, task lighting, and so on)

★ A place to store and organize shipping supplies

★ A packing table, scale, tape dispensers, and so on

★ A place to store records

★ A phone used primarily for the business

Figure 1.2 shows a typical garage operation. It's nestled into about 300 square feet.

FIGURE 1.2
A 300-square-foot PowerSeller garage operation.

The nice thing about small spaces like this is that everything is within easy reach. If many of the items you sell are small (personal electronics, jewelry, and so on), you might be able to squeeze nearly everything you need into less than a third of the space of a three-car garage. This space will be too small for many Trading Assistants as their volume grows, particularly if they need to add staff. But it is a great, affordable business incubator.

Trading Posts are typically 1,200 or more square feet, and I have seen large PowerSeller warehouse operations in excess of 10,000 square feet.

Regardless of the size of your facility you want reliable tools organized in a logical layout so that the work flows from the storage shelves through the photography process to the area where the listings will be written, and then back to the shelves. And obviously, the packing area should facilitate keeping the day's shipments from under foot, and should make it easy to get packages out the door efficiently—stairs and two-story operations can be pretty inefficient.

Even if you already have a workspace, give your floor plan some thought. Sketch it out. Play with it. Efficient workflow can mean the difference between making and losing money.

Don't neglect the human element, either. Do you like music? Add some. Can you keep the space a comfortable temperature year round? How's the lighting? Desks and chairs should be purchased and positioned thoughtfully. You and your staff will be spending a lot of time sitting at computers. Proper ergonomics will help minimize injuries and fatigue and improve throughput.

Note

Give some thought to where you can safely, conveniently, and comfortably meet customers. If you work from home, will you and your customers be comfortable meeting there? Many Trading Assistants go to their customers' homes for initial meetings and take wireless-equipped laptops for research. Some Assistants conduct initial meetings in public places—coffee shops, for example.

8. CREATE POLISHED LISTINGS AND PHOTOS

Another key to success is to create "stand out" listings. You want photos that pop and descriptions that invite, inform, and then compel competitive bidding. This will make a huge difference.

Doubt it? I did an experiment. "How much more," I wondered, "can I get for a collectible radio I had just purchased if I create a better listing than the seller's?"

Here's the original description that I saw when I bid on and won the radio. I was one of two bidders and purchased it for $10.49.

PILOT II VINTAGE MARINE/AVIATION RADIO W/CASE

Description: You are bidding on a vintage radio for marine or aviation use. It includes the original case that the radio fits into, with a shoulder strap and a compartment to hold the antenna. This item powered up but has not been tested. Sold AS IS. S/N: P2-15378.

Condition: Good

Age: 1950s

Items were photographed just before listing. Winning bidder is guaranteed to receive all items pictured. Shipping and Handling: $8.85

Figure 1.3 shows the two photos included in the original listing. Notice that the radio was only photographed in its raggedy old leather case. This is a little like having your college graduation picture taken while you are wearing the sweatshirt you use for house painting.

FIGURE 1.3

These two unflattering photos undoubtedly contributed to the low final selling price of the first auction.

A few days later I took my own photo and wrote my description. Here's the new copy, followed by the new photo in Figure 1.4:

Pilot II Nova-Tech 4 Band Radio & Direction Finder

12-transistor beauty in great shape!

Here's an unusual mid-sixties transistor radio with a swivel antenna and "sighting" system designed to enable sailors and pilots to navigate by triangulating known radio station transmitter tower positions. As you can see from the photo, the antenna swivels past compass headings marked on the top of the case, and you can peer through the flip up sights on the top. Very cool!

It receives the LF Beacon frequencies (190–400 KC), the Broadcast Band (540–1600 KC), the Marine Band (1.6 to 4.5 MC), and VHF (110–135 MC). Loaded with such features as a dial light, squelch control, a signal strength meter, three (3!) whip antennae, two sizes of earphone jacks, an external power connector, and an earphone in a leather pouch, this is guaranteed to bring Ooos and Ahhhs on your display shelf.

A very strong player with plenty of volume, selectivity and sensitivity. The plastic is flawless. No nicks, cracks, chips or noticeable scratches. Could benefit from a mild cleaning, but as you can see, looks perfectly fine as-is. All 3 whip antennae are complete and straight. Clean dial glass. Perfect meter face and dial, excellent knobs, flat, scratch-free speaker grill, Clean inside too.

The previous owner used a Dymo Label maker to add his name and address to the back. They could be easily removed, of course, but since some folks like to keep little nostalgic touches like these, I'll let the new owner decide.

You Are Gonna Love it, Guaranteed!

First, check out my store description and feedback. Still not sure? Your purchase is guaranteed to be as described in this listing. If you disagree after holding it in your hands, simply notify me within five (5) days of receiving it, and pay only the return postage and insurance for a prompt refund. The item must arrive here in the condition it left.

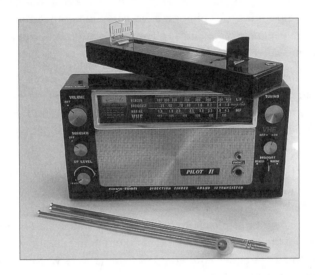

FIGURE 1.4
A new photo with the same radio out of the case makes it look much more desirable.

The radio sold for $91 at the second auction, an increase of more than $80 over the first attempt; and there were 15 bids, as opposed to 2 bids the first time.

You are probably thinking, "Yeah, but Ron, you are a collector in this category. You know about old radios." That's true to a point, but everything in the description can be found by "Googling" or by looking at the radio itself. Had the prior seller taken the radio out of the leather case s/he would have seen a very pretty radio with a nameplate containing the transistor count, bands covered, and so on.

Polished listings and photos are success key number eight.

9. PAY ATTENTION TO THE DETAILS

What's success key number nine? The devil is in the details! It creeps up on you innocently enough. At first you have a handful of items to sell in your new business, and you can keep track of everything in your head. Then one day, there are too many things to remember—dozens of auctions closing, some paid, others not. Some shipped, some misplaced, or worse yet, parts of an item have gone missing. You *know* you just saw the ear buds for that iPod. But where the heck are they now? Did we ship that necklace? Is this printer supposed to go out Priority Mail or FedEx Ground? Every time you stop the workflow to ask and answer questions like these it will cost you money.

You need to get in the habit of keeping everything rigidly organized even when it's unnecessary to do so. You, and your staff, if you have one, need to develop good working habits from the very beginning. If you are doing great marketing and giving fantastic customer service you could suddenly get really, really busy. And by then it's too late to organize. Let me share two horror stories as examples.

A Trading Post took in a bunch of camera lenses from the same seller. Many of the lenses were similar but not identical. They were to be sold separately, not as a lot. It was a busy day but, as was the policy, each lens was placed into its own plastic bag with its own paperwork. The paperwork carried a description of the lens and a unique in-house serial number. So far, so good.

The store protects small items like these lenses by placing them in numbered plastic bins, and the whole pile of lenses fit comfortably in one bin. Still no problem. The photographer was a heads-up woman, and she kept all the lenses with their right paperwork and in the right plastic bags. When she was done she placed the bags carefully back into the correct bin and moved them to the person who writes the listings. No problems here either and, after the listings were written and launched the bin full of lenses took its rightful place on the shelf, waiting to be successfully auctioned off. So far it's "all good."

A week later the first lens auction closes and the winner pays promptly. The store's shipping guy walks to the bin, and (leaving the bin on the shelf), flips open the top cover of the bin, reaches in and pulls out a lens. "Camera lens. Here it is," he thinks to himself. He flips the bin cover closed, packs and dispatches the lens to winner number-one. The problem, of course, is that he carelessly pulled just any old lens from a bin filled with lenses. So now the store is about to have two unhappy customers—the one who will get the wrong lens in a few days and needs to return it, and the rightful winner of that lens who will need to wait for its return to the store before it can be shipped to her.

The second horror story is a pretty scary variation on this theme. "Mr. Mansfield?" My cell phone crackled. "I am in deep [poop]."

Dale was the acting manager in a Trading Post while his boss was on vacation. "We screwed up bad in shipping. Somebody lined up a bunch of stuff to pack on the shipping table, and I guess the paperwork all got shoved down one item or something. A whole bunch of stuff went to the wrong people last Friday. Some of them are calling already. Is there anything we can do about that?"

Shippers are not the only folks who screw up. You can make mistakes checking stuff in, photographing it, and at every step in the process. The best bet is to get in the habit of confirming things at every step. Look at the item. Look at the paperwork. Do they match?

But don't stop there. Get anal about all the details. Is this item where it belongs? Is that bicycle going to fall over and damage the antique table next to it? Is the back door locked? Does this need to be insured? Is that a real Coca Cola tray or a reproduction? When's the deadline for the Yellow Pages ad? Are we running out of packing tape? Details. The devil is in the details!

10. DO GOOD RECORDKEEPING

The last critical key to success is recordkeeping. Some people love bookkeeping. It's a struggle for me. Regardless of your feelings about recordkeeping, it needs to be done. Chapter 21, "Check-in and Recordkeeping," has the details. For now face the fact that you will need to keep written records of inventory, money spent on items for resale, money owed and paid to customers if you are a Trading Assistant, sales tax you have collected, and more. For example, in some states law enforcement requires you to keep records for them in an attempt to thwart the sale of stolen property.

10 KEYS SUMMARY

So there you have it. Ten ways you can improve your chances of success. Can you recite them from memory? Me neither, so here's a recap:

1. Commitment

2. Sufficient Start-up Funding, Well Spent

3. Effective, Persistent Marketing and PR

4. Find Great Stuff to Sell

5. Never Sell Junk

6. Give Great Customer Service

7. Create an Efficient, Pleasant Facility

8. Create Polished Listings and Photos

9. Pay Attention to the Details

10. Do Good Recordkeeping

In this Chapter

POWERSELLING: THE 40,000-FOOT VIEW

WHY EBAY NEEDS US

Imagine owning a web-based business with more than 150 million users. Imagine welcoming an additional 100,000 brand new, mostly inexperienced customers to your web site each and every day, at all hours of the day and night. Now imagine wrangling 50 million simultaneous auction items and the related torrent of emails, payments, accounting entries; and the associated computer hardware, software, and staff necessary to keep things safely and securely spinning nonstop. You've just imagined eBay.

After coping with the nearly unimaginable infrastructure and logistics associated with a business the size and scope of eBay's, what do you suppose that company's next most critical issue is?

It's inventory. eBay needs a lot of stuff to sell, and it needs proportionally more and more of it every day. But the vast majority of eBay members never sell anything. They just shop.

Sellers are important people at eBay headquarters. If you doubt this, visit the next eBay Live convention. That's the 2005 conference shown in Figure 2.1. Walk around the exhibit floor (called the Solutions Center) or attend any of the local training workshops eBay offers. These gatherings and programs are aimed directly at sellers, as are the PowerSeller, Trading Assistant, and Trading Post programs you will be reading about in this book.

eBay loves sellers, and they want us to succeed. You see, eBay doesn't warehouse any of the items it sells; sellers do that for them. And eBay doesn't need to pack and ship the items. We do that too. We collect the money (or at least get the process started and keep an eye on it), and we even find the stuff to sell.

FIGURE 2.1
eBay values sellers, as a trip to any public eBay event will show you.

This is why eBay needs to find and groom us. Together we can keep up with the demand for new items needed by our shared, constantly expanding customer base. The good news is that eBay, one of the coolest, fastest-growing, people-friendly companies on the planet wants to get to know you and work with you to grow your business as well as theirs.

THE EBAY SELLER PROGRAMS

We will get into much more detail about eBay's seller programs as the book progresses, but for now it's enough to know that eBay has three major programs designed to grow and support sellers. They are the PowerSeller program, the Trading Assistant program, and Trading Posts.

PowerSellers are folks who sell at least $1,000 per month on eBay and meet certain feedback and other easily reached milestones. In exchange eBay provides specialized assistance, and such benefits as health insurance discounts, co-op advertising funds, and a private forum. There are multiple levels of PowerSeller status (Bronze, Silver, Gold, Platinum, and Titanium), ranked by monthly sales volume. You will learn more about this in Chapter 3, "PowerSellers, Trading Assistants, and Trading Posts."

Trading Assistants sell things for others on eBay and collect a fee for doing so. Most successful Trading Assistants are also PowerSellers simply because they sell so many items. eBay provides specialized guidance, a Trading Assistant forum, a logo you can use in your promotional activities, and more. Again, Chapter 3 will explore the program in depth.

Finally, eBay's Trading Post program is for Trading Assistants who want to have a retail presence—a drop store in a shopping center, for example. Obviously to support such a venture you will need to sell more than $1,000 worth of items each month on eBay, so Trading Post owners need to be PowerSellers.

YOUR BIGGEST DECISION AS A POWERSELLER

You are likely reading this book because you have sold on eBay and enjoyed the process. Now you want to take your selling to the next level. But what does that mean? It means different things to different sellers. Your biggest, toughest decision might be "How big do I want this to get, and can I realistically get there on my own terms?"

As you know by now, you can become an official eBay PowerSeller by successfully closing only $1,000 worth of auctions a month. You don't even need a garage to do this. It has been done on kitchen tables around the world. Perhaps you are doing it now.

Nearly a half-million people claim they work fulltime "making a living" on eBay. There are many, many eBay sellers successfully moving more than $3,000 worth of merchandise each month, putting them in the $36,000 annual gross income ballpark. After paying for the merchandise you sell, all those pesky eBay/PayPal fees, and a host of related expenses, $36,000 in annual sales will leave you with a nice supplemental income, but probably not provide what would be considered a living wage in most parts of the country.

At $10,000 a month in successful sales things look a little more interesting. With careful cost control and a lot of hard work you, and perhaps a part-time helper or three, can make ends meet. But the kitchen table will probably be too small unless you sell very small, very expensive stuff. Your garage might work, but plan on parking on the driveway (and maybe packing out there on sunny days too).

Some eBay PowerSellers move at least $150,000 worth of merchandise every month. That's nearly two million dollars in sales each year. This will require a grownup staff, a dedicated facility, and a lot of hard work, but you will likewise be able to afford a bigger garage at home and be able to fill it with a nice car or two instead of shipping peanuts and cartons.

You want more? You want fame? Fortune? These days, to get yourself mentioned in *USA Today* and on CNN as an eBay seller you will probably need to open a chain of perhaps a few hundred "clicks and mortar" eBay drop stores. You won't be the first, (which will make it a little harder to get noticed, but not impossible by any means). It will cost you a lot of money—millions for a chain. But the advantages of scale get intriguing as you fly this close to the sun. Gross incomes approaching hundreds of millions of dollars are possible at this level. The Postmaster General will want to meet you (honest)! Fed Ex and UPS will also fight for your business. And it's not impossible to open such a chain. There are folks well along the way to achieving such lofty dreams as a thousand-store, worldwide network.

You see where this is headed, right? It's time for a good hard look in the mirror, and perhaps a discussion with your significant other or business partners. What are your goals? What's realistic for you? What do you like? What do you hate?

Let's get a little more specific. It is time to pencil some goals and dreams here, and then we will see what's required to meet them in later chapters.

Note

As tempting as it is to skip the following exercise and move onto the "fun stuff" there is nothing fun about running out of money three months into the start of your new business. Or starting a business you hate. And it happens *all the time*. So please take a few moments to create an accurate baseline budget and a self-assessment.

How Much Do You Need?

Start with a pad of paper or, better yet, a computer spreadsheet. Figure out a household budget for life as it is today. Do this on your own, or use one of the many tools available today, such as the budgeting features built into many Quicken products. Here are some typical expense categories to get you started if you decide to DIY:

★ Mortgage or rent, homeowner's dues, property taxes, and so on

★ Utilities (gas, water, electricity, trash, cable, phone)

★ Home (repairs/maintenance)

★ Car (payments, gas and oil, repairs, maintenance fees)

★ Other transportation (tolls, bus, and so on)

★ Car insurance

★ Child care

★ Un-reimbursed healthcare and dental expenses

★ Tuition, books, and other childhood expenses

★ Homeowners or renters insurance

★ Food, toiletries, household items

★ Credit payments

★ Clothing

★ Savings (rainy day and retirement)

★ Eating out, entertainment, recreation

★ Hobbies (you know, the stuff you buy but don't resell on eBay)

★ Magazines/newspapers

★ Gifts/donations

★ Pets

★ Miscellaneous expenses and contingency savings

This exercise should reveal a good baseline that hopefully describes a working plan you are already comfortably achieving now with those credit card balances, if any, going down and the savings account balances going up.

If you are employed, things will change when you quit your fulltime job. Income will be unpredictable, and sometimes elusive. The health insurance that your company pays for, or at least contributes to now, will become your responsibility. Coverage similar to what you have now will almost certainly cost more than you are paying in your "day" job.

Your tax liabilities will change. True, you might be able to write off certain expenses relating to your new eBay business, but other taxes will go up. So get expert opinions on how much you will pay in taxes, and for health insurance for you and for your family if you are the provider of insurance at home.

Note

If you are thinking about quitting your corporate job to start your first business, *please* sit down with an accountant and understand how your tax, social security withholding, and insurance realities will change. Have that meeting before you tell your boss you quit. A $60,000 salary will probably leave you with much more discretionary spending money than $60,000 in net profit from your own small business. Find out why and how before you make the leap!

How Much Would You Like to Earn?

Now that you know how much you spend each month, and how changes in your tax and insurance status will affect the amount you will need to earn to continue your current lifestyle, kick around a realistic additional earnings goal if money is an important part of why you are making the leap. There is nothing wrong with keeping your financial situation status quo, but if you want more money for travel, or a big screen TV or increased savings, or whatever, this is a good time to plan for it. Write down a number. Start to imagine earning that much. Ask yourself, "What do I need to do to accomplish this goal?"

What Do You Like?

Here's what should be the fun part. The happiest people I know enjoy their work so much that they don't even think of it as work. "I can't believe I get paid to do this," they beam. Wouldn't it be nice if you could feel that way at the end of each day, even if they were exhausting days? It's possible. But first you need to know what you like and don't like.

eBay selling requires a diverse set of skills that are difficult to find in any one person. You need to be creative, but must also pay close attention to details. You need to be friendly and outgoing (in order to get stuff to sell, and perhaps find customers who want you to sell their stuff for them), but you also need to be able to plant your solitary self in front of a computer screen for hours on end.

Then there's the physical part—lifting, bending, cleaning items to make them presentable. Do you like these parts of the job too? How about photography? And spelling? Bookkeeping? Get the idea?

A few folks really enjoy all those diverse tasks, but most of us have strong preferences. Take a moment to mark up the following list. Use L for Like, T for Tolerate, D for Dislike, and ? if you have never done it:

_____ Meeting new people, small talk

_____ Finding new things to sell at flea markets and yard sales

_____ Cold calling and visiting business owners

_____ Marketing and public relations tasks

_____ Reading and answering email

_____ Talking on the telephone

_____ Doing online research

_____ Writing and proofreading auction descriptions

_____ Taking, editing, and uploading auction photos

_____ Monitoring auction progress

_____ Processing payments

_____ Packing and shipping

_____ Bookkeeping

_____ Leaving feedback

_____ Hiring and managing people

_____ Housekeeping (sweeping, dusting, inventory control, and so on)

How's it look? If there are a lot of Ds you might be reading the wrong book. If it's mostly Ls you will probably like getting up in the morning. An even mix of all three probably means you will be happiest if you can have help with your eBay selling. What you don't want is to plan a business requiring work that will be neglected because you dislike doing it. That's a recipe for failure.

If there are a lot of question marks in the list, consider interning with an established PowerSeller, particularly before committing to a store lease and the other things necessary to run a Trading Post. For most people the best way to learn is to do.

WHAT ABOUT LIFESTYLE?

I've spent a lot of time training new Trading Post Franchisees. These fine folks have paid a bundle to open their first eBay store. As you will read shortly (if you don't already know), retail requires working long hours, weekends, and even holidays.

So, on the first day of each class I ask students to share with us what they are hoping to gain by opening an eBay drop store. An astonishing number answer "I left the corporate world to have more time to spend at home with my kids," or "I want the flexibility in my schedule to coach my kids' soccer team," or "the financial freedom to travel," and so on.

Now, all of these goals are within reach of all eBay sellers eventually, but any new business requires intense focus, long hours, and the ability to juggle many things at once. Put another way, if you imagine yourself making a comfortable living by sitting at the pool with a laptop buying and selling stuff on eBay you better have deep enough pockets to hire a staff to do most of the "real" work, because most of the profit won't be generated at the pool, at least not in the beginning.

Other students are empty nesters. They are often less interested in piling up cash, but love eBay—or collectibles, or simply hanging out with other people. They are drawn to the Trading Post lifestyle because they hope it will give them a social outlet or change of pace. They frequently envision a single "mom and pop" retail store in their neighborhood. These often work out quite nicely.

Younger franchisees often have dreams of multiple stores and innovative approaches. They want to work hard and get ahead on a large scale without joining "corporate America."

Maybe your dreams are of a more peaceful life. You want a home-based business that you can comfortably mingle with picking up the kids and folding the laundry. Or perhaps you want to grow a little side business on the weekends—make some money with your hobby. You can make a great deal of money with such smaller scale approaches, but probably don't want the expense, pace, and restrictive hours of a retail business.

The point is that you need to figure out who you are, how long and hard you can work, and how much money you have to get started. Write it down. Kick it around with people you trust, and then start the business.

CHECK BACK IN

"Having lost sight of our objectives," the old saying goes, "we redoubled our efforts." Once you have a good idea of the type of business you want, keep an eye on things. When you look in the mirror each morning ask yourself if you are closer to or farther from your goals, and resolve to make it a productive, focused day.

I have a little sign on my bathroom mirror where I can see it every morning. It says simply, "Closer or Farther?" Try it.

Tip

If you don't mind engaging in a little "old school" conversation and hearing some war stories (all of which can be very valuable), the folks at your local SCORE office can be a tremendous business startup resource. Billing themselves as "Counselors to America's Small Business," SCORE volunteers will help you understand the ins and outs of running a successful business, offer to keep an eye on you, and cheer you on. It's all free. Visit www.score.org to learn more.

In this Chapter

- ★ What's a PowerSeller?
- ★ What's a Trading Assistant?
- ★ What's a Trading Post?
- ★ To Franchise or Not?

CHAPTER 3

POWERSELLERS, TRADING ASSISTANTS, AND TRADING POSTS

eBay developed the PowerSeller program to recognize exemplary sellers. This does several things. First and foremost, the program is designed to make you feel good about yourself and about your relationship with eBay. Heck, everybody likes recognition. It's human nature.

WHAT'S A POWERSELLER?

The PowerSeller program gives you extra credibility in the eBay community itself. Buyers often have more confidence in PowerSellers, reasoning correctly that experience counts. Given a choice between buying similar items from a PowerSeller or an occasional seller, especially a part-time seller without much feedback, most buyers will go with the PowerSeller. So, PowerSeller status can mean extra money in your pocket and membership in the PowerSeller program is free.

We'll also look at some other PowerSeller perks in this chapter. There are many.

Becoming a PowerSeller

People know that you are a PowerSeller because a special logo like the one in Figure 3.1 appears in your listings and next to your eBay name on search results.

The minimum entry level for eBay PowerSeller status requires you to consistently sell at least $1,000 per month on eBay. You must do this for three consecutive months to be recognized as a PowerSeller, and then you must continue at this rate or above to maintain your PowerSeller standing.

FIGURE 3.1
The eBay PowerSeller logo shows others that you know your stuff.

PowerSeller status is not just about how much you sell, however. Experience is another element. You must have been selling successfully for at least 90 days. Your account must be in good standing, which is to say, you must pay your eBay bill on time, not be suspended for eBay policy violations, and so on.

Quoting eBay here, you need to

> "Comply with all eBay listing and marketplace policies, and uphold eBay community values, including honesty, timeliness, and mutual respect."

You must also achieve and maintain an acceptable level of positive feedback. Currently, eBay requires a minimum of 100 feedback entries for PowerSeller status, of which 98% or more must be positive. Which is to say if you have only 100 feedback entries, no more than two can be negative. If you have 1,000 feedback entries, up to 20 negatives are acceptable, and so on.

Note

Feedback is discussed in detail in Chapter 28, " Feedback," but here it is worth noting that the feedback calculation used to determine PowerSeller eligibility is slightly different from the formula used for the feedback rating displayed alongside your eBay ID in your auctions. Specifically, eBay calculates PowerSeller Feedback by taking the total number of positive feedbacks and dividing them by the total number of feedbacks (both positive and negative) rather than filtering out multiple feedbacks from the same users. The reasoning is that because PowerSellers ought to have happy repeat customers, this should be recognized and taken into account.

PowerSeller Levels

There are PowerSellers, and then there are *PowerSellers*. eBay ranks us by the monthly gross sales volume achieved, and assigns us to one of five tiers shown in Table 3.1.

TABLE 3.1 PowerSeller Ranking

Level	Monthly Sales	Priority Support	Toll Free Phone	Account Manager
Bronze	$1,000	Yes		
Silver	$3,000	Yes	Yes	
Gold	$10,000	Yes	Yes	Yes
Platinum	$25,000	Yes	Yes	Yes
Titanium	$150,000	Yes	Yes	Yes

Advancing to Higher PowerSeller Levels

To advance to higher PowerSeller levels you will need to continue to comply with all of the PowerSeller program criteria. It takes three consecutive months at a new level of performance to be assigned to the next tier. So, for example, a Bronze PowerSeller will need to sell $3,000 or more each month for three months to become a Silver PowerSeller, Silvers need to sell $10,000 or more for three months to become Gold sellers, and so on.

Confirm that you have opted-in to receive advanced selling communications for PowerSellers by mail, email, and telephone. Do this by visiting the Notification Preferences area of your My eBay web page. If you have done this, eBay will automatically notify and congratulate you via email when you reach the next tier.

Note

eBay sends invitations to eligible members once a month. If you received an email and then get a "you are not qualified" message when you try to sign in, refresh your screen and try again. If you are rejected again, send an email to **powersellersinfo@ebay.com**. An eBay customer service representative will help get you going.

What If Your Sales Slip?

If your selling success falls below the level for your current tier (Gold, Silver, and so on), you will automatically receive an alert email. You will have 30 days to bring your account back into compliance. If, after the 30-day grace period, your account still falls below the criteria, your status as a PowerSeller might be downgraded to the appropriate new tier, or if you are selling less than $1,000 monthly your PowerSeller status might be revoked. You can get back in the club by reaching the necessary sales goals in the future.

Tip

If you know you will not be selling for a specific period of time—if you are going on vacation, for example—you can contact PowerSeller support and your status will be put on hold for that time period so you won't slip down a level. This must be done before the time period in question.

PowerSeller Recognition

As a new PowerSeller you will receive a welcome kit including an official certificate of achievement from the CEO. The kit also contains essential advanced selling tips.

As mentioned earlier, when you achieve PowerSeller status the PowerSeller icon will appear next to your user ID as shown in Figure 3.2.

In addition to the automatically inserted logo next to your name, you are permitted to manually insert larger versions in your item listings and on your About Me web pages.

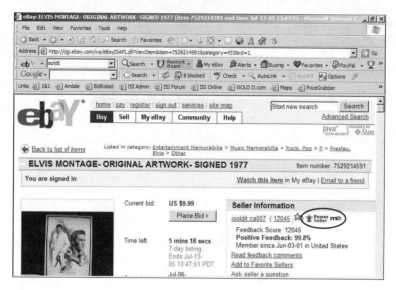

FIGURE 3.2
The PowerSeller logo will appear next to your ID in listings.

Within specific guidelines it also is possible to use the PowerSeller logo on letter-head and business card templates, in advertising, and in other customer communi-cations. You do need to follow the correct procedures, however, and in some cases obtain eBay's prior permission. A great way to study up on the latest rules and reg-ulations is to visit eBay's Help Search page and type **logo use** into the search field. You will get results similar to those shown in Figure 3.3.

PowerSeller Priority Help

eBay provides PowerSellers with priority help. The level of help varies for the differ-ent tiers. The following sections provide an overview of the various help plans and levels.

Prioritized Email Support

All PowerSellers receive priority General email support 24 hours a day, 7 days a week. Most Trust and Safety questions will be answered within 36 hours. Some examples of PowerSeller email support include the following:

★ Requesting removal of specific feedback

★ Reporting a listing violation

★ Asking why your listing was ended early

★ Reporting excessive or disruptive bids

★ Reporting other Trust and Safety issues

★ Asking general questions

★ Asking billing questions

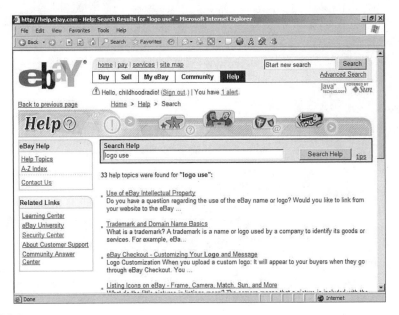

FIGURE 3.3
Search eBay's help for the latest logo use regulations.

Toll Free General Phone Support

Toll free general phone support is available 24 hours a day, 7 days a week for Silver, Gold, Platinum, and Titanium sellers. There's a separate number for Trust and Safety issues (such as feedback removal, non-paying bidder, ended listings, or suspensions). It's answered 6 a.m. to 6 p.m. PT, Monday through Friday.

Your Own PowerSeller Rep

What a godsend these folks are. Imagine having someone at eBay who will pick up the phone when you call, probably recognize you by name, and will then either answer your questions or find someone who can! PowerSeller reps work for Gold, Platinum, and Titanium sellers only. What a perk!

PowerSeller Swag

And of course there are PowerSeller shirts, and caps, and business card holders, and who knows what all (see Figure 3.4). PowerSeller collectibles should be an eBay category. In fact, if you are a PowerSeller and you attend one of eBay's eBay Live events, you will come home with tons of PowerSeller swag.

FIGURE 3.4
PowerSellers have their own shirts, caps, and other identifiers.

The PowerSeller Community

Naturally, PowerSellers have their own subculture within eBay. We get an exclusive PowerSeller-only discussion board that most folks use to trade tips, techniques, best practices, and so on. You will also find some sniveling there, as on any discussion board, but generally the folks are friendly, helpful, and encouraging.

You can also opt into a monthly PowerUp! email newsletter discussing the latest programs, special promotions, and advanced selling education. A quarterly, printed PowerUp! newsletter will be sent to you in the mail.

Reseller Marketplace

As this book is being written eBay is establishing a new feature for PowerSellers only called the Reseller Marketplace (see Figure 3.5). It will be a source of wholesale items for you to purchase and resell. The Reseller Marketplace is open to all eBay PowerSellers. You need to register to use the Reseller Marketplace.

Other PowerSeller Benefits

Additional PowerSeller benefits are discussed in detail in Chapter 29, "eBay as a Partner," but here's a peek at some of the other help you get from eBay as a PowerSeller:

★ eBay Co-op advertising—reimbursement for your advertising efforts

★ eBay Keyword ads—free banner ads up to $200/quarter

★ Health insurance solutions for PowerSellers and their employees

★ Invitations to participate in eBay events, online seminars, and more

★ Additional special values from eBay service providers

FIGURE 3.5
The new Reseller Marketplace lets PowerSellers purchase discounted bulk lots for resale.

WHAT'S A TRADING ASSISTANT?

Trading Assistants are the next step in eBay selling. A Trading Assistant helps folks who don't want to become eBay sellers sell their items through eBay. Basically, you take a customer's items and do all the selling for them—list, collect the payment, ship the item to the buyer, and so on. In return, you keep a portion of the proceeds from the sale.

The advantage is that people find things for you to sell. You can build a network of customers who will keep your shelves filled with new items for sale on eBay each week. Many Trading Assistants make arrangements with "pickers," folks who love to scour yard sales and church fundraisers for treasures. Others make arrangements with local businesses to liquidate their distressed merchandise on eBay. And, of course, the bread and butter for most Trading Assistants is provided by local home-owners wanting to reduce their clutter and get some cash in the process.

The down side of being a Trading Assistant is that you must split the profit. When you sell your own things you get to keep the entire net income. As a Trading

Assistant you split the proceeds with the item's owner. Although it is up to you to decide how much of a cut you will take, the range is typically in the 25%–40% neighborhood. So, selling an item for $100 on eBay might put $25 to $40 in your pocket before expenses.

Trading Assistant Requirements

You do not need to be a PowerSeller to be a Trading Assistant, but it's a good idea to reach PowerSeller status first, if only to gain the necessary selling experience you'll want to have as an assistant. To become a Trading Assistant, you need to meet eBay's requirements, which are detailed on its web site (http://pages.ebay.com/tradingassistants/user-agreement.html).

The minimum requirements for Trading Assistants are as follows:

★ Sell at least 10 items in the past 90 days

★ Have a minimum of 100 feedback entries

★ 97% or more of your feedback must be positive

★ Your eBay account must be in good standing

> # Note
>
> How you cover your expenses is an important consideration for Trading Assistants, and it's discussed in detail in Chapter 10, " Pricing Strategies." Obviously, someone needs to pay the eBay listing fees, eBay final value fees, PayPal or other payment processing fees, packing/shipping costs, labor, and all other associated costs. As a Trading Assistant you will need to set policies that are competitive in your community, and disclose them to customers before starting their auctions. Nothing will make your customers grumpier than watching an auction close at $100, expecting they will get a check for $60 and getting one for $50 instead.

To remain in the Trading Assistants Directory, you need to meet the following requirements:

★ Sell at least 10 items every 90 days.

★ Maintain a 97% or higher feedback rating.

★ Keep your eBay account in good standing.

If you meet these requirements, you can create a profile in the Trading Assistants Directory (see Figure 3.6) by clicking the Create/Edit Your Profile link.

Here you will describe your specialties, fees, terms, contact information, and drop-in hours (if any). Your profile will appear in search results when people look for Trading Assistants in your area.

Think of your Trading Assistants Directory entry as an electronic classified ad for your services. List your specialties, hours of operation, and any other information that might entice someone to use your services. This is a selling tool, so be professional, and brag a little, but don't misrepresent yourself. Figure 3.7 shows a copy of my Directory listing.

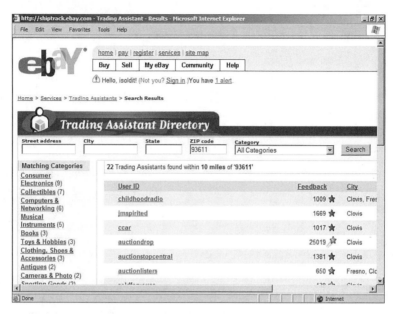

FIGURE 3.6
The Trading Assistant Directory helps customers find you.

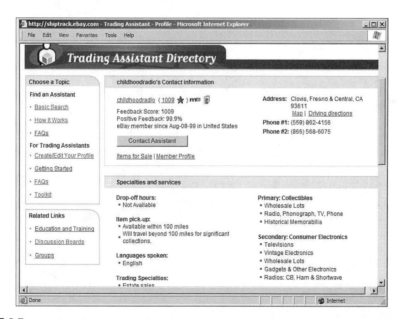

FIGURE 3.7
Here's a typical Trading Assistant Directory listing.

Do not represent yourself as an employee or independent contractor of eBay. eBay can also prevent you from posting a profile if it chooses; for example, if your clients have serious complaints about your service as a Trading Assistant.

Currently, the program is free but eBay cautions, "While eBay reserves the right to charge a fee for inclusion in the Trading Assistants Directory, there are no plans in the foreseeable future to do so. Should this change, all Trading Assistants will be notified well in advance so that they have ample time to decide whether to remain in the directory."

In later chapters we will turn our attention to the marketing, operational, and financial aspects of being a Trading Assistant, but first let's take a quick look at Trading Assistants on steroids: Trading Posts.

WHAT'S A TRADING POST?

Okay, you are a PowerSeller. You have been successfully selling stuff on eBay for your friends and neighbors. The garage is getting way too full, and it's time to think about commercial space. The knee-jerk reaction might be to rent warehouse footage out by the airport where the rents are low. But there's another alternative that's becoming quite popular. You could open a retail shop called an eBay Trading Post, also known as an eBay drop store (see Figure 3.8).

FIGURE 3.8
An eBay Trading Post in a retail setting.

Trading Posts are a relatively new phenomenon, and are now popping up like weeds all over the world. As you will see when we explore them in depth throughout this book they have a number of advantages but can be challenging to run profitably.

The big advantage is that a properly located retail store with a visible sign will attract a lot of attention, and therefore a lot of potential customers, leading, with any luck, to a lot of high-end items for you to sell for a fee on eBay. The potential downside is that retail trappings are expensive. Good locations are difficult to find, and often expensive to lease when you do find them. You will need considerable working capital to start a Trading Post, perhaps as much as $75,000 to $100,000 or more. Because you will only receive a portion of the final value of the auctions, you are going to need to sell a lot of other peoples' stuff to turn the corner financially. We'll look at some sample financial scenarios in Chapter 4, "Budgeting, Forecasting, and Cash Flow."

Trading Post Requirements

Besides having pockets deep enough to open and operate a retail business you must enter into a license agreement with eBay that includes more privileges, restrictions, and responsibilities than becoming a PowerSeller or Trading Assistant. You will be using eBay's branding (logos, name, and other identifiers) in a very public way. They want you to do it right, in order to make the company and your store look good, so the bar's quite a bit higher here than in the garage seller scenario. They also want to be sure nobody mistakes your store for an eBay-owned business.

The current license agreement can be found at_http://pages.ebay.com/tradingassistants/license-agreement.html.

The following list provides an overview of the requirements for becoming a Trading Post. Obviously, these things change over time, so you should be sure you understand the current requirements before making any financial commitments. What follows are eBay's general expectations at the time this book was written.

"To qualify to use any eBay Trading Post Branding, you must meet and maintain the following requirements throughout the term of this eBay Agreement:

★ **Account Standing**. Your eBay account must be kept in good standing at all times and you will pay all fees due to eBay in accordance with eBay's then-current, generally applicable fee schedule as posted on the eBay site. No separate charge will be assessed to you for use of the eBay Trading Post Logo in accordance with the terms of this agreement.

★ **Gross Monthly Sales**. You must meet or exceed the eBay PowerSellers Platinum Tier requirements each calendar month in terms of gross merchandise sales of product via the eBay site (such sales to occur under your eBay user ID).

★ **Feedback**. You must maintain a minimum feedback rating of 500, with at least a 98% positive rating at all times during the term.

★ **Style Guide**. You must adhere to the terms of the style guide.

★ **Customer Support**. You must meet or exceed all customer support metrics established by eBay for eBay Trading Post licensees.

★ **Program Optimization**. You must participate in secret shopper, customer satisfaction surveys, and any such other efforts proposed by eBay for eBay Trading Post licensees to measure customer experience. For instance, eBay plans to institute a secret shopper program in which independent third parties will evaluate your store and the customer experience offered therein.

★ **Agreement**. You must agree to the terms of this license agreement after reading it.

★ **Continued Membership**. You must maintain compliance with all requirements (including those enumerated here) specified by eBay for eBay Trading Post licensees for the duration of the term of this agreement. You acknowledge and agree that eBay may modify or add requirements at any time with its discretion. eBay will notify you via email (at the email address you provide to eBay) of any modifications affecting your eligibility to continue to use the eBay Trading Post branding. You will have then have a reasonable period of time as specified by eBay to comply with such updated requirements."

As you can see, opening a Trading Post is not something you can do over a cup of coffee on a napkin. You will need a lawyer. You will need a commercial real estate broker. You will need someone to help lay out the store; design, construct and install outdoor signs and indoor fixtures; and someone to help with the technology if you don't bring those skills to the party yourself.

TO FRANCHISE OR NOT?

Many successful entrepreneurs have put together wonderful, successful Trading Posts on their own. Hundreds of others have turned to franchise firms to help them along. Some of the best-known franchise firms, (listed alphabetically) include the following:

★ AuctionDrop (UPS stores)

★ iSold It

★ NuMarkets

★ QuickDrop

★ SnappyAuctions

The advantages of hooking up with a franchise organization are many. First, you get to learn from other peoples' mistakes. Hopefully by the time you join, the franchisor and its franchisees have made many of the obvious and not-so-obvious mistakes and have learned from them. Good franchisors will help train you and point out the landmines (or at least where the landmines were during their last trip through the field.)

You will have a built-in community of peers—similar franchisees who have invested a sizable chunk of their nest egg in a dream just like yours.

A good franchisor has made arrangements with vendors for such things as fixtures—counters, shelving, and so on. A few even provide "turnkey packages" where your entire store rolls up in a truck, with an installation crew. This can be a huge timesaver, and can free you up to do pre-opening marketing and the myriad other things you need to accomplish before opening day.

As franchise networks build out hundreds of stores they gain clout with shipping carriers, supply vendors, insurance companies, and others. This can often result in discounts, or at least in better customer service.

Joining a franchise can give you instant credibility, as well. If the franchisor has done a good job of establishing its brand and policing the quality of its stores, and if the firm's franchisees have a lot of well-branded auction items on eBay, your reputation will precede you. People will walk into your store and say, "Oh, I know you guys. I see your stuff on eBay all the time," or "Don't you folks have another store on the west side?" In effect you are buying the power of national and regional marketing that you could not otherwise afford.

Speaking of marketing, it's an important part of increasing any PowerSeller's business. Effective franchisors spend a lot of money on professional printed pieces, ad campaigns, public relations efforts, and much more. You'll learn about marketing and promotion in the chapters found in Part IV, "Marketing, Public Relations, and Advertising," but for now, consider this: One thing a franchise can bring to the table is a marketing and public relations team you could almost certainly not afford to assemble or maintain yourself.

Yeah, but…. Okay. You're right. There is a downside. The franchisor will want a percentage of your income—perhaps even a percentage of each auction's final ending value, even though you keep only a portion of each auction. Say, for example, that an item sells for $90 and you agree to pay its owner two-thirds of the auction's ending price, or $60, leaving you with $30. Your franchisor might want 5% of the final ending price, which is to say 5% of $90, not 5% of $30, or $4.50 rather than $1.50. This will add up and can really change a balance sheet. In return, of course, you get help from the franchisor—training, marketing, technology, and more. Just be sure you know up front what this will cost you and how it's calculated.

Read the contract before you sign it. Do a spreadsheet. Have an accountant and a lawyer help you understand the implications of your agreement. Run the numbers using realistic rent, labor, advertising, average selling prices, and other assumptions. See if it makes sense. Talk to some established store owners. Do a reality check.

Other parts of franchising that annoy some folks delight others. For example, you will probably be told quite a bit about what you can and cannot do in your store. Franchisors have an image to uphold and expect you to help them make the store conform. Some store owners love the uniformity this brings to the system. They like not having to worry about what color to paint the walls or how big a sign can be. Others bristle at being told what to do, where to locate their store, what things they can and cannot list on eBay, and so on. If you are fiercely independent, you are probably not going to be a good franchisee in any industry, be it donuts or drop stores. Think long and hard about this.

In this Chapter

CHAPTER 4

BUDGETING, FORECASTING, AND CASH FLOW

One of the most critical and challenging business tasks is getting your arms around how much money you think you're going to take in, and how much you will need to spend to reach your goals. You must estimate what it will cost to make your business thrive, and you need to project how much income the business will produce as it evolves. You also need to be sure that the money will arrive at least by the time you need to spend it, and hopefully before. Then you need to build in a cushion for the inevitable surprises along the way.

Using ballpark figures is tricky enough in an established business that has a few seasons of at-bats. It is trickier for a start-up business, especially in relatively new industries like eBay third-party selling—Trading Assistants.

In this chapter you will look at some tools and techniques you can use to begin thinking about where the money will come from, how much you will have to spend, and when to start spending. It goes without saying that this is more art than science, and that you should always hope for the best and plan for the worst when projecting business financials.

Remember, good record-keeping this year will make forecasting easier next year.

PARALYSIS BY ANALYSIS?

Before we proceed, here's a cautionary note: It's possible to get so wrapped up in budgeting and "what-ifing" that you neglect the real goal here—moving your business to the next level. You can also make a spreadsheet for just about anything, but because you create formulae and assumptions that project a million dollars in sales does not mean it will happen. So, spend a reasonable but not obsessive amount of time on these tasks, review the results with folks you trust, and then move forward with confidence.

DEVELOPING REASONABLE ASSUMPTIONS

I think the best place to start a new business forecast is to get a "40,000-foot" high view, and then zoom in closer and closer as you begin to understand which financial elements are important and which have the biggest impact on the bottom line. This is also the time to pull out those written goals you developed back in Chapter 1, "Ten Keys to Success," and use them as a backdrop for your work. Do you want to run a basic Trading Assistant operation out of your home? Open a Trading Post? Open a chain of stores?

Check Out the Competition

One way to decide what you can expect to do is to look at others around you in the same situation. For example, if you want to be a Trading Assistant working at home, you can see what like-minded folks in your community are achieving. Interested in a Trading Post? Study a few of them. As this market segment matures, it's easier to find at least a few examples of each in all but the smallest towns.

"Yeah, Ron," you might be thinking. "How many of my competitors are likely to share their numbers with me?"

You don't need to go undercover to get educated. eBay will provide most of what you want to know with a minimum of effort on your part.

Begin by visiting the Trading Assistant Directory. The easiest way to find it is probably to type "trading assistant directory" into eBay's Help feature. A couple of clicks later you should see a screen like the one in Figure 4.1.

Enter a ZIP code near where you plan to locate your business. The first time you do this don't add any of the filters (such as "show only staffed drop-off locations," and so on). You want a long list to start. The list will be displayed showing the closest Trading Assistants first, as shown in Figure 4.2. You might want to sort the list by Feedback in descending order if there are a lot of nearby competitors. This will put the bigger, more established players at the top of the list.

Ignore the TA listings that just don't make sense. For example, the nationwide chain of auctiondrop (UPS) stores all use one eBay selling ID, so if you don't look carefully you will think your local UPS store is selling a ton of stuff on eBay. Chances are, that's not the case.

Click on the sellers' names and read their write-ups. How much do they charge? What are their areas of specialization? What are their hours of operation? Click on the sellers' "Items for Sale" links and look at their auctions. How long have they been sellers? What types of items do they have listed now? How many? How nice do the listings look? How active is the bidding? How is the seller's feedback?

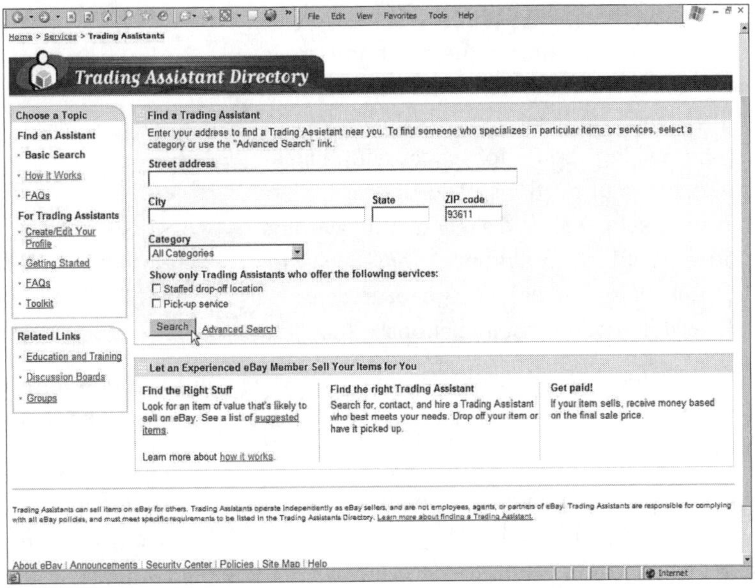

FIGURE 4.1

The elusive eBay Trading Assistant Directory.

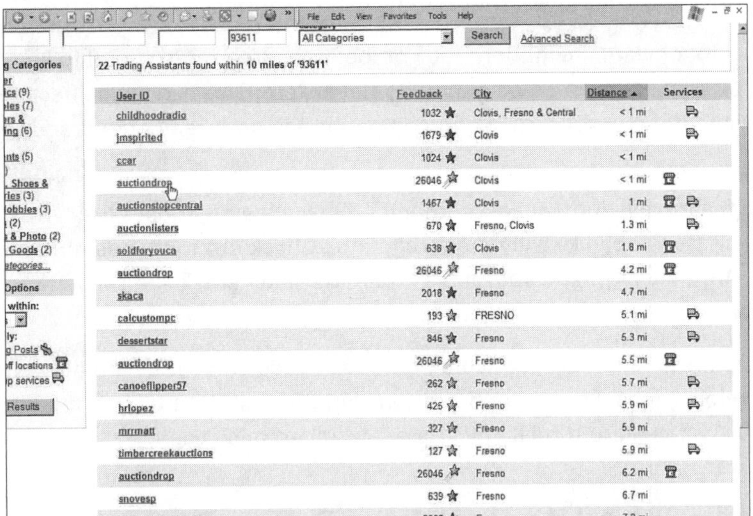

FIGURE 4.2

Local Trading Assistants selected by proximity to a ZIP code and sorted by feedback count in descending order.

Next, examine their closed listings. I like to sort by highest price first. Remember, the red numbers in the closed auctions list mean that the items did not sell. What percentage closed successfully? What's the average selling price for successful sales? Count the successful auctions. Add up the dollars from the successful sales. Calculate the average selling price (total dollars/number of successful auctions). Calculate the percentage of successful sales (successful auctions/total auctions × 100).

Note

You can either generate these numbers with a calculator or copy and paste from eBay into a spreadsheet. For this 40,000-foot view, a calculator and a piece of paper might be quickest.

Which of these local businesses are most like what you have in mind? You might even consider trying out their services. Take them something to sell for you, and see how and what they do.

Learning these facts about your competition does a number of things. First, of course you'll know whom you will be knocking heads with. But it also gives you a range of starting points for your assumptions. You will know the high and low average selling prices in your neighborhood. You will see how many items both busy and slow sellers are moving through their operations. You will know how much or how little you will be able to charge for your services. Perhaps there's a niche you can fill—selling large items that other locals refuse to take, for example.

Is there a lot of viable neighborhood competition already? It's good to know who the strongest, best-established neighboring players are. This can even affect your choice of locations if the toughest-looking competition is both really good and really close to you.

How do the top five local sellers compare? What's their feedback like? Are these folks pros or do they look like they are struggling? Check out the types of items they are selling. Are they high-end collectibles? Garage sale items? Are sellers busy liquidating inventories from local businesses?

As you will see later in this chapter, data like these can act as a reality check when you develop your own assumptions. Speaking of that, let's turn to the key assumptions you will need to model any size eBay selling business.

The Mother of All Assumptions: Selling Price and Item Count

Granted, averages can be risky, but you need them, at least in the early planning stages. Suppose you assume you can find and sell 200 items in a month and that on average they sell for either $30, $50, or $100 as illustrated in Table 4.1.

TABLE 4.1 Average Final Selling Price Revenue Comparison

Items Sold	200	200	200
Average Ending Price	$30	$50	$100
Gross Income	$6,000	$10,000	$20,000

Look at the gross incomes generated by those three different average auction ending price scenarios in Table 4.1. Which result would you rather have after a month's work? Final selling price has an extremely strong effect on profitability, particularly because it costs very little more to handle and sell a $100 item than it does a $30 item. This is yet another reason to enforce that "no junk" rule I ranted about in Chapter 3, "PowerSellers, Trading Assistants, and Trading Posts."

There are other ways to generate $20,000 in monthly gross income, of course. You could sell lots more of those $30 items each month—666.66 items, to be exact. But this would generate additional listing fee expenses, require more labor and therefore higher payroll costs, a bigger facility—you get the picture.

Note

Another option is to have slightly lower average selling prices and make it up with shipping and handling fees in excess of your actual costs. We'll play with that notion elsewhere in the book, but in my opinion, the longest, most powerful lever you have is a high selling price.

As a rule of thumb you want to have an average selling price of $75 or more, if you can maintain it, and you want to get there with a mix of mostly high-priced items. Consider the information shown in Table 4.2.

TABLE 4.2 Two Ways To Generate About the Same Revenue

Scenario One

Ending Price	Qty	Income
$30	100	$3,000
$50	40	$2,000
$100	40	$4,000
$200	15	$3,000
$300	12	$3,600
	207	$15,600
Average Selling Price		$75

TABLE 4.2 Continued

Scenario Two

Ending Price	Qty	Income
$30	0	$0
$50	0	$0
$100	50	$5,000
$200	25	$5,000
$300	20	$6,000
	95	$16,000
Average Selling Price	$168	

Selling about 200 items priced mostly under $50 can get you an average selling price of $75 and about $15,600 in gross income. Selling only 95 items all closing at $100 or more will give you about the same income with much less time and energy spent; and this approach raises the average selling price to $168.

Average selling prices approaching $200 are not unheard of, even for PowerSellers moving hundreds of items per month. But it's not always that juicy. The $75 number is a great starting point, and a reasonable goal for most new sellers.

This "do less for more" concept becomes especially important when you start selling other people's stuff as a Trading Assistant or in a Trading Post, because you only get to keep a percentage of the gross receipts.

Per-auction Costs

Another 40,000-foot estimate you need to make is cost-per-auction. Elements of auction cost include the following:

★ eBay fees

★ Payment processing fees

★ Other fees (franchise royalties and so on)

eBay Fees

If you have looked at eBay's stock or your own eBay invoice from last month you know that it charges a lot of money for its services. If you are simply a PowerSeller listing your own stuff you find at garage sales you will need to pay these fees yourself. Many Trading Assistants and most Trading Posts pass along eBay fees to their customers, the owners of the items being sold. In any case, you need to know what the fees are and how they affect your bottom line. eBay fees are feature-based, and a simple auction will cost a lot less than a fancy one. The elements are listed in the following sections.

eBay Insertion Fees

The fee eBay charges whenever you list an item is called an *insertion fee*. It is based on the starting price you pick when you list. The higher the starting price, the greater the fee, up to a starting price of $500, after which the insertion fee stays the same ($4.80 at the time this was written). Table 4.3 shows the insertion fee structure.

TABLE 4.3   eBay's Basic Insertion Fees

Starting or Reserve Price	Insertion Fee
$0.01–$0.99	$0.25
$1–$9.99	$0.35
$10–$24.99	$0.60
$25–$49.99	$1.20
$50–$199.99	$2.40
$200–$499.99	$3.60
$500 or more	$4.80

This buys you a vanilla listing in most but not all categories, with one photograph. Oh, you want a Gallery Photo? A 10-day auction? Come right this way and I'll walk you to Table 4.4.

TABLE 4.4   eBay's Listing Upgrade Fees

Feature	Fee	Feature	Fee
Gallery	$0.35	Border	$3.00
Listing Designer	$0.10	Highlight	$5.00
Item Subtitle	$0.50	Featured Plus!	$19.95
Bold	$1.00	Gallery Featured	$19.95
Scheduled Listings	$0.10	Home Page Featured	$39.95
10-Day Duration	$0.40	Quantity of 2 or more	$79.95
Gift Services	$0.25	List in Two Categories**	Double the fee

Of these options, Gallery is probably the most important feature, and you should use it on all your listings, particularly if you are going after folks willing to spend $75 or more on auction items. The other options get a little iffier. For example, you can have eBay host your photos on their servers for a fee, or do it yourself elsewhere. The various listing options are examined more closely in Chapter 25, "Listing Items," but let's keep it simple up here at 40,000 feet.

eBay Final Value Fees

Next are the final value fees—the money eBay collects if your item sells. Here too they use a sliding scale. Check out Table 4.5.

TABLE 4.5   eBay's Final Value Fees

Closing Price	Final Value Fee
Item not sold	No fee
$0.01–$25	5.25% of the closing value
$25.01–$1,000	5.25% of the initial $25 ($1.31), plus 2.75% of the remaining closing value balance ($25.01 to $1,000)
Over $1,000.01	5.25% of the initial $25 ($1.31), plus 2.75% of the initial $25–$1,000 ($26.81), plus 1.50% of the remaining closing value balance ($1,000.01 – closing value)

Caution! eBay recently changed the insertion and final value fee structure for the following selling categories:

★ Agriculture & Forestry > Tractors & Farm Machinery

★ Construction > Heavy Equipment, Trailers

★ Food Service & Retail > Concession Trailers & Carts

★ Healthcare, Lab & Life Science > Imaging & Aesthetics Equipment

★ Industrial Supply, MRO > Fork Lifts & Other Lifts

★ Manufacturing & Metalworking > Manufacturing Equipment

★ Manufacturing & Metalworking > Metalworking Equipment

★ Office, Printing & Shipping > Commercial Printing Presses

Items listed in these categories incur remarkably different, usually higher insertion, reserve, and final value fees. Table 4.6 summarizes the fees. Yikes!

TABLE 4.6   eBay's Business and Industrial Category Fees

Business & Industrial Category Specific Fees	
Insertion Fees	$20
Reserve Fees	$5
Final Value Fees	1% of the closing value (maximum charge $250)

Because most of the items in this category sell for thousands of dollars a $20 insertion fee seems reasonable enough. What you don't want to do is what a friend of mine did. He listed inexpensive trailer hitches in the trailer category reasoning that folks looking for trailers might also want hitches. He was correct, but too clever by half. Many of the hitches sold for less than the listing fee. Live and learn.

Average Listing and Final Value Fee Rule of Thumb

So, still cruising along at 40,000 feet you can develop an average listing cost and final value fee for a typical item with just the basic options selected. Let's use that $75 final value assumption from earlier in this chapter and assume you will use a Gallery shot, host your own pictures, and not get crazy with other options. And let's not use the Industrial category for this one. Table 4.7 pulls it together.

TABLE 4.7 $75 Final Value Fees

Insertion fee (start auction at $0.99) $0.25	
Gallery fee	$0.35
Fee for first $25	$1.31
Fee for next $50	$1.38
Total Fees	**$3.29**

Now look what happens if you run that same listing with a starting price of $50 instead of $0.99. Check out Table 4.8.

TABLE 4.8   Listing with Higher Starting Price

Insertion fee (start auction at $50) $2.40	
Gallery fee	$0.35
Fee for first $25	$1.31
Fee for next $50	$1.38
Total Fees	**$5.44**

Raising the starting price on your auction from $0.99 to $50 increased the insertion fee from a quarter to $2.40, an increase of $2.15. This is no big deal if you sell only a few items a year, but if you launch 200 auctions each month, that one change can cost you more than $5,000 a year! ($2.15 × 200 × 12 = $5,160). It adds up.

So, let's use $3.29 per-sold item as our rule of thumb for sold items, and move forward.

When Things Go Wrong

Not every auction closes with a winner. I know great PowerSellers who have success rates in excess of 98%. Virtually all their auctions close with a winner. Others struggle to maintain a 50% close rate. This is, as Martha would say, "a bad thing."

When an auction closes without a winner you still pay the insertion fee but no final value fee. Figure 4.9 shows the resulting damage to your wallet.

TABLE 4.9 Failed Auction Costs

Insertion Fee (Start auction at $0.99)	$0.25
Gallery Fee	$0.35
Fee for first $25	$0.00
Fee for next $50	$0.00
Total Fees	**$.60**

We all lose 60 cents every now and then without even noticing. But if you do this on a large scale it can hurt. For example, if you list 200 items a month, and only 100 (50%) sell successfully, you will be paying eBay—anyone? Right, about $720 per year for not selling your stuff. And as a Trading Assistant or Trading Post owner you are going to be tempted to not pass this along to your customers in the hopes that they will come back and try again.

It can get worse. It can get much worse. Two of the key reasons that auctions don't succeed are high starting prices and the use of reserves. Now, eBay figured this out a long time ago, and they want your auctions to succeed, so they "promote" good selling practices by penalizing you for poor ones. This is probably why they charge more for listings with high starting prices.

If you use reserve prices in your auctions (as discussed in Chapter 11, "Auction Types and Options"), eBay also charges a reserve fee that is fully refunded if the item sells. The fee applies only if the item does not sell, which is very often the case. Table 4.10 shows the reserve fee structure at the time this was written.

TABLE 4.10 Reserve Fees

Reserve Price	Fee
$0.01–$49.99	$1
$50–$199.99	$2
$200 and up	1% of reserve price (up to $100)

Suppose you start items at $50 and place a reserve of $500 on the item. It doesn't sell. Table 4.11 shows your liability. You pay the insertion and option fees even if an item does not sell.

Note

Did you catch that last line in Table 4.10? If you run an auction with a $10,000 reserve price and the item fails to sell, you owe eBay $100!

TABLE 4.11 Insertion and Option Fees

Insertion fee (start auction at $50)	$2.40
Gallery fee	$0.35
Fee for first $25	$0.00
Fee for next $50	$0.00
Reserve fee (unsold item)	$5.00
Total fees	$7.75

Remember, had you started the item at $0.99 and not used a reserve, if it didn't sell you would be out only $0.60. Moreover, an auction starting at under a dollar almost always has a winner, and usually there is enough active bidding to bring the price right up to where it belongs. We will look at this in more detail in Chapter 11.

So, the take-away here is if you list wisely you should budget about $0.60 in eBay costs for each unsold item you list.

Payment Processing Fees

The vast majority of eBay buyers, perhaps 75%+, in most categories pay with PayPal; if you are going to be a PowerSeller, you need to accept PayPal payments. Most of the rest of your winners, maybe 25%, will want to use credit cards. Payments that come to you through PayPal or credit card "merchant" accounts are discounted. Which is to say if the winner sends you $100 you don't get $100, you get something like $97.50. This is called discounting.

On top of that discounting the payment processing folks charge you a per-transaction fee, which is typically 20 or 30 cents per transaction. The higher your sales volume, and the more carefully you shop for merchant services, the lower the fees will be, but for our 40,000 foot view let's assume that PayPal and credit card fees will be 2.5% and $0.30 per transaction.

Caution

Some credit card companies ding you for the transaction fees right when the transaction occurs. Others take the funds from you at the end of the month. Be sure you know how your merchant bank does it so you don't get a nasty surprise at the end of the month.

Other Sales-related Fees

Depending on your situation, you might also be required to pay a percentage of your auction-generated income to someone else. For example, if you run a franchised Trading Post the franchisor will want a percentage of your income. Before you sign that franchise agreement you need to understand what this means and how it is calculated. For example, the franchisor might want to get a percentage of the final ending price of each auction—perhaps four or five percent, right off the top.

Some auction management services charge a percentage of your sales, or charge for each listing you launch, and so on. Be sure you understand the real cost of each eBay listing, whether it sells successfully or not.

A FIRST STAB AT INCOME ESTIMATING

We now have enough assumptions to take a first stab at the available cash generated under a series of scenarios. You can either create your own spreadsheet to do this or visit my web site (www.RonMansfield.com) and download a version of the one I used for the tables in this chapter.

Table 4.12 shows a "barebones" net income estimate assuming an average selling price of $75, 200 listings per month with a 75% success rate, and very basic listings with Gallery photos as the only option.

TABLE 4.12   A First Stab At Predicting Income—The 40,000 Foot Estimate

Monthly listings	200
Percent successful	75%
Successful listings	150
Failed listings	50

TABLE 4.12 Continued

Average selling price	$75
Total Sales	**$11,250**
eBay fees cost (successful)	$3.29
eBay fees cost (failed)	$0.60
eBay fees total (successful)	$493.50
eBay fees total (failed)	$30
Processing fee %	2.5%
Processing fee per transaction	$0.30
Total from processing fee %	$281.25
Total from processing fee transactions	$45
Other Fees	$0
Total Costs	**$849.75**
Net income	**$10,400.25**
Percent of Total Sales	**92%**

Notice that in Table 4.12 I've shown nothing for "Other Fees." If you were a franchisee., however, you might end up owing 5% to the franchisor for royalties, and perhaps advertising or technology funds or other services designed to help your business (and theirs) grow. A 5% fee off the top of the gross sales in this example would be about $563 and would lower your take to about 89% of the total sales, or $9,838 and change.

Note

If you are a Trading Assistant and charge your customers all the PayPal and credit card processing fees, you will be covered. But if you pay the fees yourself for whatever reason, remember that in addition to the 2.5% or whatever you pay PayPal for the auction items, you will pay the same percentage for shipping and handling costs, further reducing your profit!

THE "TRADING ASSISTANT EFFECT"

Before you run out and lease a Cadillac Escalade after seeing these numbers, remember that there is probably another really big mouth to feed, and it is missing in Table 4.12. If you are a Trading Assistant. you will need to give back a large percentage of the remaining money you have collected. The exact amount will vary with your contract terms, of course, but it will be substantial in any event.

In a moment we will look at getting eBay and PayPal fees back from your customers, but for now let's keep it simple up here in the clouds and decide that you are going to charge a flat 33% fee and pay the listing and payment processing fees out of your own pocket. Let's also pretend that you are not a franchisee.

TABLE 4.13   Calculating Your Commission Income

Total sales	$11,250
Net income after eBay	$10,400.25
Your commission rate	33%
Customer's percentage	67%
You pay customer	$7,537.50
You keep	**$2,862.75**
	25%

You need to pay the customers right off the top, meaning they will get 66% of the total sales ($11,250 in this example). You get to take what's left after paying all those other eBay and PayPal and merchant account fees, so you keep $2,862.75 in this example, although "keep" is a little misleading because you still might need to pay rent, hire help to find, process, list, and move all 200 of those items each month, pay the phone bill, and so on.

See where this is headed? High average selling prices and great sell-through rates rule! Table 4.14 shows a significantly improved bottom line achieved by simply selling fewer, higher-priced items and closing 85% of the auctions successfully rather than 75%. Higher average selling prices, fewer items listed, and better success rates go right to the bottom line.

TABLE 4.14   The 40,000 Foot Income Estimate with Higher Prices

Monthly listings	95
Percent successful	85%
Successful listings	81
Failed listings	14
Average selling price	$168
Total sales	**$13,566**
eBay fees cost (successful)	$5.24
eBay fees cost (failed)	$0.60
eBay fees total (successful)	$423.13
eBay fees total (failed)	$8.55
Processing fee %	2.5%
Processing fee per transaction	$0.30
Total from processing fee %	$339.15
Total from processing fee transactions	$24.23
Other fees	$0.00
Total costs	**$795.06**
Net income	$12,770.95
	94%
Total sales	$13,566
Net income	$12,770.95
Your commission rate	33%
Customer's percentage	67%
You pay customer	$9,089.22
You keep	**$3,681.73**
	27%

ESTIMATING OTHER EXPENSES

After you have an idea of the projected sales volume, variable listing, and payment fees you can turn to the rest of your anticipated business costs and potential profit.

You will need to get a general understanding of what the costs will be to run the business you have in mind. If you are planning to work out of your house you won't be paying a store lease, but you might be running the air conditioner or furnace all day. Will you need an additional phone line? Do you have room to store inventory or will you need to rent a storage locker somewhere?

Local Regulations and Expenses

Many cities and counties now tax and regulate at-home businesses. How much will the license cost, and will you even be allowed to run your business at home? What about insurance? Your homeowner's policy will almost certainly not cover your Trading Assistant activities, and simply asking your insurance company if it does could get your current policy canceled. So see Chapter 6, "Insurance and Security Issues," before picking up the phone to call your broker!

How much will advertising cost? In smaller towns radio advertising is within reach of small businesses, and can be an effective way to spread the word. Local newspapers can be effective, too, if they will take your ads.

> # Note
>
> "What?" You say? "The newspaper might not take my ads?" Some papers are so afraid that eBay will eat into their classified advertising revenue that they refuse to run ads for Trading Assistants, and especially Trading Posts. So while you are finding out how much it will cost to advertise in the paper, make sure it can be done. Chapter 15, "Advertising," goes into more detail about advertising options.

Once you get busy you will need to think about adding help. Pay scales vary from city to city, as do the costs of health insurance and other benefits you might be considering for your help.

Other nearby business people are a great source of localized information like this. Your Chamber of Commerce can help. If your area has a business development or small business incubator program check them out as well. And as mentioned in a previous chapter, SCORE (www.score.org) is a great free resource.

PROFITABILITY ROUGH CUTS: AT-HOME BUSINESS

So, with all that in mind let's put together a few "40,000-feet" projections, beginning with the assumption that you work at home, by yourself, list 95 items a month (about five new listings a day, Monday through Friday), valued at $168 each, and that 85% of them sell. You have no business landlord to pay, and your other expenses are minimal. You decide to charge your customer the eBay and PayPal fees for successful sales. Table 14.15 shows a rough idea of the potential outcome.

TABLE 4.15 Potential Sales Outcome

Income Assumptions

Monthly listings	95
Percent successful	85%
Successful listings	81
Failed listings	14
Average selling price	$168
Total sales	$13,566
After eBay & payment fees	$12,722
Your commission rate	33%
Customer's percentage	67%
Customer's responsibility for eBay & PayPal fees	100%
Customer's eBay & PayPal fee contribution	$835
You pay customers	$8,254
Cash Remaining After Paying Customers & Fees	**$4,468**

Expense Assumptions

Rent	$0
Advertising & PR	$500
Utilities	$75
Telephone	$75
Office supplies (exclusive of shipping supplies)	$50
Insurance (exclusive of personnel)	$25
Licenses and taxes (exclude sales tax)	$75
Labor (other than owner)	$0
Total Expenses	**$800**

Monthly pre-tax profit	**$3,668**
Annual pre-tax profit	**$44,019**

Well, you won't be paying cash for an Escalade SUV at this level of performance, but it's a pretty good living for a home business listing only about four items a day, Monday through Friday. The trick is high selling prices and low expenses made possible by the fact that you don't have commercial space to pay for, and that you are not paying a payroll.

Before turning to the "storefront with employees" scenario, let's peek at another way to skin this cat. Suppose you listed 10 items a day Monday through Friday, and the occasional Saturday, or about 220 listings per month, figuring 22 workdays in the average month. Let's assume each item sells for an average of $75. You will probably need a helper to pull this off, working perhaps 30 hours a month at $8.50 an hour, or $255 per month. (You will see how we got that number later in this chapter.)

This scenario requires you to have hundreds of items sitting around, so unless it's very small stuff, you will either need to park on your driveway or rent a storage unit somewhere. Let's park in the driveway for now. It's a new business.

Finally, one more wrinkle. Suppose you intentionally make a $5 "shipping/handling" profit on each successful sale. Profiting on shipping and handling is a hotly contested topic among eBayers. It is also becoming a fact of life in for many PowerSellers. You'll see why when you examine Table 4.16.

TABLE 4.16 Increased Sales at a Lower Rate with Additional Costs

Income Assumptions

Monthly listings	220
Percent successful	85%
Successful listings	187
Failed listings	33
Average selling price	$75
Total sales	$14,025
After eBay & payment fees	$12,984
Your commission rate	33%
Customer's percentage	67%
Customer's responsibility for eBay & PayPal fees	100%
Customer's eBay & PayPal fee contribution	$1,021
You pay customers	$8,375
Cash remaining after paying customers & fees	**$4,608**

TABLE 4.16   Continued

Income Assumptions

Shipping/handling profit per item	$5
Monthly shipping/handling profit	**$935**
Total monthly net income	**$5,543**

Expense Assumptions

Rent	$0
Advertising & PR	$500
Utilities	$75
Telephone	$75
Office supplies (exclusive of shipping supplies)	$50
Insurance (exclusive of personnel)	$25
Licenses and taxes (exclude sales tax)	$75
Labor (other than owner)	$255
Total expenses	**$1,055**
Monthly pre-tax profit	**$4,488**
Annual pre-tax profit	**$53,861**

So, by listing 220 items of less value, doing a heck of a lot more work with the help of a part-timer, filling your garage with stuff, and by gaining some shipping and handling surplus revenue you earn about $9,842 more a year in pre-tax dollars than the scenario outlined back in Table 4.15.

But there is another way to look at this. Back in the $168 item scenario, listing 112 items a month rather than 95, an increase of about one additional item a day, would generate about the same income as listing 220 items at $75 each, without needing to resort to the shipping profiteering, and without a helper. The longest lever is—anyone? Selling price!

PROFITABILITY ROUGH CUTS: TRADING POSTS

It gets trickier and more expensive with a retail store. The good news is, stuff will come to you every day simply because folks will drive by and see your store, which, if done right, is a big easy-to-see "billboard" for your services.

The bad news is this doesn't come cheap. You will need to sell a lot of items to simply cover the rent. More items to cover your employee costs, more to earn back the money you have spent on the facility and equipment, insurance, and so on. You will want to spend more on advertising and perhaps even franchise fees to keep your brand in peoples' minds.

Table 4.17 shows an example of what that all might look like in a simple, nonfranchised operation. Again, your mileage will vary!

TABLE 4.17 A Trading Post Scenario

Income Assumptions

Monthly listings	600
Percent successful	85%
Successful listings	510
Failed listings	90
Average selling price	$85
Total sales	$43,350
After eBay & payment fees	$40,242
Your commission rate	27%
Customer's percentage	73%
Customer's responsibility for eBay & PayPal fees	100%
Customer's eBay & PayPal fee contribution	$3,054
You pay customers	$28,592
Cash remaining after paying customers & fees	**$11,651**
Shipping/handling profit per-item	$5
Monthly shipping/handling profit	**$2,550**
Total monthly net income	**$14,201**

Expense Assumptions

Rent	$2,000
Advertising & PR	$2,000
Utilities	$75
Telephone	$150

TABLE 4.17   Continued

Expense Assumptions

Office supplies (exclusive of shipping supplies)	$100
Insurance (exclusive of personnel)	$250
Licenses and taxes (exclude sales tax)	$150
Labor (other than owner)	$1,870
Total expenses	**$6,595**
Monthly pre-tax profit	**$7,606**
Annual pre-tax profit	**$91,266**

Okay. It looks like a going business and it's worth describing some of the new numbers in more detail. Rent is pretty obvious, and will vary from one neighborhood to the next. You will probably need a minimum of 1,200 square feet to run a store moving 600 items each month. More space is always better until the costs kill you. The utilities look low because they assume most are covered by the landlord. Some leases include all utilities, some don't, or require you to pay separately for gas and water but not electricity, and so on. (Retail space is detailed in Chapter 31, "Location and Layout," and Chapter 32, "Finding and Keeping Great Help.")

The Effect of Coupons

I've assumed your commission rate is 27% rather than 30% or 33% in this exercise because you will probably need to give customers coupons in your store, thereby discounting your commission. In fact, if yours is a franchised store the franchisor might mail out coupons on your behalf, essentially obligating you to discount. Although it is possible to say "no" to customers when they walk in with a "Corporate" coupon, that's probably a bad PR move. So, when budgeting, plan for some discounting whether you do it on your own or have it done for you.

Look carefully at the sources of profit in Table 4.17. About a third of it comes from those shipping/handling fees eBayers dislike. But it's easy to see why sellers are gravitating toward them.

Labor is the trickiest thing to estimate, and Table 4.18 shows the assumptions used for this exercise. Again, this is part of the spreadsheet available at www.RonMansfield.com, so feel free to download it and modify it to fit your situation.

TABLE 4.18 One Way To Estimate Labor Costs

Monthly Labor Estimate	
Listings per hour of labor	2
Hours required	300
Owner's hours worked in production	80
Employee hours needed	220
Employee cost per-hour	$8.50
Monthly employee cost	$1,870

Opinions vary on how to compute the number of listings, and therefore sales and shipments, you can produce with an hour of labor. This obviously hinges on the skill of employees, the complexity of the listings, the layout and efficiency of your facility, and on, and on. Also, the higher your bellybutton count the less productive the team will likely be as a whole. (Pretty soon there's a birthday party every month, "Hey can I go on a break with Kenny?" moments, and so on.)

So, as a conversation starter, for the scenario in Table 4.17 I have assumed that you can process two listings per labor-hour. By *process* I mean check in, photograph, list, monitor, collect funds for, pack, and ship. I also assume you will use this same labor pool to answer emails and do all the other customer service–related tasks.

My method of estimating throughput includes unsuccessful auctions in the mix as well, because the bulk of the work needs to be done whether or not an item sells. And if it doesn't sell the item needs to be disposed of somehow—returned to the customer, donated, and so on. So unsold items count in my world.

Note

Two items per hour seems right to me. Other PowerSellers will tell you three or more per hour works for them. Others insist it takes an hour to do one right. Start out being conservative for planning purposes.

I have further assumed for this example that the owner works in the store, acts as the manager, and spends about 20 hours per week doing customer service and production tasks. Again, your mileage may vary. To keep things simple I've not assigned an hourly rate to the owner/manager's production work, reasoning that s/he will get to keep the business profits. Obviously, in a store with an absentee owner you will need to budget for a manager's salary.

I think you can see from this chapter that it's possible to make a profit in a variety of ways selling on eBay. You should also have spotted some landmines worth dodging.

And again, just because a spreadsheet or some book author tells you its possible to do something does not mean its going to be easy or even possible. So take your time, do good work, spend carefully, and have some rainy day cash handy.

CASH FLOW CONSIDERATIONS

When you first open your doors cash will be flowing out of them in a way you might not have ever seen before. Trades people will want money. The city will have its hand out. The sales tax folks might want a deposit. That employee you hired two weeks before might say to you "Hey boss. The sign guy's here, and the printer wants you to call her back." It will seem never-ending.

You also will not sell 600 items at an average selling price of $85 in the first month either. It will take time for people to notice you, longer for them to trust you with their good stuff, and even a while to remember to put their stuff in the trunk to drive it over to you.

There are other interesting cash flow quirks too. For example, when you electronically transfer funds from your PayPal and credit card merchant accounts to your business checking account they do not move at the speed of light. Funds, umm, meander, taking two or three business days to show up in your bank balance. My theory is that they go to Maui on vacation first. So don't be counting on today's PayPal transfer to cover tomorrow's payroll checks. Ain't gonna happen.

WHAT NOW?

We have covered a lot of ground in this chapter. Money is "what it's all about" in business, and you need to get it right. Test your assumptions. Sleep on them. Ask for cold-hearted opinions from people who have no need to be "nice" to you. Your significant other, relatives, and friends all want you to succeed. Many of them believe in you and think you know what you are doing.

So, find a contrarian or two. Ask for a reality check. The really negative people are probably wrong, but so are the unflappably enthusiastic. It's up to you to find your comfort zone.

FACILITIES, ACCOUNTS, AND SYSTEMS

In this Part

In this Chapter

* **Advantages and Disadvantages of a Home-based Business**

* **Location, Location, Location**

* **Sharing Space with Others**

BOSS Glass Door **OVEN**

Makes Baking Quick and Easy

While the Boss is baking crisp, brown and tempting dishes, you can be preparing the rest of the dinner. No need to worry—merely glance in thru the glass door to

CHAPTER 5

HOME BUSINESS VERSUS RETAIL SPACE

The National Bureau of Labor Statistics estimates that 3 out of 10 homeowners operate a business in their homes. I suppose everyone reading this book has had dreams of sleeping late, grabbing a lazy cup of coffee on the patio while checking email on their wireless-equipped laptop, taking a two-hour lunch without needing to explain it to anyone, and generally being "the boss of it all" while earning a living on eBay.

I know I have, and for much of my life I have worked at home. It's easy for writers and consultants. We can work just about anywhere that we can juggle a laptop and maintain reliable cell phone reception.

It's possible to make a reasonable living as a PowerSeller at home too, although it will be more challenging and resource-intensive than many other "traditional" at-home businesses.

ADVANTAGES AND DISADVANTAGES OF A HOME-BASED BUSINESS

Yes, it's true. You can go a day or two without showering or shaving and answer the phone in your bathrobe, but this is not the primary advantage of working at home. The key benefit many PowerSellers cite is economic. This is particularly true if you already have enough room at home to run your business. It means you can get started without the risks and expenses associated with signing a business lease.

You can also run the washer and dryer while earning a living. If the plumber or cable person needs to visit, you'll be there to answer the door and supervise.

To an extent you can juggle the joys and responsibilities of childcare while working at home, although this can be challenging. Being there for the kids is great, but you really need to "be there" if that's the plan.

You should budget time each day for trips to school, meals, after-school chats, and the unexpected. The great thing about being around is that you will have more interaction with your family.

The not-so-great part is that mid-day parenting will almost certainly disrupt your concentration and workflow from time to time. The simple solution to this is to plan for some non-business downtime each day. When you look at it this way it becomes a benefit rather than an annoyance or disadvantage.

Chapter 6, "Insurance and Security Issues," goes into detail about insurance for home-based businesses. For now, remember that you will need special insurance, and that you should probably not ask your current homeowners insurance company about this, at least not as the first step.

Tip

One of the delightful editors of this book, Laura, who also works at home, reminded me that a home office makes it possible to check email late at night, work all weekend, and otherwise become a workaholic if you are not careful. Make sure your office has a door. For your own sanity and for the sake of the family, keep it closed with you on the "right" side once in a while.

You also will need to carve out space for your business. It will need to be quiet enough for you to talk on the phone without being interrupted. It will need to be well lit and a comfortable temperature year-round. Ideally it should be out of the major traffic flow in your home. It's possible to split the workspace—use a spare bedroom for photography and listing and the garage for storage and shipping, for example. But spreading things out too widely will make you inefficient. And in order to make a profit selling on eBay you need to be doggedly efficient.

If you will be dealing with lots of items, particularly large items, give some thought to how the delivery folks like the one in Figure 5.1 are going to pick up and deliver items. Is there an outside area that's not in plain view and protected from the weather, or will you need to be at home every day at the right times to facilitate pickups and deliveries? Are there stairs involved? The fewer steps the better.

If you will be acting as a Trading Assistant and storing customers' valuables the "warehouse" area of your home needs to be secure, well organized, and clean, and it should give your customers reassurance when they see it.

LOCATION, LOCATION, LOCATION

Speaking of customers, where will you meet with them? As I mentioned earlier in the book some customers might not be comfortable coming to your home. You might not be comfortable inviting them into your home, and it might not be such a great idea to do that anyway.

FIGURE 5.1

Does your home have a secure area for package pickup and delivery or will you need to be home to assist?

Cruise the "used car stereo" listings on eBay, or look carefully at flea markets. See all those car electronics with the wires clipped really short, or just ripped out of the back? Some (but not all) of that stuff is, umm, stolen. And a few, probably very few, but a few of the folks wanting you to sell things for them on eBay did not come by the items legally. So, inviting strangers into your home should be carefully considered. If some folks break into peoples' cars, there's a good chance they break into peoples' homes as well, particularly homes filled with great stuff they just saw the other day....

Perhaps the best first meetings are held at Starbucks or other Internet-savvy local coffee shops like the one shown in Figure 5.2, where you can use your laptop and a Wi-Fi connection to research item prices while also sizing each other up.

Another alternative is to find a meeting room you can borrow or rent when you need it. For example, in my town there's a small business incubator organization that lets its members use a conference room like the one in Figure 5.3 for free whenever we need one. The small annual fee for membership is worth it. You can either call ahead to reserve a room on the fly, or schedule a "regular" meeting day (Mondays at 9:00, or whatever), and then schedule appointments for your customer meetings.

FIGURE 5.2
Neutral meeting places with Internet connectivity can be ideal.

FIGURE 5.3
Consider renting or borrowing commercial meeting spaces. This one's in a "business incubator" and free to members.

Advantages and Disadvantages of a Commercial Space

Commercial space comes in all shapes and sizes, from Trump Tower to strip malls to converted airplane hangers. It can be charming and inviting or downright butt-ugly and a terrible investment. The key advantages to properly selected commercial space include the following:

★ Visibility and traffic

★ Security

★ Compatible neighbors (bringing you qualified prospects)

★ Fewer zoning headaches

If you are trying to attract new customers (and you are), nothing beats commercial space with high visibility and lots of traffic. If you can find a commercial location where thousands of prospective customers must drive or walk past your business on their way to the coffee shop or supermarket or dry cleaners or movie theater, you will have an excellent shot at quickly growing your business. Let's look at some of the options in the following sections.

Shopping Centers

Busy shopping centers like the one in Figure 5.4 are arguably the best, and obviously the most expensive locations for eBay Trading Posts, but they are almost certainly too expensive for a small-scale operation. We will explore Trading Post real-estate options in Chapter 31.

FIGURE 5.4
Busy shopping centers, although expensive, often deliver great walk-by and drive-by traffic.

Specialized Neighborhoods

Many communities struggling to cope with the dollar drain from downtown retail shops to the megastores in the burbs are working hard to develop specialty shopping areas like the one in Old Town Clovis, shown in Figure 5.5. These not only offer relative bargain rates, but they also can attract the types of shoppers eBay Trading Assistants and Trading Posts desire.

FIGURE 5.5
The Old Town Clovis shopping area.

Strip Malls

Throwbacks from the '60s, strip malls are everywhere, and continue to follow new housing developments out into the wilderness. Blink and you will see the next nail salon, dry cleaner, sandwich shop—you name it. Strip mall spaces like the one in Figure 5.6 can cost less per square foot than their big shopping mall cousins. You just need to be sure that the space is visible and trafficked by folks you want to attract.

FIGURE 5.6
Here's a strip mall location on a busy street with great parking.

Parking can be an issue in some of these small centers, as well. The last thing you want is to have a customer load up her car with stuff to sell, and then drive away in frustration after finding no place to park and unload.

About the only thing that would make the strip mall in Figure 5.6 more attractive would be stronger "anchor" stores (neighbors with great appeal). For example, a Starbucks or grocery store can really increase traffic. Centers with great anchors generally charge higher prices, so it's a trade-off.

Industrial Centers and Lofts

Loft neighborhoods and industrial centers like the one shown in Figure 5.7 might work if you are going to concentrate primarily on business customers and items (liquidations and so on). Industrial centers usually don't have enough of the right foot or car traffic to sustain a full-blown "retail" Trading Post.

FIGURE 5.7
Industrial centers usually are not great traffic areas.

Some Trading Assistants are experimenting with small satellite retail spaces or even kiosks in busy retail settings. The UPS Store/Quickdrop model is a large-scale example of this approach. PowerSellers use these as promotional and "intake" points, and then use centralized, lower cost, more efficient industrial space for their warehousing, listing, and shipping tasks. This seems to work best when retail space is very expensive, such as in beach towns.

The total costs and logistics of hub-and-spoke operations such as these need to be given careful thought. There is always the risk of damaging items anytime you move them, for example. And you will need to add a truck or trucks and drivers with their associated expenses to your budget.

Office Space

Unless you are selling very small items such as tickets or jewelry, office space is probably not the optimal setting for a Trading Assistant. You will probably not be able to create the amount of visibility you need, and might face zoning and logistical problems.

SHARING SPACE WITH OTHERS

Here's an intriguing idea. Do you know any retail business owners in your desired neighborhood who have compatible customers and a willingness to share space with you? Perhaps they have a bigger space than they need and want help with the rent. Or perhaps they want to keep the space open long hours and wish they had someone else to watch the store part of the time. It might be a collectible sports memorabilia store or an independently owned packing and shipping store. Even a local car stereo dealer might work.

I rent about a hundred square feet from an antiques and collectibles consignment shop. They let me promote my Trading Assistant business and even help other dealers in the store sell on eBay. Not all consignment stores are this enlightened, and many are, perhaps justifiably, concerned that eBay in any form is the "competition." But it never hurts to ask, and these are great locations if you can get them.

Use your imagination. Pound the pavement. Perhaps you can even work a deal where you trade services for space, and have some companionship during the day as well.

In this Chapter

BOSS Glass Door OVEN

Makes Baking Quick and Easy

While the Boss is baking crisp, brown and tempting dishes, you can be preparing the rest of the dinner. No need to worry—merely glance in thru the glass door to

INSURANCE AND SECURITY ISSUES

Insuring and securing your business can be two of the most important and most frustrating aspects of any new venture. You spend money assuming that one day things will go wrong—perhaps terribly wrong—but on good days writing those checks for what seems to be nothing useful or productive will make you feel like you are betting against yourself. And even though, in a way, you are betting against yourself, it is prudent to do so.

This chapter is designed to give you a general understanding of the types of insurance and security products required of, and available to, small business owners, and it is by no means a comprehensive guide or "best practices" list. Insurance requirements and regulations vary from state to state. Your landlord might require coverage not listed here. Please consult with a local business insurance broker, and consider getting help from other local resources such as your neighborhood SCORE chapter (www.score.org). You can find links to SCORE and other insurance-related resources at my web site, www.RonMansfield.com. Another great resource is the "Business Insurance 101" page at www.iiaa.org, the site of the Independent Insurance Agents of America.

DECIDING ON INSURANCE COVERAGE

Insurance coverage will vary with the complexity of your business. If you are a PowerSeller working at home, finding and selling your own stuff, you might get by with a reasonably small package.

As you start to add workers, lease commercial space, sell other peoples' valuable items, and so on, the risks and costs can increase significantly. Sometimes careful shopping will uncover insurance that solves more than one problem for a single fee. For example, a company called Collectibles Insurance Agency (www.collectinsure.com), or simply CIA, offers a policy designed for collectibles dealers. It insures your inventory, your customers' items left in your care, and offers shipping insurance as well.

HOW MUCH IS ENOUGH?

It's a little mind-boggling what all you have to consider when purchasing insurance: arson, check fraud (employees and others), civil authority losses (actions of government), computer gear and data loss, damage from aircraft, earthquakes, embezzlement, explosions, floods, foundation collapse, fungus or mold, hail, insect damage, fire, lightning, mudslides, riots, war or terrorism, robbery and burglary, roof collapse, sinkholes, theft by employees, theft by non-employees, vandalism, windstorm, liability—general liability, errors and omissions, bodily injury or property damage caused by an employee, commercial vehicle liability, and more.

Very few policies cover all of these things, and even finding a combination that does it all can be tricky and expensive. So plan to spend some time shopping and asking professionals for advice. And don't overspend. Earthquake coverage is probably not needed in Nebraska, but hailstorms? You never know.

The other insurance buying trick is to understand what is and is not covered. This can be mind-numbing, but it *must* be done before you need to collect on a claim.

For example, remember CIA, that collectibles insurance company I mentioned previously? The coverage they sell only covers collectibles, and not all collectibles. So, if you are a Trading Assistant and break someone's lovely Tiffany lamp you would be covered. But lose an iPod and you are not insured by the CIA policy.

More confusing still, if you try to collect from CIA for gold coins, watches, statues, a vintage car, and other "collectibles" you won't be covered either— their policy excludes those items.

Note

Sometimes state regulations play a part. Some policies are not available in some states, or cost more in some places than others, and so on.

You should also understand the claims process and how items are valued. This is especially tricky for unusual collectibles and antiques where there can be important differences of opinion regarding the value of an item.

I remember once hearing about a hard-to-find painting that never reached the winner. He had paid less than $1,000 for the item but could not find another for less than $3,000, which is the amount he said he wanted in compensation, reasoning that he wanted "his" painting back, not his money back. Times like these are when it is great to have an insurance company to intercede on your behalf.

But will your insurance company help in times like this? How will it value eBay auction items? Read carefully. Ask questions.

THE BARE MINIMUM

If you are working at home alone, selling your own items, your needs might be quite straightforward:

★ Health insurance for yourself and your family

★ Disability insurance for yourself and your business

★ Life insurance for yourself

★ Coverage for loss or damage of inventory

★ Liability insurance for your home business

★ Possible upgrades to your car insurance for business use

★ Shipping insurance

As I mentioned earlier in this book, most homeowner and renter policies do not cover in-home businesses, at least not automatically. Some companies offer home-business add-ons (known as *riders*); others will simply cancel you if they find out you are conducting business at home.

Your best bet is to either work with a broker who represents multiple insurance companies, or to ask anonymously about in-home business coverage if you need to deal directly with your current carrier. If you then find out that you can't be covered, you can switch to an insurer who will cover you without having been cancelled by your current company first. Like so many other things, it's much easier and cheaper to get insurance if you already have it. Ask about which types of liability insurance you might need, and whether what you already have will cover you in the business scenarios you are likely to encounter as a PowerSeller.

If You Have Employees

If you hire employees you will need to pay for workers' compensation insurance. And, if you think you can get around this by declaring your helpers independent contractors, get a professional opinion first. You and the government might have a different view of what constitutes an independent contractor—it varies considerably from

Tip

If your employees will be driving any vehicles as part of their job be sure you understand the implications of this, and cover yourself fully.

industry to industry, and when push comes to shove the government's definition is going to be the winner.

If you hire valued, fulltime employees you will also want to consider providing or at least supplementing health and life insurance for these employees and their families.

As a PowerSeller you do have access to health coverage programs, and you should check them out through the PowerSellers' Resources links on eBay. There are other options as well. For example, Sam's Club and Costco's business memberships also offer small-business health care programs worth exploring.

If You Occupy Commercial Space

Your landlord might require insurance, and even demand a certificate of insurance before handing you the keys. So be sure you read the lease and understand the requirements up front, and then have the insurance in place before you start paying rent. I have seen a Trading Post all set to open its doors but unable to turn the key because the renter could not secure satisfactory insurance by opening day.

SHIPPING INSURANCE

There are several schools of thought regarding shipping insurance. Some PowerSellers pay for it themselves, others require winners to purchase it, and others make it optional. A brave few self-insure shipments.

The type of insurance and cost varies with the carrier used. For example, UPS offers free insurance on all items valued at $200 or less. The U.S. Postal Service will sell you insurance for items valued at up to $200 on a sliding scale ranging from $1.30 to $3.20. You can purchase the insurance online at time of shipment. For items more valuable than this you need to visit the post office branch to insure through them.

But there are alternatives. For example, stamps.com offers competitive rates on shipments through the U.S. Postal Service. There are restrictions, of course. The limit is $2,500 per item. You can't ship from Wyoming because the insurance company's not authorized to do business in that state, and there are restrictions precluding the insurance of certain items such as coins, event admission tickets, and so on.

A growing number of third parties are offering insurance including PayPal, DSI (Discount Shipping Insurance), Endicia, and others. This is an exploding field at the moment, so visit my web site where I will try to maintain an up-to-date list of links.

FACILITY SECURITY CONSIDERATIONS

Security is obviously an issue, particularly as your business grows and your inventory becomes more attractive to thieves. Besides picking a good neighborhood for your business and making sure the areas around your business are well lit and patrolled, there are other things you can do. Some of these will help reduce your insurance costs. All of them make sense for your safety and the safety of your employees. Here are 10 suggestions:

1. Install an alarm system connected to a central monitoring service. Display the service's sign in the front and back of your location. Install alarm "chime" options on all doors so you'll know when people come and go. Change the alarm code whenever you terminate an employee.

2. Install video security cameras and make sure they are visible. Post signs warning visitors that video surveillance is in use.

3. Install a safe, and use it for small, valuable items (jewelry, event tickets, cameras, and so on). Gun safes work great and are available locally at Costco and Sam's Club, among other places. Bolt the safe to the floor.

4. Don't accept cash from people picking up their items, and don't have a cash register at your location. Consider posting a "no cash on premises" sign at your door.

5. Get to know your local law enforcement officers. Introduce yourself, make friends. Describe the nature of your business and its contents.

6. Get to know your neighbors. Introduce yourself, make friends. Ask about any problems or troublemakers.

7. Lay out your space so that access to the inventory is limited. If you work in a garage, consider shielding inventory from view when the doors are open. In a store, when planning the location of a public lavatory, make it accessible without walking through the item storage area.

8. If you have a back door keep it locked at all times. Consider window security gates that can be pulled closed and locked at night.

9. Instruct employees to keep customers and visitors on the "public" side of the counter.

10. Consider having a "no solo" employee policy, especially after dark.

SECURING YOUR COMPUTERS

Computer security is a crucial task in an eBay-based business. This is especially true if you are collecting customers' personal information. Here are 11 tips for securing your computers and accounts:

1. Install antivirus software on every computer and keep it current. Make this someone's specific responsibility. Do not leave it to chance. Schedule regular full disk scans at least weekly and log them.

2. Install eBay's toolbar on all your browsers and use the Account Guard feature to sniff out bogus web sites pretending to be official eBay and PayPal sites. Make certain everyone in your operation knows how this works.

3. Get in the habit of checking your My Messages section of your My eBay page. My Messages is the only place you will receive secure, relevant messages directly from eBay and other eBay members. All messages originate from eBay systems and are guaranteed to be authentic. If you get a message through your regular email tool (Outlook, or whatever), and can't find a copy in the eBay My Messages box, it is almost certainly fraudulent.

4. If you use Outlook for email add Cloudmark's Safety Bar feature (www.cloudmark.com) and pay for a subscription.

5. Create a list of items to back up, and maintain a written backup schedule/log. Store backups off-site, ideally in a different Zip code.

6. Use difficult-to-crack passwords (no words, mixed case, include symbols if possible, and so on), and change them regularly, especially whenever you terminate an employee. Don't write down passwords and leave them in view of visitors.

7. Do not use wireless Internet connections in your operation at home or in a store setting. These are not secure enough to safely handle credit card information and your customers' personal data, even when encrypted.

8. Install standby power supplies on all computers.

9. Give access to accounts on a need-to-know basis. For example, most store employees should not know your PayPal or Merchant Account logon information.

10. Do not give customers access to computers. Customer "surf stations" in the lobby designed to let folks check on your auctions, and perhaps even bid on your items, are a very bad idea. Besides risking viral infections that can spread networkwide, customer surf stations can create the appearance of

shill bidding back at eBay, and in extreme cases can cause all of your auctions to be shut down with little or no warning (see Chapter 29, "eBay as a Partner").

11. Keep all paperwork containing customer sensitive information locked at all times. Shred when disposing of these documents.

GETTING IT ALL TOGETHER

Here's a checklist to help you get organized and ensure that you cover all your bases:

✓ Meet with business insurance agents. Explain operation and growth plans.

✓ Compare quotes. Be sure you understand what's covered and what's not.

✓ Create a shipping insurance policy, and pick the vendors you plan to use for the insurance.

✓ If you have employees, arrange for workers' comp insurance.

✓ Provide landlord/franchise with proof of insurance.

✓ Create and implement a physical security plan. Include alarm, alarm service, video monitoring gear, security warning signs, a properly installed safe, lockable file cabinets, and so on.

✓ Secure all computers and task someone to keep them current.

✓ Make certain that employees are trained not to fall for spoof emails.

✓ Devise an effective password policy and adhere to it.

✓ Have a document retention and destruction plan.

In this Chapter

★ **Incorporation, Licenses, Agreements, and Accoun**

★ **Getting Started**

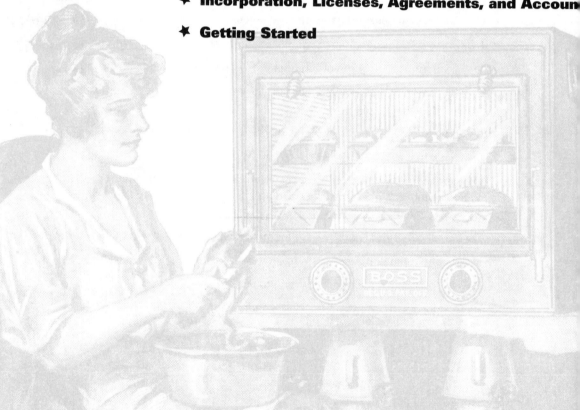

BOSS Glass Door **OVEN**

Makes Baking Quick and Easy

While the Boss is baking crisp, brown and tempting dishes, you can be preparing the rest of the dinner. No need to worry—merely glance in thru the glass door to

STARTING YOUR BUSINESS

Picking a great name for your business and a related eBay ID can help people figure out what you do and remember you. Spend some time on this. Look at what others have done, not only so you don't pick a name that is already in use but also to get a sense of what works and does not.

A lot of the obvious names have already been taken, so it's going to require a little work to stand out. Avoid vague names like "Dave's Place." You want something that says "auction help" or "cash for your stuff," or maybe "online auction expert."

Your official business name should not include "eBay" but you might be able refer to eBay in your signage and promotional materials. For example, if your business was called "Unload Your Stuff," your signs and brochures might be able to say "Unload Your Stuff on eBay" if you carefully follow eBay's guidelines.

Try to make your eBay ID reinforce your business name. "UnloadYourStuff," for example, would be a great eBay ID for a business by the same name.

INCORPORATION, LICENSES, AGREEMENTS, AND ACCOUNTS

As your business evolves from a dream to a reality you will be presented with a pile of papers held in the hands of perhaps a dozen or more folks with smiling faces saying "Sign here...and here...and here." Or worse yet, you might not put yourself in front of the right person holding a pen and form, and find yourself in hot water down the road. Let's look at some of the paperwork involved in starting a grown-up business.

What Type of Company Is Best for You?

The simplest type of business is probably also the riskiest. It's called a *sole proprietorship*, and it's what you will automatically be running if you don't opt for something else. Sole proprietors and partners accept unlimited personal liability for business debts and lawsuits. Creditors can attach your homes, cars, savings, or other personal assets.

Incorporating or forming a *limited liability corporation (LLC)* can help, but probably won't totally separate your personal identity from your business identity. In theory, at least, only the money you put into your LLC venture is at risk.

There are other ways to incorporate, such as *S Corporations*, and many considerations when incorporating. For example, you don't necessarily need to incorporate in the state where you live. The timing of your incorporation can save or cost you money as well. There will be additional expenses involved at the time of incorporation, and on-going expenses for the extra accounting and filing steps necessitated by these slightly more complicated business types.

> # Note
>
> This single chapter can't possibly lead you through the entire thicket of incorporation, taxation, licensing, and all of the other concerns for running an eBay business. The required steps can vary widely from PowerSeller to PowerSeller, and even from one city or county to the next. Get professional, local help, and use the information in this chapter as a conversation starter. Don't be afraid to ask questions.

If this is your first real business (not counting that lemonade stand in third grade), you definitely need help with these decisions. Start with a visit to SCORE or your local small business incubator or advocate. Chances are you will still need to pay an attorney and accountant, but by getting some knowledgeable free advice first you will be better prepared. You might also be able to get attorney and accountant referrals from these mentors. By the way, just because your Uncle Fred filed bankruptcy twice does not mean he is an expert.

Partnership Agreements

Partnerships can be great. One of you can be the idea person, the other the detail hound. One brings a sense of humor and is full of optimism; the other is the worrier and level head.

Balances like these can be powerful, and there are many examples. Jobs and Wozniak (of Apple Computer fame) spring to mind of course, and they raise another interesting point. Partners, like lovers, can be best friends one minute and dark enemies awhile later, especially when the business hits a rough patch. New business ventures always have rough patches, and unless this is the second Trading Post (or restaurant or hobby shop) you have opened with the same partner, neither of you has a clue how well you will work together, if at all.

A dear friend of mine with lots of eBay selling experience opened a store with a partner. These are both bright, capable, accomplished businesspeople. But they failed to create a written document detailing who was putting in how much money, which of them would provide the bulk of the sweat equity, how much all of that hard work was to be valued at.... You see where this is headed.

One partner ran out of cash, hated the whole concept of being an eBay seller, and wanted out. The other partner was faced with all the ugly options—could the business remain open? Did the partner expect to be bought out? How much was all that freely given labor worth, and how would it affect the valuation of the business assets? Were they both still liable for the reminder of the computer leases? And on it went.

In short, it was a train wreck made worse by the lack of a concrete written agreement and the complete absence of a bookkeeping trail that clearly showed who put in how much of what.

If you are going to create a partnership get a lawyer—no, make that two lawyers—and write stuff down! And if you think partnerships are tricky, imagine inviting multiple investors to the game. Put it all in writing while things are still rosy.

Franchise Agreements

Some of you are exploring franchise arrangements, and you already know I think these can put you a leg up on the competition if you pick the right franchisor and strike the right deal. Once again, having a solid written agreement and understanding what it means will be critical to your long-term success and happiness.

Visit with established franchisees in their stores and ask them what they wish they had understood about their agreements before they signed them. Most will tell you there were some pleasant and unpleasant surprises.

It is your responsibility to perform something called *due diligence*. This simply means you need to do enough research to convince yourself that you have all the necessary information to make an informed decision. This probably involves meeting with the franchise company employees, of course, but also with a number of other folks including owners of franchise stores, customers of the stores, your accountant, insurance experts, web content creators, and anyone else who can provide insight.

In other words, you need to do your homework. Here are just a few of the things you need to understand about your franchise agreement:

★ How much is the up-front fee?

★ How much are the ongoing fees, and how are they calculated?

★ How much will it *really* cost to build out your store(s)?

★ What territory, if any, do you own?

★ Will there be a map attached to the contract with your territory clearly marked?

★ How close can another franchisee build to your store(s)?

★ How many stores are you expected to open, and by when?

★ What happens if you don't or can't open them all on time?

★ Will the company be building its own stores near you?

★ Who has final say regarding the suitability of a site?

★ What type of help will you get from the franchisor?

★ Will you be charged for the help? How much? When?

★ Must you purchase supplies, printing, insurance, and so on from specific vendors?

★ How much control, if any, do you have over the appearance of your store (paint colors, fixtures, signage, and so on)?

★ When an auction ends, where does the money go—to your account or to the franchisor's?

★ Who pays your customers—you or the franchisor? How quickly?

A professionally run franchise company expects you to ask questions like this, and will think less of you if you don't. But remember, the first people you are likely to encounter when exploring franchise opportunities are salespeople. And their job is to sell franchises. It's your job to understand what you are buying.

In any business transaction there is the risk of what I call "optimistic selling and selective hearing." As a buyer you very much want to find a quick solution to your problem, and the seller is eager to make sales. So if you ask, "Is the whole patch from the river to the freeway still available?" and the salesperson replies in the affirmative causing you to ask, "So I can have that whole territory, right?" a nod of the sales rep's head simply means that it's not out of the question, rather than it's a done deal. You need this stuff in writing, and you need a lawyer to look it over carefully with you.

Business Licenses

Even if you are simply PowerSelling from your garage, chances are you will need a business license from your city or town. This will certainly be the case if you open a store. Cities need revenue to survive, and one of their favorite sources is the business community. Plan for it. Budget for it. Apply for it. Keep your license current.

You will also be expected to file a *Doing Business As* or *DBA filing*. This usually requires publishing your business name, address, and other vital statistics in a local paper. You often need to refile if you move, and renew (refile) at some time in the future.

Tax Collection Paperwork

Most states and many, many counties and cities expect you to collect sales tax for them. Although much of what you sell as an eBayer will be sent out of state, and therefore will not be taxable in your state under current law, some percentage of the items will sell to residents of your state. Chances are your state will want you to collect and forward on to them sales tax on these sales.

It gets even messier when someone in your neighborhood wins an item and comes to you to pick it up. In this case you might be responsible for state, county, and even local tax collection, reporting, and subsequent payment.

You will be expected to obtain a tax identification number, and in many states, need to submit a deposit up front. The deposit will be based upon the expected amount of tax you will collect over some specified period of time. You will be asked to estimate your first year's sales, and this is no time to be bullish or brag. You should also remember that in a typical eBay business only a small percentage of the sales made will be to people in your own state, since you are selling in all 50 states and perhaps internationally. So do your best to get the deposit based on as realistically low an in-state sales number as you can honestly estimate, rather than on your total estimated eBay sales.

Special Business Licenses and Permits

America, being the bureaucratic country that it is, allows (and perhaps even encourages) states and counties and cities to invent a chaotic array of rules and regulations. Licensing and permitting is a great revenue source, and a way to protect citizens from themselves while demonstrating to us how hardworking our local officials can be.

Recently, legislators (after some encouragement from the pawn brokers' industry) have turned their eyes toward eBay drop stores. These stores, pawn brokers contend, could be hotbeds of stolen property, and therefore should be forced to register as secondhand stores, fingerprint customers, hold inventory for extended periods of time, and even send lists of serial numbers and other descriptors to the local peacekeepers.

This is by no means a nationwide movement yet, and I am guessing that eBay's lawyers and lobbyists and campaign contributors have bigger, umm, guns than the pawn brokers, but you still might find yourself in a time and place where you are required to do some pretty convoluted things, including applying for another expensive permit, and giving lists of camera and MP3 player serial numbers to desk sergeants who would rather not have more papers to file.

One web site tracking this relatively new phenomenon is www.beantowntrading-post.com/ebay_regulation/states.php. There will undoubtedly be others, and I'll try to keep my web site (www.RonMansfield.com) links current as this evolves.

Bank Accounts

Early on you probably just dumped those PayPal payments and money orders right into your household checking account. As an active, professional PowerSeller you will need at least one business checking account, and possibly more. Why might you need more than one account?

If you are a franchisee, and if your franchisor pays your customers, as is the case with at least one of the biggest, they will want access to a business banking account they can "sweep" when they need funds to pay your customers.

It works something like this: PayPal and your credit card merchant bank deposit funds directly and automatically into your "sweep" account. The franchisor has access to this account, and can electronically withdraw the funds necessary to send checks to the folks who brought things into your store. The franchisor will also take the funds owed to it for royalty fees, check processing charges, advertising funds, and other agreed upon expenses. (You did read that contract carefully, right?)

So, at the end of this if everybody is doing his job right there will be money left for you to pay your bills. Now you could just do that right from your sweep account, but it makes much more sense to set up a second account and move money from your sweep account into it for paying the rent, payroll, and so on. Besides the fact that it makes the financial reporting and auditing a little cleaner, it gives you some control over at least some of the funds you collect, since you won't need to give the "keys" to this second account to anyone else.

PowerSellers with multiple eBay accounts (discussed next) often set up separate checking accounts for each eBay account. This can help keep the books straight.

Do You Need Multiple eBay Accounts?

Many, many PowerSellers have multiple eBay accounts. There are a number of good reasons to join them. For example, some sellers use a separate account for buying, reasoning that it will be harder for bidders to learn how much you paid when buying items to be resold. I think a better reason is this: If you specialize in something particular—collectibles, let's say, or iPod accessories, you don't want to clutter up searchers' "See Other Listings" searches or your eBay storefront with the occasional oddball items you find at yard sales. You want to present a focused, uncluttered appearance to your regulars, and to folks looking for a particular category of items.

A second eBay account can give you a place to dispose of this stuff, and "dump" less than perfect merchandise without devaluing the good stuff.

If you have multiple stores, or company names, multiple eBay accounts make sense. If other family members use your current account you definitely want a new one for your business. If you are an avid collector and buy things that you don't intend to resell, a second account can be useful too.

Do You Need Multiple PayPal Accounts?

Multiple PayPal accounts make sense for all the same reasons as multiple eBay accounts, but they are a little trickier. Anyone can have two PayPal accounts—a personal account and a Premier or Business account. PowerSellers should have either a Premier or Business PayPal account because you need one of these to accept credit card payments.

You can have up to eight separate eBay IDs for your personal account and another eight for your Business PayPal. You can attach up to eight bank accounts to each of your two PayPal accounts. Beyond there be dragons. If you want more than two PayPal accounts (one personal, the other business), or more than eight eBay IDs or bank accounts you will need to convince PayPal. It has been done, but not easily.

Merchant Accounts

Five minutes after you have filed your DBA your phone will ring off the hook. People will show up at your door holding credit card swipe machines under their arms. This isn't a cloud of locusts, but simply merchant account bank sales reps, and they want your blood.

Although it is possible to take credit card payments only through PayPal, many PowerSellers opt for a second stream through processors like VeriSign or Authorize.net and their partners, bank credit card merchant account banks. These services make it easier for some people to pay you, and might actually be required if you use certain auction management software packages.

Having a merchant account, and possibly a card reader, in your store or home will make it easier for walk-in winners to pay. It also makes it easier for employees to steal from you, but we will go there in a moment.

If you decide you want to sign up for a merchant account so that you can directly take Visa, Master Card, American Express, Discover, and possibly Diner's Club cards, you should shop around for the best rates. This is a lot like shopping for insurance. There are rates for easily verified transactions—when the card holder brings you the card, you swipe it and type in the secret code printed on the card—and another, significantly higher rate if you take the card info over the phone or get careless while typing the cardholder's information into your computer instead of using the machine. There are also per-transaction fees, minimum fees, setup fees, "because we are the bank and we say so fees." Shop, look, and listen.

Again, several unusual sources are worth considering, including Sam's Club and Costco. Your local banker might or might not be helpful too. If you are using auction management software—ándale, for example—make sure you get the correct card processing (verification) service. VeriSign and Authorize.net are the best known. There are others, but they don't all work universally. Start with the software company, then pick your verification service, and then hunt for compatible merchant banks with the best rates.

Now, about those card machines and employees stealing from you. Card machines do not require you to tie a refund to a specific sales transaction. So, retail employees and their partners in crime are tempted to do things like this: The employee's significant other walks in when things are quiet, and the employee takes his or her card, swipes it through your machine, and issues a credit for a purchase that was never made. Scary, huh?

The best way to avoid this is to not have a machine, and do all of your refunding through the computer, using a "terminal" program provided by VeriSign or Authorize.net or whomever. These require employees to at least reference the "selling side" of the transaction.

Other Business Accounts

If you aren't suffering terminal writer's cramp by now, sign up for other business accounts, such as those offering an affordable line of credit. See if you can find a shipping supply vendor who will offer you discounted prices on boxes and peanuts in exchange for a long-term loyalty promise. Sign up for annual contracts for XM or Sirius satellite radio feeds if that's how you plan to get your tunes. Will you be cleaning your own windows or buying that service too? Shop around. Sign them up, remembering to keep it simple and as cheap as possible without being unprofessional.

You will also need postage and shipping accounts, but they are discussed in Chapter 27, "Packing and Shipping."

GETTING STARTED

Here's a summary checklist of things you'll need to at least consider doing as you start or expand your eBay business:

✓ Create a meaningful, memorable company name and eBay selling ID or IDs.

✓ Pick the desired type of business (sole proprietorship, LLC, and so on); execute the necessary papers.

✓ Draw up partnership agreements if you have partners or investors.

✓ Read, understand, modify, and sign franchise and territory agreements, if any.

✓ Arrange for all necessary business licenses.

✓ Understand and implement sales tax collection procedures, licenses, and so on.

✓ Make sure any specialized local permits are obtained, such as a consignment store license.

✓ Open one or more business bank accounts and a business PayPal account.

✓ Consider merchant accounts for credit card processing. Be sure they are compatible with any auction management tools or services you plan to use.

✓ Set up other business service accounts (box supplier, cleaning services, and so on).

✓ Set up postage and shipping accounts compatible with any auction management tools you will employ.

In this Chapter

BOSS Glass Door OVEN

Makes Baking Quick and Easy

While the Boss is baking crisp, brown and tempting dishes, you can be preparing the rest of the dinner. No need to worry— merely glance in thru the glass door to

CHAPTER 8

COMPUTERS, OFFICE EQUIPMENT, AND MORE

You'll need hardware to be a PowerSeller on eBay—everything from computers to printers to phones, shipping scales, cameras, lights, and much more. Here's what it takes to trick out your workspace.

COMPUTERS

The backbone of any online business is its computer system. eBay does most of the heavy lifting for you with its acres of servers and related hardware. But you will need one or more computers yourself. What you buy will vary with the size and scope of your business. Let's take a look.

Which Platform?

Okay, let's get this one out of the way first. I use Windows XP machines but love Macintosh computers, and envy my friends who use nothing else. If you plan to only use web-based selling tools such as My eBay or ándale online, you can probably survive using Apple computers. But if you want to use fancier auction tools such as ándale Lister Pro or eBay's Turbo Lister, or most of the other mainstream selling and inventory management tools, you are going to need to get in bed with Mr. Gates. Even if you never use specialized software and employ only web-based tools, browser compatibility issues raise their ugly heads from time to time when using a Mac.

Profitable eBay selling requires productivity and the ability to quickly evolve with the industry. Your safest alternative, albeit perhaps the most frustrating and boring, is Windows.

Which Machines?

If you will work by yourself at home, a laptop computer makes the most sense. This way if you write your listings in the den and do your shipping in the garage you can use the same computer both places with a minimum of fuss. By adding the right wireless card and service, discussed later in this chapter, you can use that same laptop to do research in the field, as well.

As the business grows and you hire additional workers, you will probably need more computers. Those computers will need to be networked, and the data thereon will need to be shared in an organized, secure way.

It's going to be cheaper to purchase "traditional" processors with desktop displays rather than laptops, at least for the second and subsequent "everyday" machines you will use for shipping, photo editing, listing, and so on.

Virtually all of today's Pentium class computers come with big enough hard drives for all but the bulkiest photo libraries, and remember, except for inventory items that you sell over and over, auction images have a very short half-life. A month after the auction ends you can easily delete, or at least archive, those old photos. Moreover, dirt-cheap USB2 and FireWire external hard drives make disk storage upgrades quick and painless, should they become necessary.

> **Note**
>
> Here again, digging out that set of objectives you created in Chapter 1, "Ten Keys to Success," will help you pick the right computing resources and help you plan for growth.

> **Note**
>
> Processing horsepower does matter for at least some tasks. Photo editing can go much more quickly with the right processor, a fast graphics card, enough RAM, and a quick hard disk. It's my opinion that you need at least a Pentium class machine with 1GB of RAM to do photo editing, particularly if you will be doing a lot of it every day.

Your hardware choices might be affected by the auction processing software you choose. For example, if the package you sign up for requires a SQL Server (pronounced see-quill), be sure you buy at least one machine hefty enough to handle the task. As with photo editing, you want a high-end processor, as much RAM as you can afford, and at least one large fast hard disk or better yet, a disk array. Look to the software maker or your franchise company for the necessary computer specifications.

It's best to shop for the software first if you plan to run high-end seller software, particularly in a Trading Post setting. By the way, some franchisors will not only specify exactly what computer gear you need to work with their proprietary software, but they also will insist that you let them buy and set up the computers for you. So if you are thinking about investing in a franchise, don't buy your own computers without the franchisor's guidance.

Which computer manufacturer you choose is a little like deciding between Ford and Chevy these days. We all have our favorites and our horror stories about the "other guys." I tend to be a brand-name kinda computer buyer. My vendor of choice at the moment rhymes with hell, but there is any number of other solutions, including custom machines assembled by reliable local integrators. You want fast, sturdy, and reliable, whatever the source.

BROADBAND AND WIRELESS

I can't imagine being a PowerSeller without a quick, dependable broadband Internet connection. Many, if not most of you, will also want wireless options to use while doing field research.

> # Note
>
> If you get a knot in your stomach when someone says "USB," or just don't have the time or inclination to tinker with computers, consider purchasing yours from a local system integrator who will sell you preconfigured computers and provide paid after-sale support on a much more satisfying level than you'll get from a big chain seller. Expensive up-front, but this approach could save you money down the road.

Broadband connections simply speed up your Internet access. Files that would take minutes to send or receive over a dial-up connection appear almost instantly over broadband. Wireless connections let you cut the cord and give you Internet access on your laptop, PDA, or even a web-savvy cell phone anywhere you can receive a useable signal. Let's look at both technologies.

Broadband

Broadband comes in five basic flavors: DSL, cable, T1, microwave, and satellite. Again, I have been privy to more than one rowdy debate on the pros and cons of each technology, often with beer involved. There is no shortage of strong opinions. Here's mine.

I have seen perhaps a hundred PowerSeller workplaces, and my experience tells me this: Use cable if you can get it, DSL if there is no cable, microwave if it's available but cable or DSL are not, and a T1 line as a last resort (in which case you better hope you can share the expense with some other local businesses).

"What about satellite, Ron?" I love satellites. Great movies, swell music, satellites are perfect for choreographing a war or snapping the occasional picture of my house from way, way up. But satellites just don't work well for PowerSelling. First of all, most of the solutions have painfully slow upload capabilities and weird latency delays. Since you will be doing a lot of photo uploads or, more correctly, waiting forever while the satellite connection chokes on all those pixels, listing via satellite will take forever. Some software vendors (like ándale) either really dislike or flat-out refuse to support satellite connectivity. So just say "No" to satellite, at least for the present.

Note

Here's a handy site to help you find and evaluate broadband options in your community: www.dslreports.com.

Wireless

There are two types of wireless connectivity of interest to PowerSellers. The first is hotspot Wi-Fi technology. You can purchase monthly, annual, or "as-needed" Wi-Fi services from companies such as T-Mobile, Boingo, and Verizon. All you need to use these services is a laptop or Pocket PC with a Wi-Fi (802.11b) wireless electronics and, of course, proximity to hotspots providing Internet access. Many new computers come equipped with Wi-Fi hardware, and if yours didn't you can add it for less than $10!

To use this type of Wi-Fi service you need to be within range of compatible Wi-Fi hotspots hosted by a provider that has an arrangement with the service to which you have subscribed. So, for example, if you want to hang out at Starbucks and do research with your customers over a latte, you will need an account with T-Mobile. Sit down in an airport terminal and you might need a Boingo account, and so on. Wi-Fi, while very useful, can be frustrating if you move about from one part of town to the next. And it is unlikely that you will find a useable hotspot in someone's garage or at a flea market.

This is why after giving Wi-Fi a long trial I have switched to the cellular technology. Most cell phone companies offer these options now, as do some ISPs such as Earthlink. For example, Verizon sells under the brand names BroadbandAccess and NationalAccess. Figure 8.1 shows a PCMCIA card that plugs into your laptop

You will also need a new cell phone account (but not necessarily a new phone), and you will pay a monthly flat fee or a flat fee plus use-based charges for the connect time and the data that you sling.

Although you can purchase all this online it might be a better idea to visit a local wireless phone retail store and let them walk you through the pricing, installation, and testing processes.

This cellular-based coverage is much wider than today's Wi-Fi hotspot technology, and although the speed is not breakneck, it's good enough for everyday research, checking your eBay auctions, and so on. You could even limp along with this as your only PowerSeller connection for a day or two if your wired service failed.

FIGURE 8.1

Cellular-based wireless Internet access services offer nearly omnipresent coverage in most cities.

If you shop for used PCMCIA cellular interface cards on eBay, remember that while most of them come from one or two different manufacturers and even have the same model numbers, minor variations in the service provider's configuration of the cards can render them useless on a competitors' network. Your service provider might even refuse to help troubleshoot issues like this, as I found out the hard way. Bite the bullet. Pay a little more the first time.

Note

Some new cell phones can be used both for web browsing and as wireless modems. For example, I am currently using a PalmOne Treo 650 phone with "PdaNet" software that lets me plug my phone into my laptop's USB port and use the phone as a wireless modem. Zoom zoom!

NETWORKING

If you have more than two computers in your workspace you will almost certainly want to network them. Because of the sensitive nature of the data you will be handling (winners' credit card numbers, customers' addresses, your PayPal password, and so on), I recommend that you do not use wireless as the technology to interconnect your workplace computers.

I have watched a 14-year old break into a supposedly secure wireless connection in less than two hours. And even if your computer installer swears that every available security measure has been enabled on your wireless gear, the first time you or one of your employees make a tech support call, the help desk will probably walk you through disabling all those protections in the name of "narrowing things down," and then forget to walk you through putting the barriers back up. Wired networks are generally faster than wireless ones, too.

> **Note**
>
> Besides recommending that you not set up a wireless network in your PowerSeller workspace, I also suggest that you disable your laptop's wireless network cards when not using them out in the field for research.

What I do recommend is a router compatible with your broadband provider's modem, a high-speed switch, if you have more computers than your router supports, and CAT5 or faster Ethernet wiring for your entire workspace.

Routers simply allow you to connect your broadband modem to multiple computers. A *switch* interconnects your networked computers, printers, and other networked devices. A hardware *firewall* adds an extra layer of security to your local network making it harder, but not impossible, for hackers to access your systems. (You'll learn more about these in a moment.) Some broadband providers will give you (or sell you) a single device that does all of these things. Larger installations (such as Trading Posts) might need more complex hardware than most ISPs provide. When in doubt, pay for an expert opinion.

You probably do not need a wiring patch panel or wall jacks even though many network wiring vendors will encourage you to add them. *Patch panels* contain rows of connectors that let you interconnect wall jacks and other network devices in a virtually limitless fashion. Perfect for large enterprises, patch panels are overkill for all but the biggest Trading Posts.

Simply ask for "home runs" from each computer and other networked peripheral to a central location back near where the broadband service enters your workspace. Have the installer crimp plugs on both ends of each wire run. Plug the resulting network cables directly into your router or switch.

> **Caution**
>
> Systems that work perfectly without them are often made useless when a new firewall is introduced. These problems can usually be overcome with some tweaking and head scratching, but troubleshooting can be time-consuming and expensive.

Many consultants recommend standalone firewalls for commercial workplaces instead of, or in addition to, the ones built into most broadband modems today; and you should consider one. Firewalls help frustrate many outside "hacking" attempts, a fact of life with 24/7 connectivity. Do realize that these firewalls can be a source of frustration to you as well as the bad guy, however.

So, if you decide to add a firewall be prepared to deal with your broadband provider, the firewall maker's helpdesk, and perhaps the tech support folks at a software vendor or two. Again, if you have contracted with a good franchise it will handle these details for you, so don't just go out and buy the first firewall you see at your local Socket Circus store. Figure 8.2 shows a typical simple network without a separate firewall.

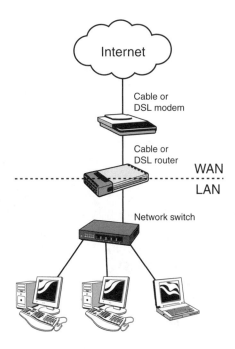

FIGURE 8.2
A simple wired network without a separate firewall.

If you decide to add a firewall it would be connected between the modem and the switch.

PRINTERS

PowerSellers do a lot of printing. We create packing lists and shipping labels, of course, but other things as well. You might want to print small quantities of brochures and coupons, for example, or

> # Note
>
> Plan for growth when doing the initial wiring, especially if building out raw space. And, if you will be using networked security cameras, printers, or credit card machines, be sure to wire for them as well.

employee handbooks, reports, accounting documents, accounts payable checks, customer check-in forms, inventory control tags, work schedules, and more. To do this properly and economically you will want a reasonably fast, economical printer. This pretty much rules out inkjet due to the high cost of supplies and relatively slow speed offered by most.

When comparison shopping for laser printers be sure you understand the supply costs. Some printers use technology that combines the drum, toner, and developer all in one cartridge. Other designs require you to purchase and replace these items separately. Be sure you understand the cost and yields of all the necessary supplies, and any other expendables such as fuser rollers, keeping in mind that manufacturers can be pretty optimistic about the yields you will get.

I also suggest that you purchase printers with readily available, local supply sources. Running out of toner or needing a replacement drum that comes from out of town can bring your business to a halt.

Color or black-and-white is another consideration. Color laser printers have become pretty affordable now, and they are handy for printing eye-catching business cards, brochures, coupons, and so on. Supplies can cost three to four times as much when you print in color. For example, my color laser printer's drum is consumed four times faster when I print in color. If you do purchase a color printer be

Tip

If you are running a Trading Post you might want two printers—one at the check-in counter and another near the shipping station. Besides preventing people from tripping over each other when it gets busy, this gives you backup if one printer fails.

sure the black toner can be replaced without throwing out unused color toner because in a PowerSeller setting the bulk of your printing will be in black.

Here are some more printer suggestions:

★ Purchase a printer with two paper trays. Load one tray with preprinted paper containing your terms and conditions. Print customer receipts on this T&C paper stock.

★ Purchase printers with Ethernet ports to simplify networking. (If you choose to share USB-connected printers instead, you will need to leave the "host" computers powered up.)

★ Some printers offer automatic two-sided printing as an option. This feature might make sense if you plan to print two-sided marketing materials or lengthy reports.

★ I advise against printer/fax/scanner combo devices in all but the smallest, most cramped PowerSeller operation. Besides the fact that these devices don't usually perform tasks such as printing or faxing as well as their standalone counterparts, most can do only one thing at a time. Even those $10,000 washing-machine-sized behemoths can't necessarily print from your computer while a fax is lumbering in over the phone line. Dumb.

★ Although many PowerSellers use small thermal label printers for shipping labels, the trend seems to be away from these devices. Most shipping software, including PayPal's latest offerings, can conveniently print combined shipping labels and packing lists on a single sheet of letter-sized paper. Fold the page in half, tuck it in an inexpensive clear plastic pouch, slap it on the box, and two jobs are done at once. It's very efficient. I have a thermal label printer, but when it dies it won't be replaced, or even missed.

★ Be sure the printer you purchase is compatible with any auction management software you intend to buy.

★ When opening a franchise, let the franchisor advise you about required and supported printers.

SCALES

You will need at least one shipping scale in your operation, and it needs to be able to accurately weigh both the lightest and the heaviest items you plan to sell on eBay. When working at home one scale will do. In a Trading Post you might want more than one scale—one near where the person writing listings sits and another in the shipping area.

Digital scales are recommended, and if your listing and shipping software support scales that interface directly with computers, this feature might be worth the extra expense. Some scales have USB connections that tell your computers how much items weigh. This can prevent typos and speed up throughput somewhat but will not be a huge labor saver, and again, your software and scale will need to be able to talk with each other for the extra investment to make any sense. Buy the software first.

CASH DRAWER?

If you run a Trading Post and decide you want to take cash payments for local pickups, advanced listing fees, and so on (something I strongly discourage for safety reasons), you might want to add an electronic cash drawer and software to the manager's computer. Do realize that cash in the store makes you vulnerable to walk-in holdups and employee pilferage.

DIGITAL CAMERAS

The choice of useable digital cameras is overwhelming. Models come and go overnight. Pixel counts grow and grow, seemingly without stop. Currently I am using, and love, a Nikon CoolPix 8800, but I have also worked successfully with much lower-priced and less fancy Canon PowerShot point and clicks. Here's a list of things I think you should look for in a camera:

★ A minimum of three megapixels

★ A good close-up capability for small objects and details

★ The biggest LCD display you can afford

★ An efficient way to move images from the camera to your computer, probably USB2

★ A way to run the camera on AC, or removable batteries, so you can recharge one set while using another

While little pocket cameras take mighty fine shots, often perfectly acceptable for eBay listings, sometimes bigger, bulkier cameras have an added "wow" factor that prospective customers notice. They say to themselves, "Wow. That's better than my digital camera. I bet it takes nicer pictures."

Nine times out of ten though, your real secret weapon will be good lighting.

PHOTO LIGHTING AND BACKGROUNDS

Photo quality is something that sets PowerSellers apart. Great photos can generate better bids. In this day of affordable digital photography there is no excuse for you to have anything less than catalog photo quality in every one of your listings.

The big trick is great lighting. You want to flood your items with soft, even, flattering light. The least expensive way to do this is with "umbrella" lights, but there are other options as well. For example, I like Cool-Lux Hollywood Soft Lights like the ones shown in Figure 8.3.

These are expensive if purchased from a photo dealer, but they do show up from time to time on eBay if you have time to wait, and in my opinion, are worth the money in the long run, even if purchased at retail prices.

Note

Although it is possible to use flash lighting instead of always-on incandescent lighting, I believe you will find it trickier to work with flash, and you will find yourself reshooting items due to unexpected glare in the photos. This is particularly true when shooting close-ups.

FIGURE 8.3
Cool-Lux Hollywood Soft Lights provide compact, flattering light.

Another way to bathe objects in soft light is to surround the items with a translucent tent, or dome. One popular manufacturer of these lighting accessories is Cloud Dome, Inc., located in Colorado. Figure 8.4 shows Cloud Dome's tent approach. You place the subject in the tent and shine light through the translucent tent material, creating soft, "cloudy day-like" lighting.

Alternatively, you can use a plastic dome with a hole cut out in the top and a bracket for your camera. Figure 8.5 shows an example of this approach, again from Cloud Dome, Inc.

As you can see by comparing Cloud Dome, Inc.'s "with" and "without" shots in Figures 8.6 and 8.7,

FIGURE 8.4
A typical tent-style light diffuser.

FIGURE 8.5
Cloud Dome, Inc.'s
dome lighting diffuser.

these diffusers can really perk up difficult-to-shoot items such as jewelry.

My preference is for the "tent" approach, or simply shooting with the diffuse light available from products like the Cool Lux lights, but domes do give you more control over extraneous light than either of the alternative solutions. The big disadvantages of domes, in my opinion, are that you must mount and dismount your camera; it's a little tricky to stage items under the globe; and globes work best with relatively small objects only. Nonetheless, domes are used enthusiastically by PowerSellers and crime scene investigators worldwide.

FIGURE 8.6
Without diffused lighting.

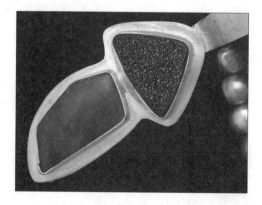

FIGURE 8.7
With diffused lighting.

Photo Backgrounds

Another trick is to create a seamless backdrop for your photos. This can simply be a large sheet of seamless paper or a more expensive commercial gadget. Figure 8.8 illustrates the concept.

FIGURE 8.8
A commercial seamless background.

This small tabletop unit from Cloud Dome, Inc. curves up in the back, making the background disappear in photographs. You can do something similar with an inexpensive pad of easel paper purchased from an office supply store—the kind used to making big notes in group discussions.

These are great for small objects, but as a Trading Assistant you will probably be photographing larger items that would dwarf most tabletop backgrounds. Clothing on a mannequin, guitars, and snowboards are all pretty big objects. The solution to shooting large items like this is to purchase photographer's background paper available at any local photography dealer who caters to the commercial crowd. Rolls can be four to eight feet wide or wider, and long enough to be the background for anything you can fit in your building. You can also purchase photographer's background rolls in a variety of colors, white and black being the most popular choices. Black works great for glassware and other sparkling objects. Owens Originals, Inc. (www.owens-originals.com) is one popular source for backgrounds and holders. Check local prices too; shipping can really add up on large items of this type.

Some folks use cloth curtains instead of paper as well, or purchase velvet cloth to use for backdrops. We'll look at this more closely in Chapter 23, "Photography."

SECURITY CAMERAS

Video security cameras serve several useful functions in retail settings. First, they discourage the walk-in criminal element. It's much easier to go down the block than to risk being videotaped doing evil deeds. Customers bringing you their stuff will be reassured to see that you have installed security gear to watch over their items. They will feel safer leaving things with you than with an unprotected competitor.

Cameras can help put most of your employees at ease too, especially the honest ones, since they understand that cameras do deter walk-in crime. Cameras will give dishonest employees something to think about, but employee dishonesty still does occur in areas under video surveillance.

Most systems have a host of options you will need to sort through. It is possible with many systems to sit at home by the pool and watch live video feeds from your store on your laptop. I can tell you first-hand this is incredibly boring video. Sending all that video out of the store over the Internet does add to the load on your broadband service, and can slow things noticeably under certain circumstances. So unless you really need to keep an eye on things remotely, don't overspend on fancy versions of this feature.

What you might want is a way to record video to disk under specific conditions—motion in the store after the alarm is set, motion in the neighborhood of the safe, and so on.

Tip

Video storage can be disk-intensive, so plan for this when computer shopping if you want it.

Many cameras let you record audio as well. This is a bad idea if you are recording during the workday, and might even be illegal under some circumstances. But if the cameras can be set to record audio when there is motion after hours, or when a panic button is hit, the feature might be useful.

Your "Video Surveillance In Progress" signs are at least as important as the cameras themselves. Post one at the front and back doors, one over the check-in counter, and so on. Oh, and if you are thinking about some of those $29.95 dummy cameras with the flashing lights, forget about it. Nobody will be fooled.

Alarm Systems

You need a decent alarm even if you are simply acting as a Trading Assistant in your home. Again, warning signs are probably as important as the electronics, but you should have a working alarm and use it. Your insurance company will give you a discount if you have an approved alarm system.

In retail spaces be sure your alarm has a door chime feature (for all doors), and enable it. You will also appreciate an alarm monitoring service with a human available to call you when the alarm goes off. That said, if there is any indication that there is movement in your store, do not be the first person to arrive at the scene. Leave that to the pros as well. It's only stuff in there.

CREDIT CARD MACHINES

I dislike in-store credit card machines, and I won't spend much more ink on them here. They create an enormous opportunity for employee fraud because it is possible to issue credits without tying them to specific transactions. But if you decide to get an in-store machine, be sure it is compatible with your merchant bank service provider, and consider getting one that connects to the Internet via your broadband connection rather than the phone. It will be quicker.

PHONES

I think that home PowerSellers need at least one separate line for conducting business. In a retail setting you will likely need two or even three lines to deal with outgoing, incoming, fax, and credit card machine traffic. Many of the inbound calls will fall into a handful of categories. "What are your hours?" "Where are you located?" "How does it work?" "I live in town. If I win an auction can I pick up the item in your store?" You and your staff will get very tired of answering these questions, and they will distract you from the online portions of your business, including answering emails along the same lines of questioning.

One solution is to record a long outgoing voicemail message that answers the common questions. A better is to use a message tree approach—"To hear our hours of operation and location, press one," and so on.

The remarkably low cost of Voice over IP (VoIP) phone systems from Vonage, Packet8, and the like make them very attractive, and worth considering. Do realize that VoIP is very bandwidth-intensive, however, and you had better have a smokin' broadband connection if you plan to talk on a couple of phones while sending up photos and receiving a fax.

Tip

Speaking of fax machines, VoIP does not always do a good job with fax transmission and reception, although the technology seems to be improving as I write this. Sometimes fax machines won't even connect if you are using VoIP. Ask vendors about faxing if this is important to you.

In this Chapter

- Auction Management Solutions
- Auction Management Solutions for Trading Assistants and Trading Posts
- Examples of Third-Party "Consignment" Solutions
- Proprietary Software
- Custom/DIY
- Photo Capturing
- Photo Editing
- Contacts

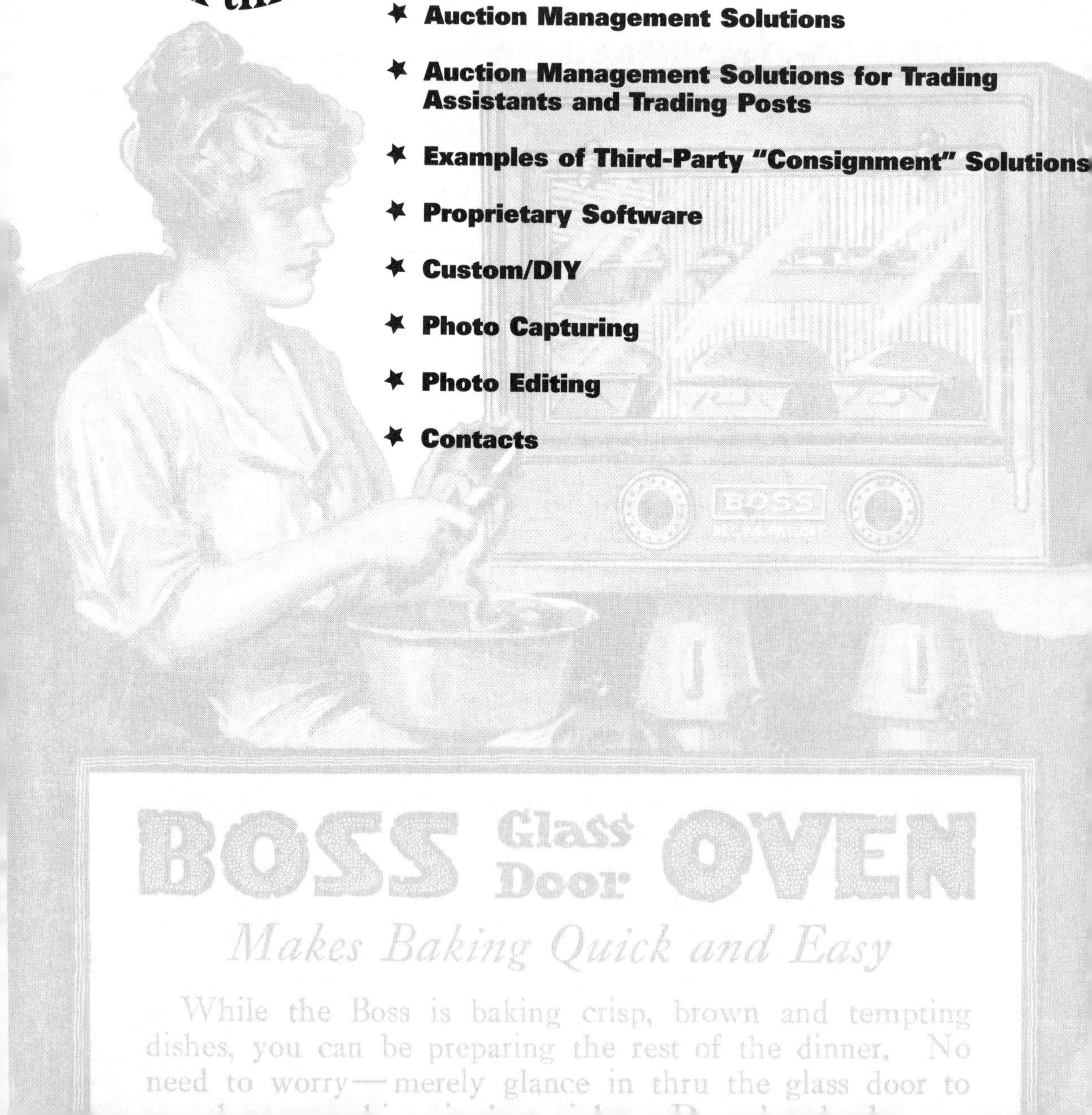

BOSS
BOSS Glass Door OVEN
Makes Baking Quick and Easy
While the Boss is baking crisp, brown and tempting dishes, you can be preparing the rest of the dinner. No need to worry—merely glance in thru the glass door to

CHAPTER 9

SOFTWARE

Software is at the heart of any e-commerce venture, and PowerSelling is no exception. Some of the software you'll use will be web-based; some of it will reside on your local computers.

There are a number of options for "pure" PowerSellers selling inventory they own. Those of you doing consignment work—Trading Assistants and owners of Trading Posts—have fewer specific products, although the options are increasing as Trading Posts explode all over the landscape, making the market more interesting for software developers. Let's take a look at some of today's choices. You will find contact information for the vendors at the end of this chapter.

AUCTION MANAGEMENT SOLUTIONS

It's pretty easy to juggle a dozen live auctions in your head, but when you have hundreds or even thousands of auctions and store items in various stages—waiting to be listed, listed, closed but not paid, ready to ship, and so on—you need help. Moreover, even a solo PowerSeller needs to interface with a number of entities—eBay, the item's winner, a payment processor (PayPal or whomever), shipping services, tax collectors, accountants—you get the idea.

If you are a Trading Assistant or run a Trading Post you also need to deal with customers, which adds another whole layer of information and complexity. Let's look at the simpler of the two problems first.

eBay Selling Manager Pro

eBay Selling Manager Pro is my current favorite solution to PowerSelling on eBay, particularly if you are not a Trading Assistant. It's simple, powerful, web-based, and integrated with your "My eBay" page (see Figure 9.1).

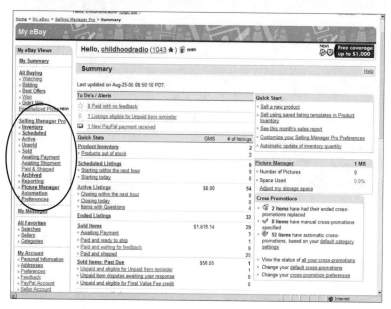

FIGURE 9.1

Selling Manager Pro is integrated with My eBay.

Loosely quoting from eBay's propaganda regarding this product, it

★ Helps you track your inventory and get alerts when you are out of stock

★ Provides listing statistics, including your products' success ratio and average selling price

★ Offers bulk features and automation for such tasks as email messaging, feedback management, and invoicing

★ Helps you understand your business thanks to monthly sales, cost, and fee reporting

★ Keeps an eye on problem bidders and helps you wrangle your nonpaying bidders, unshipped items, and more

★ Provides additional free listing templates

I have been using Selling Manager Pro for a while now, and am blown away by how nicely everything is integrated. You really can take care of most of your business with this tool. For example, Figure 9.2 shows a typical auction status screen. Note the little icons on the right.

You can tell at a glance who has checked out, who has and has not paid, which items have shipped, feedback status, and so on. Then if you click on a specific record link, you get details like the ones shown in Figure 9.3.

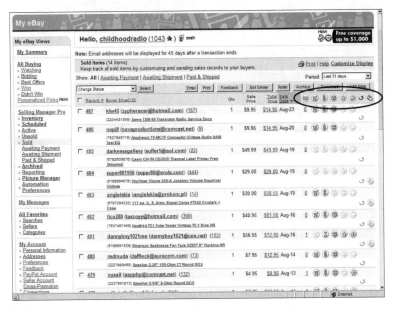

FIGURE 9.2

Selling Manager Pro shows the status of all auctions.

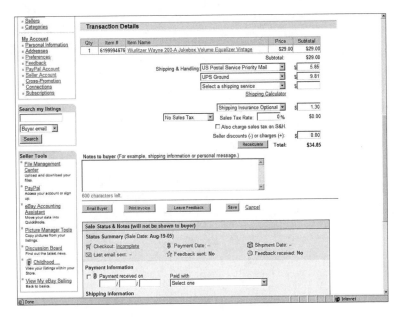

FIGURE 9.3

Item details in Selling Manager Pro.

This is where you can see details about the winner, shipping options, and much more. You can also print an invoice or manually record payment information if it was from a nonautomated source (a money order, for example). You can email from here, and so much more.

Figures 9.4 and 9.5 give you a glimpse into Selling Manager Pro's reporting features. You can see a roundup of final selling prices, the amount of shipping you charged, fees, and profitability if you take the time to manually enter cost data. There are even a few charts.

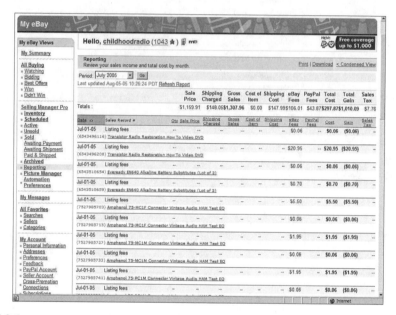

FIGURE 9.4

Selling Manager Pro reporting.

In my mind, one of the coolest things is how Selling Manager Pro lets you spot problems such as slow-paying bidders. For example, Figure 9.6 shows how you can filter the display to show only unpaid auctions.

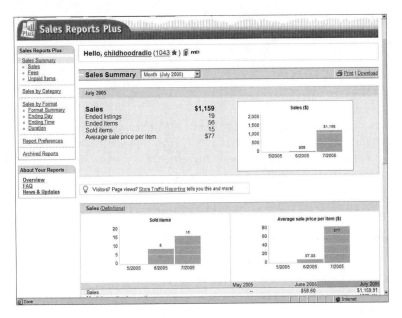

FIGURE 9.5
Selling Manager Pro Sales Graph.

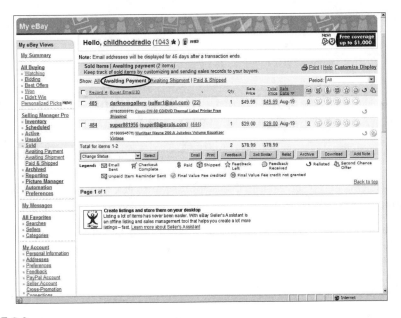

FIGURE 9.6
Selling Manager Pro helps spot problems such as unpaid auctions.

eBay Seller's Assistant (Basic and Pro)

eBay Seller's Assistant Pro is an older, desktop-based sales management solution that does many, but not all, of the things Selling Manager Pro accomplishes; and you can work mostly offline, but do need to remember to synchronize regularly via an Internet connection. Quoting eBay exactly this time, Seller Assistant Pro helps you

★ *Create professional listings: Easy to use HTML templates produce professionally formatted listings for auctions, fixed price, or Stores listings. Set up your payment terms, tax, shipping and any other information to be inserted into each listing automatically.*

★ *Track sales information: Track your bids received, emails, feedback, and items shipped.*

★ *Advanced Email Management: Create standard email messages for all your key customer correspondence.*

★ *Efficient bulk processing: List hundred of items at a time or easily relist groups of items. Leave all your feedback with the click of a button. Send email correspondence to all your buyers at once.*

★ *Easy listing process: Schedule your listings to start up to three weeks from today.*

★ *Advanced post-sale processing Print shipping labels and reports.*

Having used both, I'd vote for the online Selling Manager Pro solution. It will change the way you work. As Martha says, "It's a good thing."

AUCTION MANAGEMENT SOLUTIONS FOR TRADING ASSISTANTS AND TRADING POSTS

For the moment at least, Selling Manager Pro does not deal with the "customer side" of Trading Assistant and Trading Post operations. Although it is possible to export eBay sales data and import it into QuickBooks, where you can issue seller checks, it's not quite as automated as it could be, at least not yet.

A handful of software companies offer solutions to this problem and, of course, franchisors create their own proprietary solutions, which are often mandatory.

What to Look For

If you decide to use a third-party solution to auction management that facilitates seller payments, often referred to a *consignment* features, here are some shopping tips:

★ Be sure you understand the total costs. Some vendors charge a flat fee, others monthly fees, and some even want a percentage of your sales!

★ Check references, including some not given to you by the vendor if you can find them. (You can often spot additional customers by looking for the software vendor's logo at the bottom of auction listings.) Ask users if they are happy. Is support quick and helpful? Does the vendor keep up with eBay's evolution? For example, when a category's Item Specifics change, can the vendor keep up? If web-based, is the system responsive enough, even during busy times? What's the uptime like? Would they choose this solution again?

★ How much of what you see in marketing materials and demos is final code, and how much of it is only planned or in beta?

★ Does the solution support all the venues and sales types and eBay features you plan to use, such as eBay stores, non-eBay venues, retail walk-in, and so on? For example, don't assume that because a tool can run 7-day auctions it can run 10-day or "until sold" auctions. Ask.

★ Does the solution support all the shipping options you plan to use, such as USPS, Fed Ex, UPS, DHL, International carriers, insurance vendors, and so on?

★ Is this a seamless integration, or will you need to use other programs for photo editing, HTML editing, printing shipping labels, and so on? Get a list of compatible products, if possible.

★ How long has the vendor been around?

★ How easy and affordable is it to set up a trial?

EXAMPLES OF THIRD-PARTY "CONSIGNMENT" SOLUTIONS

As I mentioned earlier, this is a burgeoning field, still in its infancy. I'll provide brief descriptions of a few vendors' products here, and will add additional links to my web site (www.RonMansfield.com) as I discover and explore them.

Another great resource is eBay's Solutions Directory, found in Seller Central. Choose the Complete Selling Solutions link and search for "Consignment," or "Trading Assistant," or "Trading Post." You will get results similar to those shown in Figure 9.7.

Besides the brief descriptions, you will find user ratings, pricing information, and links to the solution providers' web sites.

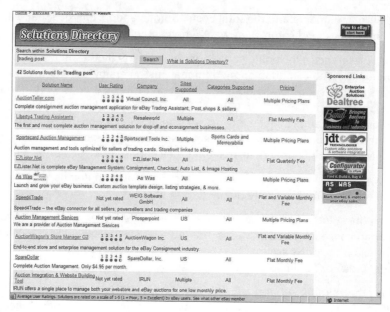

FIGURE 9.7
Searching for solutions in eBay's Selling Solutions neighborhood.

Although these user opinions can be helpful, dig deeper. As with all such web-based community gatherings, some of the information is old or doesn't pertain to your situation. It's not unheard of for competitors to leave less than glowing opinions, either.

AuctionTeller

AuctionTeller's makers claim they developed their consignment tool from scratch for the specific needs of eBay Trading Assistants and Trading Posts. They say it is "completely integrated with eBay and PayPal so all the auctions and consignments are automatically updated and moved for next stage such as Awaiting Payment, Items to Ship, Consignment Check to be printed," and so on.

It also allows sellers to communicate with the buyers, and consignors, (sellers)

"Through all stages, keeps track of all auctions and unsold items, created different consignment plans for sellers based on flat or sliding commissions (including minimum or upfront fees), generates detailed reports for each item and consignment, prints checks for partial or final amount of the consignment balance, etc."

There is access control, making it possible to manage availability of confidential information on a need-to-know basis, something I think is critical in a Trading Post environment, or in any operation with multiple employees.

The AuctionTeller folks say they are working on adding many more features and hope to remain a leader in consignment auction management software. AuctionTeller offers a three-week trial period to review features and manage test auctions and consignments. After that, you prepay per auction listing.

AuctionWagon

AuctionWagon claims its Store Manager G2 solution is the result of a year-long effort to solve the "overwhelming logistical demands of eBay consignment stores."

It also claims that Store Manager G2 is

> "An end-to-end solution, that prints contracts, barcode and readable inventory labels, handles sophisticated rate structures and discounts, offers copy spell checking, live photo editing, launch scheduling, shopping cart checkout, UPS, FedEx, and USPS shipping integration, QuickBooks accounting integration, seller payments, inventory management, auto re-listing, and buyer and seller communication, among other things."

Kyozou

Kyozou offers a variety of solutions designed to "quickly and easily consign products, issue drop forms for your consignors, and set up detailed and scalable commission plans." Kyozou will then print all your consignment reports, help you resolve payments to your consignors, and provide them with an easy interface through which to track their products.

Liberty4

Resaleworld offers a product called Liberty4 that it claims will allow you to "track consignors and their inventory, post auctions, manage orders, pay consignors what they are owed, and much, much more. "

Resaleworld says they have been developing consignment software for more than 12 years, have a client base of more than 5,000 bricks and mortar consignment stores worldwide, and is dedicated to delivering the very best consignment software possible.

Liberty runs on your desktop and does not require a constant Internet connection. It uses a local Microsoft SQL Server.

TAM

TAM's makers claim their software has been designed from the ground up to handle auctions, e-commerce, and retail (POS), and that one of their users runs a million dollar–plus operation with only three employees.

Features supported include automated question alerts, second chance offers, galleries, counters, cross-selling, direct tie-ins to your eBay store, make an offer, unlimited free image library storage, batch uploads, global changes in all specified auctions including HTML, easy relists, item specifics, and more.

TAM provides free tech support from its U.S.-based headquarters and charges a percentage of your auction revenue on a sliding scale from 0.25% to 1% based on your sales volume. Discounts are available for big customers.

PROPRIETARY SOFTWARE

If you are a franchisee, chances are your franchisor will provide proprietary software, and it might even require that you use it so that a portion of your auction proceeds will automatically flow back to the corporation. When researching franchise opportunities, be sure you understand the software requirements, pricing, and functionality. Before investing in a franchise, it's also a good idea to ask existing franchisees for their opinions about the software, reliability, support, and so on.

CUSTOM/DIY

Although it is of course possible to roll your own auction-related software, it will be expensive, time-consuming, and probably not worth doing unless you have envisioned a huge, specialized operation that can't be served by today's off-the-shelf solutions.

If you go that route, be sure to join eBay's Developers Program. Read more about it at http://developer.ebay.com/index_html. As you can see from Figure 9.8, eBay provides a number of technical tools and runs a lively community of friends and competitors.

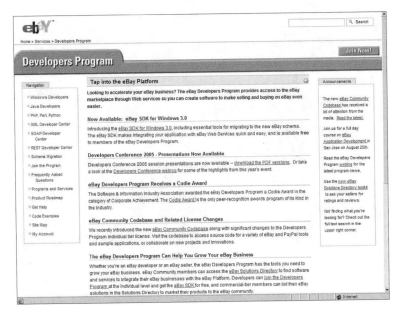

FIGURE 9.8
The tip of eBay's Developer Program iceberg.

PHOTO CAPTURING

There are several photo capturing and editing tools worth considering. They can speed up your photography workflow considerably and make photos look better. Perhaps the most intriguing category is camera remote control software (see Figure 9.9).

This software connects your camera directly to your computer and lets you control the camera from the computer. You can zoom, change color balance, change exposure options, even click the shutter release using your keyboard and mouse without jiggling the camera. It also lets you automatically name and dump photos directly onto the hard disk, saving an additional step. It's quite possible to go right from shooting to listing photos this way without separate editing steps.

Perhaps best of all you get to see really big previews of photos on your computer screen rather than those postage stamp–sized camera display images, so you can tell whether they are in focus. This can all but eliminate the need to reshoot.

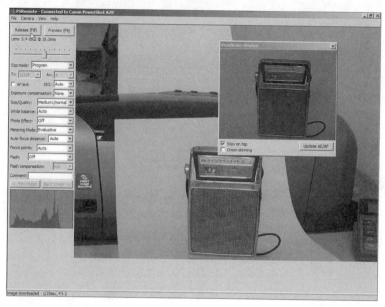

FIGURE 9.9
Remote camera control software.

The program shown in Figure 9.9 is PSRemote from Breeze Systems (www.breezesys.com). Breeze specializes in software for popular Canon cameras, but there are other makers of similar software for other brands. Nikon offers its own programs for selected models, for example.

Caution

Be sure you check for compatibility before purchasing software, or worse yet, buying a camera only to discover there is no software for it.

PHOTO EDITING

Sometimes photos can use a little tweaking. You need to crop out unwanted background objects, adjust the color balance, or perhaps enhance the sharpness. There might be a thousand or more tools available to do this. My favorite high-end tool is Adobe PhotoShop, which is probably overkill. Then there is its less fully featured, but still mighty, cousin Adobe PhotoShop Elements, and a lesser-known low-cost program called PhotoLightning, shown in Figure 9.10.

It's a pretty complete little package that lets you crop, resize, and correct images quite efficiently. You can even resize images in batches, add logos or other watermarks to your eBay listing photos, and much more. There's a "one-step-fix" future that does an impressive job of figuring how much color correction, brightness, contrast, and sharpening work is needed, and then makes the changes. It's a real bargain at less than $40 (www.PhotoLightning.com).

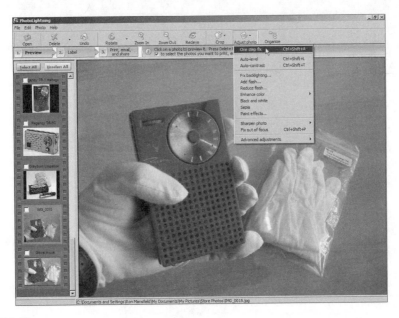

FIGURE 9.10
PhotoLightning: A photo editing bargain.

CONTACTS

Here is the contact information for companies and products mentioned in this chapter. I will update and add to the list on my web site at www.RonMansfield.com.

eBay: www.ebay.com

eBay Selling Manager Pro: http://pages.ebay.com/selling%5Fmanager%5Fpro/

eBay Selling Assistant (Basic and Pro): http://pages.ebay.com/sellers_assistant/

eBay's Developers' Program: http://developer.ebay.com/

Auction Teller: http://www.auctionteller.com/

Auction Wagon: http://www.auctionwagon.com/

Kyozou: http://www.kyozou.com/

Liberty4 (ResaleWorld): www.resaleworld.com

TAM: http://www.cdbsystems.com/

PSRemote (Breeze Systems): http://www.breezesys.com/

Nikon: www.nikon.com

Canon: www.canon.com

PhotoLightning: www.photolightning.com

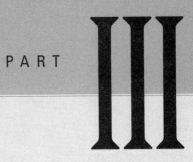

PART

FINE TUNING YOUR OPERATION

in this Part

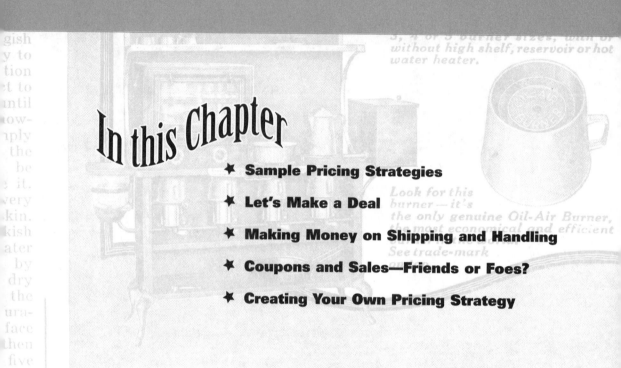

In this Chapter

CHAPTER 10

PRICING STRATEGIES

Successful businesses learn how to charge as much as possible for their products and services without losing too many desirable customers by overcharging. You can learn what to charge by trial and error, of course, but it's a good idea to do some local research first. This will help you figure out what works and doesn't in your neighborhood, and what you are up against.

Don't fall into the trap of meeting or beating the lowest price offer you find, however. Sometimes "discount price" businesses fail to thrive because their costs aren't met. They subscribe to that old school of thought "lose money on every sale, but make it up in volume." Predatory pricing might work to get people in the door, but not in the long run. (Remember the dot-com bust?)

SAMPLE PRICING STRATEGIES

Let's look at the pricing structures advertised by 10 Trading Assistants all located within five miles of each other. Keep in mind that these are all taken word for word from the listings, so any grammar and punctuation errors are found in the original listing:

Trading Assistant #1

I charge a flat fee of 33% of the final auction price, so you get two-thirds of the final selling price. For example, if an item sells for $300 you will get $200. NOTE: Unlike many Assistants I pay ALL the eBay listing fees, PayPal fees, etc. You pay nothing up-front and nothing if the item does not sell. When individual items sell for more than $2,000, and for large collections, inventories and estate sales we can make special reduced fee arrangements.

Trading Assistant #2

We charge a commission of 20–38% of the final sale price of the item, plus eBay fees. We accept items with a minimum eBay value of $75.

Trading Assistant #3

I pay all eBay listing, final value and PayPal fees. For auctions under $100.00 my commission is 30%. Over $100.00 my commission is 25%. RESERVE auctions require a deposit of the RESERVE auction fee. This fee is refunded if the item sells. Unsold auctions: I split the fees with you. You pay half, I pay half. (Normally less than a dollar on most items.)

Trading Assistant #4

Item value: $50–$1,000 30% of selling price, above $1,000 depends on the item. I prefer to sell items with an estimated value of no lower than $50.00. I have a $5.00 minimum fee.

Trading Assistant #5

Small dollar items are commissioned at 38% of the final sale price. Large dollar items are commissioned at a smaller percentage of the final sale price. There are no hidden eBay or PayPal fees, complicated formulas or special charges to you. Call for further details!

Trading Assistant #6

My rates are negotiable, but right now I charge 25% of whatever the item sells for, and the person I sell the item for pays the listing fees. I will handle the shipment of the item.

Trading Assistant #7

First, my clients reimburse my eBay fees including optional feature fees. I then charge $15 per item I list regardless of whether each item ultimately sells or not. I reserve the right not to list items I believe won't sell on eBay. I'm really in this more for the fun than the money, so if you have particularly interesting items to sell (particularly Computer Parts)...I'm the Trading Assistant for you!

Trading Assistant #8

I charge 40% of everything that I sell. There is no charge if the item doesn't sell. Basic listing fees, including gallery fees and picture fees are included in my fee, if you want extra features, I will charge for those. Items will be listed up to 3 times.

Trading Assistant #9

You are responsible for all eBay/PayPal fees related to each particular item. I am only asking for 25% of the final sale price of each sold item, which will include eBay/PayPal fees.

Trading Assistant #10

You will pay all sellers fees for listing and if sold you will be responsible for the ebay fees as well as any pay pal fees.My normal listing fee that i am charged is .70 cents,because I do all my own pitcures and html.And it will depend on the final sale price for my fees as well.Which I will explain in full before ever putting a item up for bid.The lower the final sale price the lower my fee,but I will analize to deterimine if it is worth my time and your money before ever being put up for bid.I do not want anyone to feel like they were cheated including me.

The "final value" percentage fee in my unscientific sample ranges from 20% to 40%, which is quite a spread. One seller (Trading Assistant #7), appears to charge a flat $15.00 fee, rain or shine, sold or not, with no final value percentage calculation.

But final value fees are only part of most Trading Assistants' pricing schemes. Plans range from very simple (Trading Assistant #1), to unintelligible (Trading Assistant #9 and #10). What does Trading Assistant #9 mean? The customer pays 25% plus eBay and PayPal fees, or does the 25% includes the PayPal and eBay fees?

Some sellers want all the eBay and PayPal fees paid for by their customers as separate charges, others build the fees into their percentage. We will take a closer look at all of these strategies, but before moving on, take another look at Trading Assistant #10's listing with your proofreader's glasses on. Come on folks! A big part of what Trading Assistants do is write advertising copy for their customers. Spelling, capitalization, punctuation, and grammar count. Make sure your promotional materials, and even your price sheets, reflect the quality of work you intend to do for your customers.

LET'S MAKE A DEAL

It's human nature. We almost all like to be able to predict outcomes and not be disappointed or feel misled. I can still remember my first disillusionment as a consumer even though it happened decades ago. I must have been seven, or maybe eight years old. I saw this huge submarine bathtub toy advertised on the front of a cereal box. The sub looked to be about six inches long and four inches tall. Heck, the photo took up half the front of the box. I sent off my lunch money and a box top then ran to the mailbox every day after school for weeks in anticipation. When the toy finally arrived it was about an inch long and perhaps half as tall. The picture on the box was "not to scale," as advertisers now need to say.

You don't want your customers to have experiences like that. You want them to know what to expect, get what they had hoped for, and come back for more. You begin this process by clearly explaining "the deal."

Suppose, for example, you are a seller using the plan that Trading Assistant #4 uses, and I bring you a jacket to sell. You tell me that, as a Trading Assistant, you "prefer

to sell items that sell for $50.00 or more," and that you "charge 30% of the final value fee, with a $5.00 minimum."

This 30% fee (and the $50.00 minimum value) sticks in my head. I walk out figuring some eBayer will bid fifty, maybe sixty bucks for my jacket and, after your 30%, I will receive a check for a minimum of $30.00 (60% of $50.00). If the jacket sells for $60.00 as I am secretly hoping it will, I'll get $36.00. Cool.

You put my Dale Earnhardt jacket up for auction, and you start it at $4.99 as we agreed. There are a lot of Earnhardt jackets up that week, many like mine. The jacket doesn't sell for $50.00, never mind the $60.00 I was hoping to get. There are only two bids and it sells for $5.49. I shrug and expect to get a check for about $3.30, which is 60% of the final selling price.

The mail comes. I rip open the envelope and find a check for—figured it out yet? Yup. I get a check for $0.49. You charged me the $5.00 minimum, so I really got charged a lot more than 30%, didn't I? As a Trading Assistant you not only lost money on this one, you also lost a customer.

I am not a big fan of minimum fees because, if an item won't sell for $50.00, or $100.00 we probably shouldn't be listing them for people as Trading Assistants. And if we screw up, we should pay the price, not our customers.

Who Pays for What?

For you to make a profit, your customers are going to need to pay your eBay and PayPal fees for you, one way or another. You can arrange this through a convoluted pricing structure that places vague demands on customers and leaves them wondering how much they will really get after the items sells. Fine print like this is very "old school." Today's consumers hate ambiguity and weasel words. They have much more sophisticated BS detectors than their parents and grandparents.

My recommendation is to be both up-front and uncomplicated where pricing is concerned. That's why I use a structure like the one used by Trading Assistant #1. In fact, that plan is my pricing structure. I wrote it.

What's a Fair Percentage?

This leads us back to determining a "fair" percentage. You need to be profitable, of course, so you will need to dust-off your spreadsheet to determine what it will cost you to sell items. In a small scale, carefully run operation with high average selling prices and good sell-through rates you can probably make a profit at 33% or less, even if you are covering the costs of basic auctions and payment fees out of your take. But if you are doing lots of reserve price auctions, or going crazy with optional listing features, or if you have franchise fees to pay, or are selling only a small percentage of what you list, flat fee pricing without charging customers for the extras will bite you in the butt.

Sliding Scales

It's tempting to offer deep discounts as the final ending price goes up. After all, it takes the same amount of effort to list and sell a $500.00 item as it does a $50.00 item, right?

True, but this thinking can severely erode your bottom line, and I'll bet there's not single customer who will walk away from you if you charge the same percentage across the board until the price gets pretty high—usually above $1,000 dollars or more.

People simply don't do sliding discount math in their heads. They don't say "Lemmie see, 30% of the first $500, that's $150.00, then 25% of the next $500.00, that's $125.00, so my total is $275.00." They might do the math at a flat 33% and conclude that your fee will be $330.00, and then either tell you your prices are too high, or agree to your terms. In this example a standard sliding discount would cut you out of $55.00 in revenue on each $1,000 auction, probably without customers even appreciating the "favor" you have done for them.

Standard and Platinum Pricing

Increasingly, Trading Assistants are saying to customers "Look. I'm the expert. I like to start items at low prices to attract bidders. We don't use reserves because they have been proven to stifle bidding. We don't use eBay's "high-end" listing options for most items. If you agree with that line of thinking I will list your item for a flat fee of X%. If you want me to start at what, in my expert opinion, is an excessively high opening price, or use reserves and so on, I will do that for you but it is going to cost you a non-refundable $19.95 listing fee." This has led rise to what I call "Standard and Platinum" pricing packages.

Variations on this abound. Some Trading Assistants only charge the fee if the item does not sell. The upside is you get to cover your costs on items that don't sell.

But the downsides are considerable when you think about them. Suppose you use a reserve, charge the customer $19.99 for it, and sell the item—but for thousands of dollars less than it would have without the reserve. Both you and the customer have lost money on this approach. Moreover, if the item doesn't sell the customer is not happy for two reasons—her item didn't sell, and she's out twenty bucks.

The jury is still out on "Platinum" pricing schemes, in my mind at least. I think they do more harm than good.

MAKING MONEY ON SHIPPING AND HANDLING

By now you know my ambivalence about handling fees and marked-up shipping costs. Making a $5.00 "handling profit" on each item you sell can add up if you sell a lot of items. It flows quickly to your bottom line and pushes some of the costs to the buyers' side of the equation, allowing you to perhaps streamline your customers' pricing while spreading around the costs of doing business.

But a lot of eBay buyers hate these markups, and not only avoid bidding on items with such markups, they often leave negative feedback when they accidentally encounter them. Some folks will even report you to eBay if they don't like your shipping fees.

Although eBay has policies against excessive shipping mark-ups, even numerous complaints will probably not result in eBay shutting you down, unless Trust and Safety thinks the high fees are designed to reduce eBay fees. For example, if a DVD sells for $24.95 on eBay and ships for $1.99, eBay gets $1.91 in fees. If the same DVD sells for $1.99 on eBay and you charge $24.95 for shipping and handling the winner pays you the same amount but eBay earns only $0.70 and feels cheated. This will get you in hot water.

Note

Chapter 18, "Customer Service," looks at better ways to overcome customers' demands for reserves and high starting prices.

Tip

Your pricing structure for selling cars will need to be different from the one you use for other items. It is unlikely that you can get a car owner to pay you 33% (or even 5%) of the selling price of a $30,000 car. You will most-likely want to have a flat up-front, non-refundable listing fee, and then perhaps a second fee if the car sells. Again, check your neighbors, but these fees are probably in the $200–$500 range for most cars and localities.

Tip

A great way to protect your margins while encouraging good customers to return is to create special pricing for them. Start a Platinum club, for example, where they get better prices, or perhaps bold listings or expedited listings, or some other little perk.

COUPONS AND SALES—FRIENDS OR FOES?

Coupons can be effective tools. They can be calls to action: "Bring in an item in the next 10 days and get half off." "Refer a friend, and your next auction's free." We will look at specific types of coupons and strategies in Chapter 14, "Public Relations," but for now remember this. Coupons can kill your profit.

If you get in the habit of handing out (or mailing out) discount coupons month after month after month they not only lose their impact, they will significantly lower your bottom line. You might as well just hand everybody a $5 bill when they bring you something to list. Coupons need to be special. They need to get something done that you want done: new customers, return visits, higher-end merchandise. And usually, everyday low prices are better than frequent discounts.

We have two grocery stores in our neighborhood. One has everyday low prices (that actually are low). The other store has a membership card, double coupon deals, and non-stop sales on selected items. You know what I am talking about. I personally enjoy low prices without fumbling for coupons or waiting for the best day to buy your favorite brand of wine, or whatever. How about you?

CREATING YOUR OWN PRICING STRATEGY

Based on what you've read in this chapter, I've created a quick checklist to follow when creating your own pricing strategy:

✓ Research other sellers' strategies and their results.

✓ Pick a strategy that meets your needs and apply it uniformly, while monitoring results and customer questions.

✓ Decide who pays for what (fees, listing upgrades, and so on) and make sure customers understand the impact of your decisions up front.

✓ Develop a separate pricing strategy for cars, RVs, and other big-ticket "titled" items.

✓ Consider discounts for special customers, but don't go overboard.

✓ Design coupons to accomplish specific tasks (build traffic, increase average selling price, and so on) but use them sparingly. It's not special if the customers see it every day.

In this Chapter

CHAPTER 11

AUCTION TYPES AND OPTIONS

The number of listing options available has increased steadily as eBay evolves. For example, you can easily add multiple photos or pay to make your auctions stand out when eBay browsers search specific categories or keywords. You can run traditional auctions or let eager shoppers purchase and pay for items immediately. Naturally, there are fees associated with these fancier auction types and options. Let's take a look.

ENHANCED LISTINGS

Enhancements to listings, such as boldface, subtitles, and so on, are designed to make your item stand out on computer screens when potential buyers visit eBay. You will see some examples of these enhancements in the illustrations that follow.

There are always additional listing fees for these enhancements, sometimes substantial ones. Adding enhancements to listings increases your costs regardless of whether the item sells. This makes it critical that you understand the fees, use features prudently, and make sure most of your items sell, particularly if you have paid for enhanced listings to describe them.

You also want to use features that make sense. For example, using eBay's $39.95 Home Page Featured fee probably does not make sense if you are selling a $19.95 DVD unless, of course, you have dozens, or perhaps thousands of them to sell.

Occasionally, eBay puts enhancements on sale (free bold listing days, for example), which is a good time to test their effectiveness. Ironically, because the whole point of enhanced listings is to make them stand out from everyone else's plain listings, if you test during the time eBay is promoting them your enhanced listings will stand out less because so many other sellers will be using the enhancements along with you. Put another way, if enhancements work for you even in these crowded conditions, they are probably worth using every day.

Some sellers use enhancements on just a handful of their auctions to get browsers' attention, and then cross-promote their non-enhanced listings from within the enhanced listing and their eBay store (see Chapter 12, " eBay Stores," for more on eBay stores).

Enhancement Fees

Table 11.1 contains a summary of eBay's charges for various enhancements at the time this book was written.

Note

Some categories and communities "respond" better to enhancements than others. If you are selling rare, desirable collectibles in a sleepy category you might not need to spend much money on listing enhancements to get noticed. Specialists will find you because of your great title and excellent description. In crowded categories, it's harder to stand out, and enhancements might be more effective.

TABLE 11.1   eBay Enhancements

Feature	Fee
Gallery	$0.35
Listing Designer	$0.10
Item Subtitle	$0.50
Bold	$1.00
Scheduled Listings	$0.10
10-Day Duration	$0.40
Border	$3.00
Highlight	$5.00
Featured Plus!	$19.95
Gallery Featured	$19.95
Home Page Featured	$39.95
Home Page 2 or more	$79.95

Because eBay does change its pricing sometimes, be sure to check for updates every now and then by simply doing a search for "eBay fees" using eBay's help search feature (see Figure 11.1).

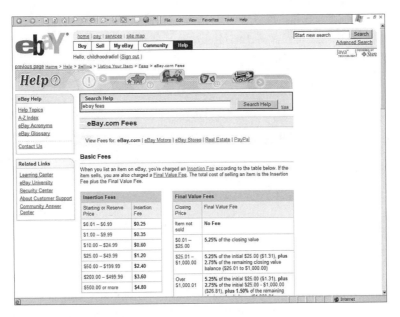

FIGURE 11.1
Find eBay's current fee structure via the Help feature.

Enhancement Options

The following sections give you details about the enhancements shown in Table 11.1.

Gallery

The *Gallery* feature puts a small "thumbnail" image above your listing title when searchers choose Picture Gallery view. Figure 11.2 shows an example of items with and without the Gallery feature. Always use the Gallery feature unless an item is expected to sell for a pitifully low price, in which case you should probably not be listing it. Figure 11.2 shows listings with and without the feature. Which would you look at first?

FIGURE 11.2
The gallery feature draws browsers in.

Notice also in Figure 11.2 that items with Gallery shots appear before items without, even if the "non-gallery" auctions have photos available within the listings. Not using Gallery can put your items way back on the last few search pages, particularly in crowded categories. My advice is to use gallery photos every time you list.

Listing Designer

The *Listing Designer* helps you add some decorative features to your listings and specify photo locations without knowing HTML. It's an option you will encounter while building your listing, as shown in Figure 11.3. You accomplish this by choosing one of eBay's predesigned themes and specifying the desired location of your photos. You can preview as you go, giving you some idea of how your chosen theme and photos look together.

As you can see in the preview generated for Figure 11.4, the results are decorative, but nowhere near as eye-catching as the results most PowerSellers obtain by creating and using their own templates.

The other disadvantage is that no matter which eBay template you choose, thousands of other sellers are using the same one. This waters down the visual impact of your listing and any branding you are trying to accomplish. (Branding is discussed in Chapter 13, "Marketing.") If you are going to be a serious PowerSeller you should either learn template design and do it yourself, or hire an expert.

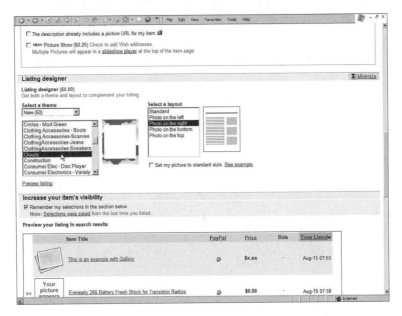

FIGURE 11.3

The Listing Designer adds borders and arranges photo locations.

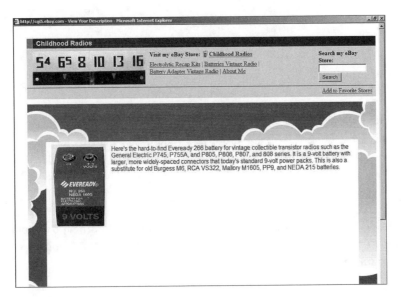

FIGURE 11.4

You can preview the effect of the Listing Designer as you work.

Bold Title

Bold title makes your auction's titles slightly darker in eBay search results lists. It costs $1 to use the Bold option. You can see an example in Figure 11.5.

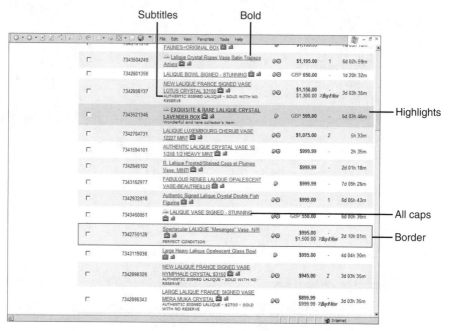

FIGURE 11.5
Bold, highlights, subtitles, borders, and all caps at work.

The auction titled "Lalique Crystal Ropes Vase Satin Trapeze Artists" at the top of the figure is in bold. Bold doesn't stand out very much, especially by itself on some computer monitors. It's not my favorite choice for getting attention on a cluttered screen.

Border

Items using the Border feature stand out a little more. Figure 11.5 includes a bordered item, titled "Spectacular LALIQUE 'Mesanges' Vase, N/R." Your eye is clearly drawn to this one.

Highlight

The Highlight option costs $5 and adds a colored band to help your listings stand out. It's also illustrated in Figure 11.5 with the item titled "EXQUISITE & RARE LALIQUE CRYSTAL LAVENDER BOX."

Subtitles

I like subtitles in crowded categories because they get you a little extra real estate, and they offer an opportunity to differentiate yourself from the rest of the pack. The seller offering the "NEW LALIQUE FRANCE SIGNED VASE LOTUS CRYSTAL $3100" in Figure 11.5 uses subtitles effectively for this purpose.

All Caps (IT'S FREE!)

Typing your titles in all capital letters is a cheap and often effective trick. It costs you nothing, and our eyes are naturally drawn to the somewhat bigger letters. The listing in Figure 11.5 titled "LALIQUE VASE SIGNED - STUNNING" doesn't get any points for best use of 55 available characters (the title should have been longer), but it does illustrate how all caps can stand out a bit from the crowd.

Combine Enhancements for More Impact

Finally, if you want to spend the money, you can combine these enhancements to make really eye-catching browser listings. The listing titled "EXQUISITE & RARE LALIQUE CRYSTAL LAVENDER BOX" combines all caps (free), highlight ($5), and subtitle ($0.50).

These options add $5.50 to the cost of the listing. Opting for a border costing $3 more might have been overkill because the listing does pop out on its own without it. With a border, the listing enhancement add-on costs would have been $8.50. If you do that a hundred times month your eBay bill will increase by $850, so again, use some restraint here.

Enhancements in List View Versus Gallery View

So far we have been discussing eBay's List View. The listing embellishments have a different impact in Picture Gallery view, as you can see in Figure 11.6. Border, for example, stands out more in Gallery view, while subtitles seem to disappear and highlights are a little more noticeable. That's my opinion, at least.

Because the illustrations in this book are black and white, you won't see the full effect of the listing enhancements on the printed page. Browse your competitor's listings on eBay and see which options they are choosing, how they look on your computer screen, and how this affects their success rate, if at all.

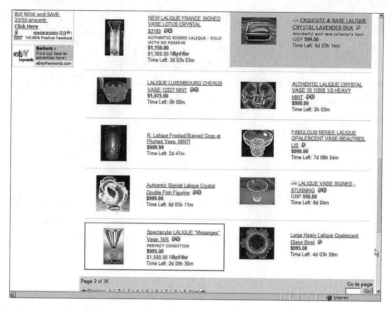

FIGURE 11.6
Features have different impacts in List View and Picture Gallery View.

FEATURED PLUS!

Search results can be organized by the listing end date, price, or other options that the viewer can choose. There are 50 results per page in List view, fewer in Picture Gallery view.

Your Featured Plus! item will appear at the top of the page it naturally falls on in the search results list. The Featured Plus! package costs $19.95 and combines several options to help your listing stand out in both category lists and search results. For example, your item will be shown prominently in the Featured Items section of its category list.

It will also appear in the regular, non-featured item list (Figure 11.7 shows an example). The key advantage of Featured Plus! is that you will always fall in the first few search screens, which is helpful in crowded categories. But because it is an expensive feature it should be used only with high-ticket items or to draw attention to a lot of related listings you have running at the same time.

Note

Featured Plus! is only available to sellers with a Feedback Rating of 10 +.

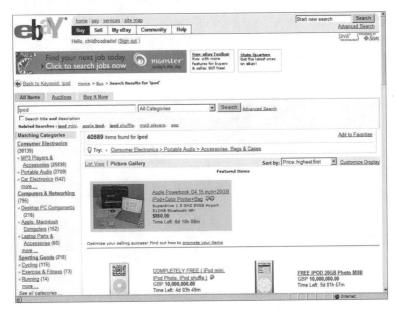

FIGURE 11.7
Featured Plus! puts you on the first few search pages, with an embellished appearance.

HOME PAGE FEATURED

The rather expensive Home Page Featured options give your listing a chance to rotate into a special display on eBay's home page. Your item is very likely to show up on the home page, although eBay does not guarantee that your item will be highlighted in this way. It could even show up in the middle of the night when nobody is shopping, so there is a bit of a risk. Also, the eBay home page is valuable real estate, and now is so cluttered that featured items almost disappear. That's them, on the bottom there by the little hand pointer. See them in Figure 11.8?

Your item will also have a chance to rotate into a special display on eBay's Buy Hub page. Finally, your item will also be listed in eBay's special Featured Items section.

Home Page Featured is available for $39.95 per listing (single quantity listings) or $79.95 per listing (quantity of two items or more in a single Multiple Item Listing).

Note

You need a feedback score of 10 + to use Home Page Featured.

FIGURE 11.8

The rotating featured auction list shown by the mouse pointer near the bottom of the illustration.

Home Page Featured cannot be used with the following:

★ Adult listings

★ Listings for services or the sale of information

★ Promotional or advertising listings

★ Listings for novelty items of questionable taste

★ Auction utility software

★ Listings that do not offer a genuine auction by eBay listing policies

★ Certain prohibited, questionable, and infringing items

PICTURE HOSTING AND FEATURES

Realizing that sellers are willing to pay for enhanced photos, eBay has added some to its bag of tricks and is continuing to add more as I write this book. Currently, they include the following:

★ Picture Manager

★ Picture Show (Slide Show)

★ Supersize Pictures.

Picture Manager

Picture Manager is eBay's picture hosting service. You upload photos to eBay's servers, and eBay pops them into your listings when viewers visit them. There are fees, of course.

If you add pictures one at a time to each listing your first picture on each listing is free. Additional pictures cost $0.15. If you sign up for a Picture Manager subscription you can upload pictures in bulk, eBay stores them indefinitely, and you can add them to multiple listings, if you choose. This is great for stores, or items you sell repeatedly. The introductory pricing is $9.99 for 50MB, $19.99 for 125MB, and $39.99 for 300MB. This might increase over time, so check before signing up.

Note

Although eBay's new picture hosting service is handy, and it integrates well with eBay's other picture features, it is not cheap, even at introductory prices. If you have even minimal web hosting experience, or know someone who can help, you can probably host your own photos for less money, although not as conveniently.

Picture Show

Adding Picture Show lets buyers "flip through" multiple Preview Pictures or play them in a slide show. When combined with Supersize, it lets buyers browse or run the slide show with Supersize versions of your pictures in the Picture Viewer.

Supersize

Adding Supersize lets buyers click the Preview Picture to view a larger version of your picture in a Picture Viewer. This enables fast initial listing downloads, and enables interested bidders to display pictures at sizes up to 800×800 pixels (800 pixels on the longest side). It costs $0.75 to add this feature to a listing, and you must use eBay's hosting service.

Tip

Again, PowerSellers have been doing things like this without eBay's help, and you can too, if you like. Even if you don't want to write the code yourself there are dozens of third-party photo hosting companies. Google "eBay picture hosting service" or visit my web site (www.RonMansfield.com) for links.

Although excellent pictures are a valuable listing tool, I fear that fancy photo display products can get in the way of folks—especially unsophisticated shoppers—seeing your photos. Sometimes simple is better, especially when trying to reach a broad, nontechnical audience.

TYPES OF AUCTIONS

Although many PowerSellers simply work with traditional auctions and add the embellishments we've just looked at, you should consider at least experimenting with eBay's growing list of new auction types and venues. As the eBay community grows so does its needs and preferences. These new auction types are eBay's response.

> **Tip**
>
> Picture Packs are combinations of the various eBay photo features sold at a discount. For example, $1.00 buys you Picture Show, Gallery, and Supersize for up to 6 pictures, while $1.50 gets you Picture Show, Gallery, and Supersize for up to 12 pictures.

Standard Auctions

Standard auctions are most PowerSellers' bread and butter. They can run from 1 to 10 days, start at any dollar amount you specify, and will always have a winner if at least one person bids. As you learned back in Chapter 4, "Budgeting, Forecasting, and Cash Flow," the starting and ending prices affect your eBay fees.

Buy It Now

Buy It Now (BIN) auctions can be used by sellers two different ways. In either case impatient shoppers are able to get an item without waiting for a specified auction ending time, or risk losing the item to another bidder.

When Buy It Now is added to a standard auction the BIN button disappears once anybody has made a bid or, in the case of a reserve auction, when the reserve price has been met. Sellers complain to eBay all the time about the disappearing BIN choice, but at least at the moment, eBay refuses to budge.

Another variation on BIN is to run fixed-priced listings as opposed to auctions. In this way the BIN

> **Note**
>
> The primary thing sellers dislike about disappearing BIN options is that it is not uncommon for bidders to make a lowball bid simply to remove the chance that someone else will come along and pay the BIN price before the auction ends. Because eBay charges for BIN, sellers feel they often do not get their money's worth out of the feature when used in auctions.

stays in play until the item sells or the listing ends. This is a great way to sell "commodity" items with a known value. BIN is the way eBay store items are sold, for example.

As security features, BIN purchasers must meet several criteria. They must have feedback greater than or equal to 0, or have a credit or debit card on file, or have had their ID verified. If they don't qualify and click the Buy It Now button, buyers will be asked to do one of these things to qualify.

BIN auctions also have an option some sellers find attractive. It is possible to force buyers to pay immediately via PayPal after clicking the BIN button. Unless you are selling in a fraud-rampant category, I suggest you avoid this feature because it precludes folks paying by check or money order, and can complicate credit card payments. There is also the remote but real chance that a winner can lose the item to someone else while trying to pay for it.

Dutch Auctions

A *Dutch auction*, also called a "multiple item auction," is one of the most confusing eBay features on the planet. They confound sellers, and especially new buyers. I dislike Dutch auctions, but here are the basics in case you decide to try them.

You create auctions offering two or more identical items. A single auction of this type can have multiple winners. So, for example, if you have five George Bush T-shirts you can list them all in one auction and up to five bidders can win one apiece. Or one bidder could win all five. Or one bidder could win two and another three. You get the picture.

When a bidder bids on a Dutch auction, she specifies the number of items desired and the price she is willing to pay per item. Bidders cannot use eBay's automatic bidding system to enter a maximum (or "proxy") bid.

Winning bidders will all pay a price equal to the lowest winning bid. Winning bids are selected in order of bid price per item. Using eBay's online help example, a bid for 5 shirts at $12 per shirt is ranked above a bid for 10 shirts at $11 per shirt. If two bids have the same price per item, the earlier bid is given priority.

Bidders cannot lower their "total bid value" (the bid price per item times the number of items on which they are bidding).

Here's another example from eBay: For a listing with 10 available items and two bidders: Bidder A bids for 8 items at $5 each, and bidder B bids for 3 items at $6 each. In this case, the lowest successful bid is $5. So the outcome of this listing is that bidder B wins 3 items at $5 each while bidder A wins 7 items at $5 each.

Winning bidders have the right to refuse partial quantities. This means that if they win some, but not all of the quantity they bid for, they don't have to buy any of them. In this example, bidder A bid on 8 items but won only 7 of them. Bidder A can refuse to complete the purchase because bidder A did not win the quantity he bid on.

Bids are displayed when you click on the "Bidders list" link. Bids that are not currently winning show their bid prices, but bids that are winning show the price that they would pay if the auction ended immediately. This means that, in the Bid History, all winning bids show the same price per unit—the lowest winning bid. To place a winning bid (a bid that wins at least some units), bidders need to exceed this price.

Got it? I didn't think so. Another way to sell five shirts is to post five listings. Besides simplifying things for bidders you can learn a lot by trying different categories, different starting prices, different ending times, and different listing features on each of the five auctions to see what works best.

Reserves

Reserves are usually bad for business. Buyers dislike them. Reserves usually lower final selling prices, and often result in unsuccessful auctions. They are mentioned here because they are a type of eBay auction worth considering for unusual, high-ticket items, if at all.

eBay Motors

Motors is more of a venue than an auction type. (eBay calls Motors a "specialty site.") It's where and how you sell vehicles and accessories. Figure 11.9 shows the home page of eBay Motors.

When starting a listing that falls into a motors-related category you will be automatically taken to Motors.

Real Estate

Selling real estate on eBay is possible, but not for the novice or faint of heart. If there isn't a book about selling land and condos and timeshares on eBay there should be one. It is clearly beyond the scope of this book. To get an idea about the rules, regulations, and techniques you'll need to master before selling real estate online, use eBay's help feature. Search for Real Estate, as shown in Figure 11.10.

FIGURE 11.9

eBay Motors.

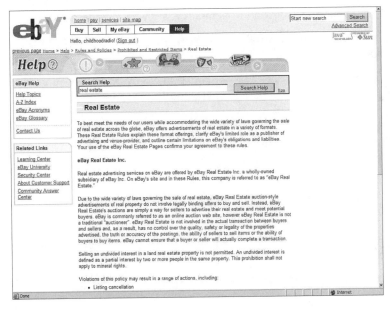

FIGURE 11.10

Real estate rules and restrictions.

Travel

Travel is another intriguing eBay market segment. Again, it is fraught with rules and regulations. Here, from eBay's Help feature, are some examples of who can and can't sell what.

Businesses that actually provide travel services, such as airlines, trains, hotels, resorts, and cruise ships, may list items such as their own gift certificates, airline tickets, lodging, cruises, or vacation packages. As providers of the actual travel service, they are often exempted from seller-of-travel laws and need not provide travel licensure information. However, they should clearly identify themselves in the listing as the actual provider of the travel services offered.

The restrictions are many, and they change. If you plan to sell travel or real estate–related items, you should most definitely check eBay's online help, and probably discuss your plans with your eBay PowerSeller rep before launching auctions.

TIPS AND TRICKS

★ Always use the Gallery feature.

★ Using ALL CAPS in titles costs nothing and grabs attention.

★ Forget about eBay's Listing Designer. Create your own templates.

★ Subtitles work best in crowded categories where they give your listing extra "real estate."

★ Experiment with borders and highlights on some of your auctions to see if they are effective in the categories where you sell the bulk of your items.

★ Save Featured listings for special items. They are expensive.

★ Although eBay's new picture hosting features are convenient and effective, explore alternatives, particularly if you are computer savvy and use a lot of photos.

★ If you use big photos, provide smaller thumbnails to speed auction browsing for buyers with slow connections.

★ If you have multiple identical items, sell some at auction and list others as Buy it Now items for folks in a hurry.

★ Avoid Dutch auctions (unless you are Dutch, of course).

★ Try to avoid reserve auctions.

★ Learn the rules before selling real estate or travel items.

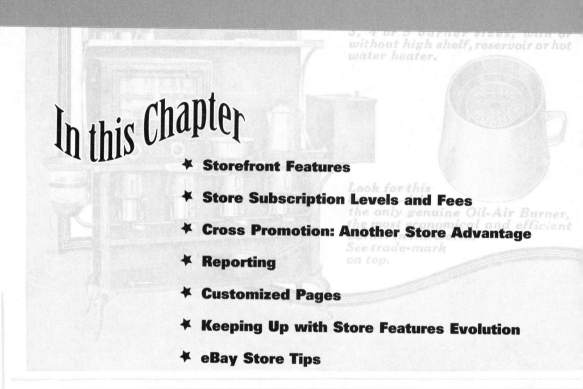

In this Chapter

CHAPTER 12

EBAY STORES

"Back in the day," eBay stores were these wimpy little things that nobody wanted. Like everything else on eBay, stores have evolved. To be a PowerSeller these days you probably need one. Besides reducing costs, showcasing your items, and helping you manage inventory, stores can be real traffic builders. Stores are no longer simply places to "park" Buy it Now inventory. Stores also showcase auctions and more, as you will see in a moment.

If you don't have a store you need to rethink this. If you do have a store you might want to retool it. Figure 12.1 shows my evolving store in Picture Gallery view.

This is a pretty typical, unembellished storefront using eBay's standard tools. As you will see in a moment, your storefront can look much fancier if you choose to spend some time and money. First, let's look at the basic features.

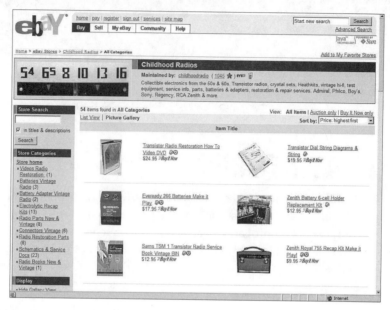

FIGURE 12.1
A typical store in Picture Gallery view.

STOREFRONT FEATURES

Starting at the top, the custom storefront header contains my logo and store name, (Childhood Radios). It contains a link to my feedback, and a link that lets shoppers contact me through eBay's "My Messages" feature. There's also a link to my "About Me" page. The little door next to "Me" in Figure 12.1 is a store door, and if you have a store, this door icon appears in various searches and in your listings along with the name of your store as a hyperlink. This tells shoppers that you have a store, and lets them click to visit it (see Figure 12.2).

Custom Listing Header

Figure 12.2 shows another important store feature called the *Custom Listing Header*. It contains my logo, a link to the store, a way to search across just the items I am selling (as opposed to eBay's entire universe), and links to any store categories where I have items listed. These headers appear in all your listings including auctions, but you must enable them. If you have a store, but have not created and enabled a Custom Listing Header, put down this book and do it now. It will drive people to your store and increase your sales, I promise. Here are the steps:

1. In My eBay, click Manage My Store.

2. Choose Listing Header.

3. Choose Show My Listing Header in My Listings.

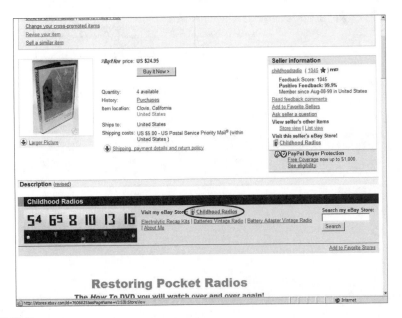

FIGURE 12.2
Store owners have links to their stores inserted automatically into each eBay listing.

Store Categories

You can arrange items by category in your store, and you get to pick the category names. Currently, eBay offers a maximum of 20 store categories, although the buzz at eBay Live! 2005 was that this might increase.

I have assigned names to all 20 categories, and you should too. Use the Categories feature in the Manage My Store feature found in My eBay to add this feature. Figure 12.3 shows part of that category management screen. Notice that you can specify the order in which categories appear.

> ## Note
>
> Even if you create 20 store categories for your store, only categories containing active items (store inventory, auctions, BIN listings, and so on) show up as links in your store. You should always have items in all categories, although I didn't when I wrote this. As soon as I finish this book I'll get my store whipped into shape. Promise!

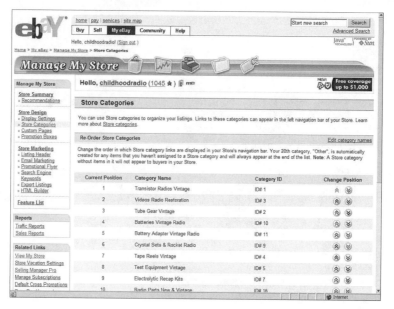

FIGURE 12.3

Some of my 20 store categories.

Moreover, when creating listings—auctions, BIN, and so on—you must remember to specify at least one and as many as two store categories. This ensures that store visitors get to see your auction items organized by category in the store. For example, when I auction transistor radios I specify "Transistor Radio Vintage" as the store category, BIN batteries get set to "Batteries Vintage Radio" when I list them, and so on.

Tip

Store category names are indexed by search engines, and you should create them with this in mind. Unique, descriptive store categories will get you additional hits from Google, Yahoo!, and others.

STORE SUBSCRIPTION LEVELS AND FEES

Before looking at additional store features let's look at the store pricing structures offered by eBay when this book was written. You have a choice of three store subscription levels:

★ *Basic Store* ($15.95/month) is for lower-volume sellers.

★ *Featured Store* ($49.95/month) includes full product features; probably best for most PowerSellers.

★ *Anchor Store* ($499.95/month) includes increased marketing support, maximum exposure on eBay, and 24/7 tech support.

Of these, the Featured Store level is probably appropriate for most PowerSellers, especially as you start out.

Store Feature Level Comparison

Let's take a little closer look at the key features and which levels get you which features, as shown in Table 12.1.

TABLE 12.1   Key Features

Features Provided	Basic	Featured	Anchor
Additional Pages in your store	5 pages	10 pages	15 pages
Promotion boxes	Yes	Yes	Yes
Store inventory format	Yes	Yes	Yes
Vacation hold	Yes	Yes	Yes
Online sales management	Selling Manager	Selling Manager Pro	Selling Manager Pro
Promotion on eBay cross-promotions tools	Yes	Yes	Yes
Custom listing header	Yes	Yes	Yes
Free eBay keywords (see Chapter 14)		$30/month allotment	$100/month allotment
On eBay Increased Exposure		Yes	Yes
Off eBay store referral credit	Yes	Yes	Yes
Email marketing	100 emails/ month	1,000 emails/ month	4,000 emails/ month
Create collateral for your store	Yes	Yes	Yes
Sales reports plus	Yes	Advanced data	Advanced data
Traffic reports	Yes	Advanced data	Advanced data
Accounting assistant	Yes	Yes	Yes

TABLE 12.1 Continued

Features Provided	Basic	Featured	Anchor
Customer support 6 a.m. to 6 p.m. PST 6 a.m. to 6 p.m. PST	Mon. through Fri. Mon. through Fri. Dedicated 24 hour support		
Store price	$15.95	$49.95	$499.95

All three levels provide promotion boxes, the store inventory format (items organized by categories), vacation hold (great for solo sellers), a subscription to Selling Manager or Selling Manger Pro, and cheaper FV fees if shoppers come from non-eBay sites, discussed later.

The primary differences in the plans are the number of free eBay keywords you get, the number of free marketing emails you can send, and the depth of sales reporting. Anchor stores get 24/7 tech support while other levels can get answers from 6 a.m. to 6 p.m. PST.

Featured stores also let you minimize the size of the eBay header in your store. You can see the difference in Figure 12.4. Use the Display Settings page in Manage My Store to reach this option.

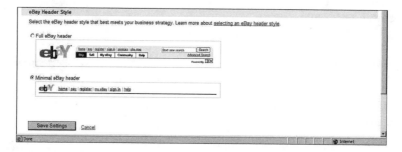

FIGURE 12.4
Featured stores can minimize the eBay store heading to get more space for themselves.

Store Listing and Final Value Fees

For the time being at least, store inventory creation is a bargain. Even with flap over price increases, store fees seem reasonable to me. And if you bring shoppers from outside eBay to your store, Final Value Fees can get dirt cheap. Have a look at Table 12.2.

TABLE 12.2 Insertion Fees

Duration	Insertion Fee	Surcharge	Total
30 days	$0.02	N/A	$0.02
60 days	$0.02	$0.02	$0.04
90 days	$0.02	$0.04	$0.06
120 days	$0.02	$0.06	$0.08
Good 'Til Cancelled	$0.02/30 days	N/A	$0.02/30 days

The insertion fee covers any quantity of items with a single listing, whether you list 1 or 1,000 of the same item. The insertion fees vary based on the duration of your listing, not on quantity. Good 'Til Cancelled listings will be charged the relevant fees every 30 days.

By now you should know that eBay charges sellers a percentage of the final selling price when an auction succeeds. Table 12.3 shows the rates at the time this book was written.

TABLE 12.3 Final Value Fees

Closing Price (in U.S. Dollars)	Final Value Fee
Item not sold	No Fee
$0.01–$25	8.00% of the closing price
$25.01–$1,000	8.00% of the initial $25 ($2), plus 5.00% of the remaining closing value balance ($25.01 to $1,000)
More than $1,000.01	8.00% of the initial $25 ($2), plus 5.00% of the initial $25.01–$1,000 ($48.75) plus 3.00% of the remaining closing value balance ($1,000.01–closing value)

To explore these options in more detail visit http://pages.ebay.com/storefronts/subscriptions.html

Saving FV Fees with Your Store

Store sellers can earn a store referral credit and save 75% off final value fees of store inventory listings when they drive traffic to their store. Go ahead, reread that sentence.

If a buyer comes to your store from outside eBay, and then buys something from your store, you save 75% off the eBay Final Value fees. This should be reason enough to consider setting up a private web site (like my ChildhoodRadios.com) and using it to "push" buyers to your eBay store.

CROSS PROMOTION: ANOTHER STORE ADVANTAGE

Still not convinced stores are worth it? If you have a store, eBay can automatically help you cross-promote your auction and store items by placing thumbnails and links to other items you are selling in every listing you launch. eBay's computers will pick related items for you or you can specify them.

In Figure 12.5, for example, eBay has inserted links to four similar connectors of different sizes at the bottom of a listing for a fifth connector type I sell. Current auctions also show up in these cross promotions, another good reason to add the proper store category when creating auction listings. This helps eBay pick the right items to highlight for each of your live listings.

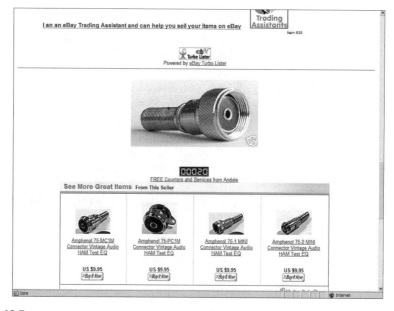

FIGURE 12.5
Store owners can have automatic cross promotions added to all listings.

REPORTING

Stores, and especially featured stores, come with an impressive array of reports designed to help you understand what sold and did not, where your visitors are coming from, and so much more. Figure 12.6 shows one small example of this.

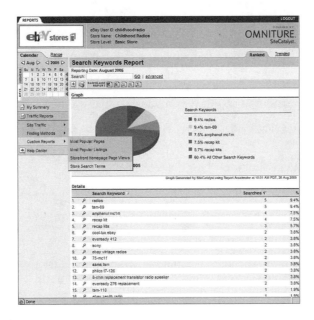

FIGURE 12.6
Reporting features can give you new insight into what's working and what's not.

CUSTOMIZED PAGES

You can add custom pages to your store. Use these to promote sale items, talk about your experience, and so on. To create and manage custom pages

1. Click the Manage My Store link in the left-hand navigation bar.

2. Click the Custom Pages link in the left-hand navigation bar.

3. Click the Create New Page link.

4. Step through the process of naming your page, selecting a layout, and adding any desired pictures and text.

You can also edit, hide, and delete pages here. Standard stores can have up to 5 pages, featured stores 10, and anchor stores 15.

KEEPING UP WITH STORE FEATURES EVOLUTION

Stores are evolving at an extremely quick pace these days. One way to keep up is to visit the store forums reached this way from the eBay home page: Home, Community, Discussion Boards, eBay Stores, Discussion.

EBAY STORE TIPS

Here's one last tidbit on stores to help you on your merry way:

★ Open a store if you don't already have one.

★ Turn on the custom listing header made possible by your store.

★ Choose store categories carefully. Think of them as aisles in a brick and mortar store.

★ Go for a featured store level for the extra features.

★ Drive buyers from private web sites to your store to reduce FV fees.

★ Learn to use the store reports. They can be quite informative.

★ Customize your store pages.

★ Consider using advanced web coding on your store pages to stand out from the crowd. (See http://stores.ebay.com/Period-Paper for an extreme example of this.)

MARKETING, PUBLIC RELATIONS, AND ADVERTISING

in this Part

8/38

In this Chapter

★ **Elements of a Marketing Plan**

★ **Creating a Marketing Plan "Rough Cut"**

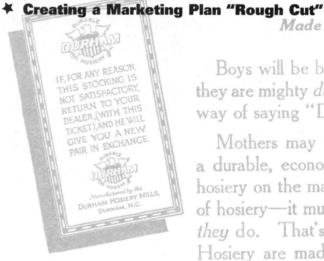

KIRT. No. 8168—Cut in
inches waist.

DRESS. 8138—Cut in
inches bust measure.

CHAPTER 13

MARKETING YOUR BUSINESS

People define marketing in many different ways. Some confuse it with advertising, which is an important part of any marketing effort, of course, but by no means the primary marketing task. I like to think of marketing as "planning and executing strategies that maximize your success rates with audiences you intentionally target."

To start, you should create a marketing plan. If you are working alone on a small business, or informally with a partner or two, you can scribble out a plan on a legal pad. If you have bigger dreams, you might want something more formal and flashy to be used with lenders and other investors.

ELEMENTS OF A MARKETING PLAN

In my mind, a marketing plan needs to answer these questions:

★ What is your target audience?

★ Where are these folks found?

★ What are the best ways to reach them?

★ What do they like and dislike?

★ What's the competition doing?

★ Where are your key opportunities?

★ What pricing strategies make the most sense?

★ What are your goals here (short-term and long)?

★ How much should you/can you spend on marketing?

Let's take a look at these elements in the context of eBay PowerSelling.

What Is Your Target Audience?

If you are a PowerSeller planning to sell only items from your own inventory, as opposed to being a Trading Assistant, the answer to the "audience" question might be pretty simple. Your audience is eBay shoppers. But even at this simple level you should sharpen the point a bit. Will you sell internationally or just in the states? Are you going to sell general merchandise to anybody who will view your listings, or are you going to specialize?

For example, do you want to specialize in vintage transistor radios? Perhaps you want to cast your specialist's net a little wider and sell all types of vintage electronics from the 1950s and 1960s. Or how about wider still? Maybe you should offer collectible electronics of all types. Which of these specialties do you know the most about? Is a narrow focus going to produce enough customers and revenue to meet your needs?

If you are a Trading Assistant you need to consider your other audience too. Besides reaching eBay buyers you will need to reach potential sellers, or sources of merchandise for you to sell. For a Trading Assistant, this is probably the more important of the two audiences. It will require localized efforts in your neighborhood (ads in papers, public relations campaigns, and so on), which brings us to the next step.

Where Are These Folks Found?

The next question you need to ask yourself is where are your customers located? If you are just selling, the answer is "on eBay in America," or perhaps all over the world. But as a Trading Assistant you need to discover where your customers will reside. For example, if you wanted to help old radio repair shops liquidate their vintage parts and service documents, these items might be scattered all over the country rather than just in your town.

What Are the Best Ways To Reach Out?

Reaching general eBay buyers by creating snappy auction titles is a little like a kid yelling for his dad at the other end of the ballpark. There are many dads in the audience, and a few will hear the youngster, but the chances of the right dad hearing are pretty slim.

As a seller you will probably want to drive buyers to your auctions from outside eBay. Today, this requires a website with some non-commercial educational content along with links to your auctions or eBay store. If you specialize you might also want to make alliances with specialty sites run by other enthusiasts, write articles for focused magazines, even appear on radio talk shows aimed at your buyers.

The best ways for Trading Assistants to reach local sellers might be by advertising in local newspapers, chamber of commerce newsletters, and so on. Even direct mail might work. In other words, you need to decide which folks you need to reach and what they will most likely respond to. Some avenues to explore include

★ Word of mouth

★ Web-based advertising and promotion

★ Direct mail (postcards and so on)

★ Printed brochures

★ Signs

★ Big visual tricks (car wraps, inflatables, human sign wavers, and so on)

★ Local radio and television advertising (surprisingly affordable in many markets)

★ Yellow Page and other directory advertising, where affordable and proven

★ Public speaking (at the local chamber of commerce, for example)

★ Fundraising projects

★ Sponsoring local sports teams

★ Freebees (pens with your logo, Post-It note pads, and so on)

★ Ads in local papers, printed programs for local school plays, and so on

What Do They Like and Dislike?

Your success with both buyers and sellers will be determined by how well you get to know them. Who are they? Are they bargain hunters or more interested in quality than price? As a Trading Assistant do you want to focus on people needing some quick cash or customers who like to trade up expensive items every year or two? Which group in your town is likely to become repeat customers?

Knowing this will alter your approach and the tools used to reach them. If you are smart, it will also change the look and feel of your image—the appearance of your eBay listings, business cards, signage, location, everything.

What's the Competition Doing?

Once you have defined your audience find out what your competition is doing. How are they positioned? What pricing and advertising strategies have they employed? To the extent you can learn it, what has been working for them?

Where Are Your Key Opportunities?

After you have defined an audience and understand that marketplace and the competition, you will hopefully be able to spot opportunities. Perhaps you can sell vintage radio enthusiasts specific restoration items or information found nowhere else. Or maybe you can strive to be the place people turn to for World War II vintage posters of women, or video game hacks. Find a niche or two that seems under-exploited, and then exploit the heck out of it before the competition follows you there.

Any business needs to change over time. One of the speakers at eBay Live 2005 told us about a million-dollar niche that competitors started nibbling away at almost as soon as he developed it. Things move quickly in cyberspace. Not only do you need to set out a timetable in your plan that encourages you to move quickly, you need a Plan B as well.

What Pricing Strategies Make the Most Sense?

Marketing plans need pricing strategies. For PowerSellers this can mean picking auction starting prices and listing options that work for your audience. If you sell gift items, for example, Buy it Now, gift wrapping, gift card insertion, and marked-up express shipping options might make sense because so many gift givers wait until the last minute to shop.

If your market niche is crowded with competitors already marking up shipping charges left and right, maybe you should find a way to include free shipping in your offerings. Put on your buyer's hat. What appeals to you?

I've already discussed some pricing strategies in Chapter 10, "Pricing Strategies," that you can use with customers if you are a Trading Assistant. What's your neighborhood like? What are other Trading Assistants charging for their services? Are they charging too little? Too much? Can you be more attractive by simplifying your fee structure? Make a plan. Write it down, or at least implement it consistently.

What Are Your Short- and Long-Term Goals?

We are back to goal setting again. Do you want to be the preeminent seller of transistor radios on eBay? Do you want to have the coolest Trading Post in the state? Would you like 50 Trading Posts statewide? Create your marketing plan with these goals in mind.

How Much Should You Spend on Marketing?

An important part of any marketing plan is a budget. How much can you afford to spend, and how much do you think it will cost to do a proper marketing job? The answers to those two questions might make you rethink the whole plan. It's not unusual for business to spend 20% or more of their gross income on marketing-related costs.

Importance of Branding

Think of Starbucks. What comes to mind? You can almost see the logo, right? The look of the store comes to mind. The light wood, the angles. The uniformed team members. Tall, Grande. Get the idea? They have successfully packaged a brand image and brainwashed us. You can do something similar on a smaller scale. The following sections outline some key elements.

Easy Recognition

You want to be recognized quickly. When people surf through a ton of auctions you want yours to stand out. That's why some sellers make their photo watermarks so

noticeable in their listings. It's not so much about discouraging image theft as it is about hitting you in the face with their logo time after time after time. They are using their eBay listings to build brand awareness. For example, I put the logo in Figure 13.1 together using Microsoft Word's clip art feature.

FIGURE 13.1
Logos need not be expensive. This one was created in Microsoft Word.

Consistent Look and Style

It's not enough to splash your logo all over town; you also want it to look the same everywhere. You want the "corporate" colors to look right on your business cards, brochures, letterhead, in listing templates, on signs, and so on. For example, Figure 13.2 shows a business card using the logo and envelope derived from Figure 13.1.

Reputation

The other key element to branding is reputation. You want your brand to be reassuring. You want people to see your auctions and think, "Oh yeah. Those guys! They shipped quickly. The item was just as described—better, maybe. And their emails were so nice."

FIGURE 13.2

Use your logo consistently.

This is why McDonalds employs secret shoppers. They ensure that the company's standards are being followed. When big companies talk about protecting their brand, what they are really saying is that their good reputation is important because it adds value to their company.

You can and should build and protect your brand, too. If you have multiple locations, besides the obvious use of consistent logos, adhering to standards, using similar listing templates, and so on, consider such simple ideas as setting up a separate selling account for items that might detract from your primary marketing effort and brand. The founder of Sharper Image wouldn't try to sell his garage sale items on the Sharper Image web site. It would water down the brand. You shouldn't do this to your brand, either.

CREATING A MARKETING PLAN "ROUGH CUT"

Take a few moments to jot down answers to the following questions, and then kick them around with your partners or advisors. You will be well on the way to developing a marketing plan.

Our target audience ranges in age from ____ to ____

They live within ____ miles of our location

They are most interested in:

    ____ Getting cash

    ____ Clearing clutter

    ____ Trading up to new or different items

The price of our services will be:

    ____ Very important to this audience

    ____ Somewhat important

    ____ Less important than quick, convenient service

Our biggest competitors will be (specify) _____

Our biggest competitor's strength is (specify) _____

Our biggest competitor's weakness is (specify) _____

The most intriguing niche market in our area is (specify) _____

We want to be known as a PowerSeller with a reputation for:

    ____ Low-priced service and a variety of items

    ____ A seller of mid- to high-priced items

    ____ A seller specializing in (specify) _____

    ____ A "high-end" seller with a "prestigious" reputation

The best ways to reach our target customers include:

    ____ Signs (where?) _____

    ____ Newspaper advertising (specify) _____

    ____ Other print ads (specify) _____

    ____ Local radio/TV (specify) _____

    ____ Web-based ads (specify) _____

    ____ Direct mail (specify) _____

    ____ Handouts (specify) _____

    ____ Sponsorships (specify) _____

    ____ Fundraisers (specify) _____

____ Free promo items (specify) _____

____ Giving informational talks/classes (specify) _____

____ Joining local organizations (specify) _____

We have about $ _____ to spend for our first 6 months of marketing

We expect to spend about $ _____ per month thereafter

We plan to design and produce our marketing materials:

____ In-house (specify) _____

____ Outside (specify) _____

____ Some of each (specify) _____

We:

____ Are happy with our current logo and image

____ Need to change a few things (specify) _____

____ Need to start from scratch (specify) _____

The next two chapters look at how public relations and advertising fit into your overall marketing plan. Let's forge ahead.

In this Chapter

CHAPTER 14

PUBLIC RELATIONS

Public relations, or PR, is often misunderstood. It's not simply "free advertising." It's a series of ongoing activities designed to build awareness of your brand and generate community goodwill for your business.

WHY GOOD PR IS SO CRITICAL

The cool thing about PR is that if you do it right other people will be singing your praises. Rather than telling everybody in town how cool your business is, a local television reporter will do it for you. PR often generates great third-party praise, which can be much more credible than advertising, something we all think of as self-serving. So, yes, it's potentially low cost, but it is much more than that.

What are some examples of great PR? Here are just a few:

★ Free "Just open" articles in your local newspapers

★ A television news story about spring cleaning with your Trading Assistant services featured

★ A fund-raising event where you get to introduce an entire church congregation, chamber of commerce membership, or all the parents in a local school to your business

★ A local radio station doing a remote broadcast from in front of your store

★ A collectibles newsletter article that you have written (or perhaps have paid someone to write with your help), mentioning your web site and eBay listings

★ An eBay "how-to" class with you as the instructor or guest lecturer

★ A picture of the mayor or other known celebrity cutting the ribbon in front of your new store

★ Praise in a popular blog or on a specialty web site

★ A sponsorship sign with your logo at local school sports venues

★ Your sponsorship logo on local school sports team uniforms, fundraising T-shirts, and so on

★ A well-attended grand opening party

DO IT YOURSELF OR HIRE A PRO?

If you have never done PR you might want to hire some local gunslingers, especially until your business becomes known well enough in town that you have your own entreé with the local television, radio, and print producers. You can learn quite a bit by watching a PR pro at work, and the good ones can easily earn their keep. It takes time to write good copy, buttonhole busy TV news producers, and so on. Paying someone to do this for you can make a lot of sense.

If your dream is small, however, and the budget smaller, you can, and should do PR yourself. It's not impossible.

WRITING A GOOD PRESS RELEASE

It's an old saw, but press releases should cover five things: What, why, when, where, and who. Keep releases simple, and one page long if at all possible. (Microsoft Word has some Press Release templates you can use, or create your own.)

Be sure the first sentence in your release is killer. One sentence is the attention span of a busy media person today. Draw them in. "Why?" is usually the best hook. The following are other tips to keep in mind:

★ The information must be newsworthy.

★ Start by focusing on the newsy aspect, and then mention yourself later.

★ Don't be wordy—stick to the facts.

★ Provide as much contact information as possible, and then make sure the contact information works.

★ Typos at this point will kill you.

★ Tell readers the name of the individual(s) to contact, relevant addresses, phone and fax numbers, and, of course, email and web addresses.

SPREADING THE NEWS

If you are using a PR pro he will already know techniques and resources for getting the word out, but if you are on your own here are some tips:

★ Find out which outlets will be interested in your story. (Read the paper, watch some television, cruise the Net.)

★ Find out which writer/editor/producer follows the topic.

★ Learn how each of these people likes to be reached. (Some will prefer email, others the phone, and some like good old snail mail.)

★ Start by phoning or emailing the various outlets and asking the receptionist how to best send releases to their desired targets.

★ Many outlets now have "How to Reach Us" information on their web sites. Read it!

★ Know the outlet before you talk to its employees. Don't embarrass yourself by not knowing the content, style, and point of view expressed by the outlet.

★ Keep notes in your contacts database using Outlook or whatever suits your style.

★ Begin by mailing and emailing, and then follow up with a phone call or two if you don't hear back.

★ Be sensitive to deadlines. If someone asks you to call back, ask when and make a note to follow up.

★ Keep records. Which releases worked? Which media outlets, editors, reporters, and producers liked or shunned you?

WHEN TO START

You want your public relations activities timed to match the situation. Obviously, some things need more advanced planning than others. If you are going to sponsor a school soccer team you will need to work through the details and make the commitment long before the season begins.

Sometimes PR can be "hot topic-driven." The next Harry Potter movie might be a good excuse for a local television station to do a piece on Harry Potter collectibles, for example. How cool would it be to have them come to your store or home to do it?

Reporters, especially in small town markets, love story ideas like this, and they are often surprisingly easy to reach by phone or email. For example, a nearby paper in my neighborhood serves a

Tip

If you need the local weekly news sources to cover your upcoming grand opening you'll want to delay those press releases until a few weeks before the event date. Sending releases too soon will guarantee that they will get tossed in the "round file." But if there are monthly or quarterly publications in town their deadlines will be farther out, and those reporters and editors need to learn about your opening before the dailies.

population of more than a million, and each reporter's articles end with the phrase [journalist's name] can be reached at [journalist's name]@[newspaper's name.com]. And ya know what? They can be reached that way, and they return email queries.

KEEP IT COMING

Don't think of PR as a one-time thing you do when you open your business. Your marketing plan should include some PR activities every month. And don't be discouraged if you miss an opportunity or if a competitor gets noticed first. Most media repeat news cycles, particularly seasonal topics. If you read a spring cleaning article featuring a competitor this year, make a note to pitch a similar idea next year, perhaps with a slightly different twist.

PROMOTE YOUR BRAND AS WELL

If you have developed a logo and other branding images, be sure to use them in your PR efforts. Add your logo to your signature in emails. Send along photos of your facility, truck, or other items with the logo in view. And of course, as shown in Figure 14.1, if you send printed releases and faxes, include your logo.

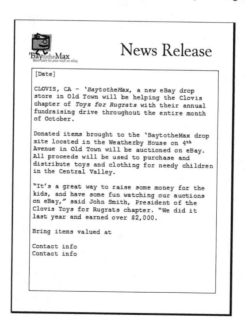

FIGURE 14.1

Use your logo in PR campaigns

WHY DO READERS CARE?

When trolling for PR, local PR especially, keep in mind that editors and reporters want to know what's in it for their readers and viewers. They know you want some free ink or airtime, you and hundreds of other business owners. What really makes a difference, and is likely to get a "go," is an idea that offers something helpful to their readers and viewers, while also making the editor or producer or journalist look good.

So while an article or television segment about selling on eBay will be nothing new, if you pitch something like "how to get the most money for your items on eBay" you might get some ink or air. You'll need to share the obvious tips, of course—clean most things except antiques, include owners manuals and accessories when selling electronics, take great photos, and so on—all the while working in the notion that these things take time and can be handed over to pros if the reader/viewer is too busy to do things right.

FUND-RAISERS

When done correctly, fund-raisers can be awesome PR tools, and a real benefit to your community. They can also be a source of income. But perhaps best of all, fund-raisers can be a source of loyal, repeat customers.

It works like this. You approach large, sympathetic local charities such as schools, children's hospitals, and so on, and offer to help with an eBay fundraiser. To do this credibly you will need to prepare some hand-out materials, perhaps draft a letter to parents or the charity's general membership, and so on. You will also need to demonstrate your ability to sell effectively on eBay, so you should wait until you have some representative auctions under your belt before approaching any large charities.

Offer to help educate the members of the organization. Offer to be on, or at least meet regularly with, the fund-raising committee. This is an important step because things can go wildly out of hand in your absence.

Carefully set realistic income expectations. The good news is that many of the candy drives and other traditional fundraising resources typically take 50% or more of the proceeds. Even if you offer your standard fee arrangement they will likely get more than with most other activities.

Tip

Work out a plan for getting donors letters for tax purposes. Who will write these, you or the charity? It's important to know what the charity expects in this regard. Some will hand out their own receipts to each donor, others will want you to do that, or at least provide them with a breakdown showing how much each donor's items sold for.

The bad news is that eBay fundraising drives almost always unearth tons of junk. And you know how I feel about junk. So you need to be brutally honest about how important it is to filter out the junk before it gets to you, and what you will do if it comes anyway. Say it over and over again. Put it in writing. The organizers and members need to understand that they should not be running a flea market or garage sale on eBay. Show them what sells best on eBay and what doesn't. Consider running a contest to see who can bring in the item or items that earn the most for the charity.

There are two schools of thought regarding how the items you will sell for your charities should physically move into your possession. One theory encourages fund-raisers to define a "donation day" where folks bring their items to the school or church or hospital parking lot where you triage it, and accept the acceptable while turning away the junk.

Charities love this because it's an "event." Folks get to see each other, they get to bond, check out each others' contributions, and basically have fun. The advantage to you is that you get to head off the junk before it gets to your location. You can also hand out informational pamphlets in the parking lot and perhaps coupons in hopes that folks will bring their "really good stuff" to you for private sale after the fund-raiser. That's okay, but not ideal.

The other disadvantage of this "donation day" approach is especially huge if you have a Trading Post and want people to see it. Many times when people walk into a well-run Trading Post for the first time they say (literally), "Wow! This is so cool!" You live for those moments. You have paid the landlord, and the sign guy, and maybe your fran-

> **Tip**
>
> If you do a "donation day" give some consideration to how all that stuff is going to get to your location at day's end. If it's just you and your Chevy Nova hatchback you will be in big trouble. Beg, borrow, or steal a truck or trucks, and some muscle to do the loading and unloading. Done right, a charity brings you a ton of stuff. Done at an event, it brings it all at once.

chisor a bundle to generate these moments. The best way to have more of them is to get more prospects into your store. So, it is probably a good idea for Trading Post owners to run fundraisers where folks bring their donations directly to the store.

By the way, especially for large fundraisers, it might be tempting to have the charity store the items for you while they are on auction, and you might be tempted to go to their storage room do the photography, and perhaps even the listing and shipping. I vote "No." There is a very good chance some of the things you sell will come up missing or damaged at auction's end.

You will be the recipient of negative feedback if this happens. So, if you don't have room in your own garage or store, plan on paying for a secure storage space for the event, or run the event over a longer time period in hopes that items will dribble into your possession.

BE CAREFUL ABOUT MENTIONING THE CHARITY'S NAME IN AUCTIONS

This is important! eBay has very strict guidelines about naming charities in auction listings. Put simply—don't do it and your life will be simple. Do it, and you need to do it right. They would prefer that you run charity auctions through their "eBay Giving Works" program. There are fee reductions and other benefits (read more by searching for "eBay Giving Works" on eBay's Help page).

But the process of getting charities recognized by the program can be time-consuming and, some would argue, daunting. You avoid this by simply not mentioning the charity in your auctions. Chances are nobody is going to bid more for an iPod just because the money is going to a charity, anyway.

> # Note
>
> A word about publicizing fundraising events is in order. These are a great opportunities to get three mentions in the press:
>
> ★ Children's Hospital to Fundraise on eBay Next Month
>
> ★ Local "Unload Your Stuff" Store Is Accepting Donated Goods for Children's Hospital This Week Only
>
> ★ Children's Hospital Has Record-Breaking Fundraiser on eBay!

Quoting eBay, here are the requirements for doing charity auctions outside the Giving Works program:

Sellers may only list items for charity without eBay Giving Works if they are soliciting on behalf of recognized tax-deductible charitable organizations (for example, 501(c)(3) status or equivalent with the IRS), and receive advance written consent for the solicitation from the benefiting nonprofit.

To verify you received permission, you must include a scanned copy of the consent in your listing. It must appear with the nonprofit's letterhead, signed by an officer and include the nonprofit's tax-deductibility status as well as your name or eBay User ID, dates of event/listings, and donation amount (percentage of the final sale price).

In this Chapter

CHAPTER 15

ADVERTISING

Advertising is the next logical step in any comprehensive marketing campaign. These days, to stand out you will need to use a variety of media from print to electronic to car wraps, and anything else you can imagine. The goal is to keep your business in peoples' minds. For PowerSellers this means that when people think of selling on eBay you want them to immediately think of you.

The amount you will spend on advertising will vary with your location and ambitions, but it is not unusual for a small retail store of any kind to spend more than $1,000 per month, sometimes substantially more. If you don't have a storefront you will still need to advertise. In fact, it will be more critical because folks won't discover you by simply driving past your house.

TIMING

I once stood with a friend staring out the front window of his "too quiet" retail store. He had his arms folded, obviously worried about his lack of customers. "As soon as business picks up a bit," he said, "I am going to do more advertising."

It doesn't work that way, of course. You need to advertise to get the customers to come. They will pay for your next round of advertising, and so forth. Advertising needs to be a steady drumbeat that can be heard throughout your kingdom. Think about your own experience as a consumer. How long after you first hear of something do you try it? Even if it sounds great, it takes a while to get organized, motivated, and driven to action.

As a PowerSeller you should probably spend more on advertising when the business is new, starting with some "coming soon" messages, but you should keep plenty of startup cash earmarked for the first three to six months of advertising, because it might take that long to get things rolling to the point where ads will pay for themselves, and you want to be advertising all the while, even as business picks up.

Stopping your ads when business is good is like stopping medication because it is working. The old (and I do mean old) saying goes, "The forgotten man today stopped advertising yesterday." Corniness and chauvinism aside, it's the truth.

TARGETING

Savvy advertisers know to place their messages where they will be seen by the desired audience. Tonight spend a while watching your local CBS television station. You will see ads for motorized wheelchairs, pharmaceuticals, and other things used by folks in their 50s, 60s, and later years. Switch to the WB and you will find fashions, amusements, and other products aimed at much younger consumers. Why? Because young people watch the programming on the WB network, and older folks watch CBS.

As a Trading Assistant, your audience probably watches the Home and Garden cable channels, the Discovery Channel, the History Channel, and so on. The cool thing about this is cable providers make it surprisingly affordable to reach local viewers of this very specialized programming.

Television is not the only place to target advertise, of course. It's done in print, on radio, via the Internet, and so on. In the next few sections we'll look at some options.

TRADITIONAL ADVERTISING

We've all grown up with traditional advertising, and it's not going away. If anything it's getting more forceful and competitive. Signs, print ads, handouts, direct mail pieces, and advertising over the airwaves are all commonplace. Internet advertising, a rarity slightly more than a decade ago, is now considered not only "traditional," but mandatory for many businesses.

Signs

Obviously, if you run a Trading Post you will have at least one sign, and perhaps many located on, in front of, and at the rear of your store. But you do not need a storefront to tap into the power of signs.

In smaller markets billboard advertising can be affordable enough for Trading Assistants to try. You can sponsor one of those "Adopt a Highway" signs in your neighborhood to promote your business. Car washes and other local businesses might have advertising kiosks where you can pay for placement. Many of these high-traffic signs even have business card holders so that viewers can take away a reminder. You can't even close the door to your stall in a public restroom these days without being confronted by this "traditional" form of advertising.

The type, size, and even style of signs you can employ are often regulated by local governments, so before plunking down a lot of money for a fancy "sandwich board" (or "A" frame) sign, or neon sign, or inflatable flying sign, make sure you can do it legally. Most cities enforce their sign ordinances, and some regulations can be pretty convoluted. You might be told how often (and when) each year you can put up a banner. Holiday signs might be restricted to specific date ranges...the list goes on. Chances are your city or town has sign ordinances, requires permits, and should be contacted before you make expensive mistakes.

Note

Hiring local sign makers and installers can reduce your chances of breaking the law, since hopefully these pros know your community's ins and outs. But remember, the responsibility is ultimately yours, so get those plans reviewed before you pay to have signs made and installed.

Brochures

Brochures are terrific advertising tools. They can get your whole concept across in a very small space. You can hand brochures to people, mail them, and enclose them with shipments.

There are a number of low-cost color brochure printing companies on the Internet, or if you have access to a color printer you can manufacture your own. This is a particularly good way to test and refine your materials before paying for large quantities.

Either pay to have a local professional develop your brochures or, if you have the time and inclination, try some yourself. Microsoft Word, Publisher, and other programs have templates for tri-fold brochures that work great as mailing pieces, counter takeaways, and handouts. Figure 15.1 shows just a few of the formatting possibilities available in Microsoft Publisher.

Caution

Everyone makes mistakes. Printed errors can be costly, embarrassing, and totally negate your efforts. A wrong phone number, address, or date is very expensive, if not impossible to undo once the ink dries. Demand a printed proof before going to press. Get as many people a possible to double and triple check it with you!

Consider developing multiple brochures—one for traditional Trading Assistant auctions, perhaps another for selling cars on eBay, and maybe a third business liquidation brochure.

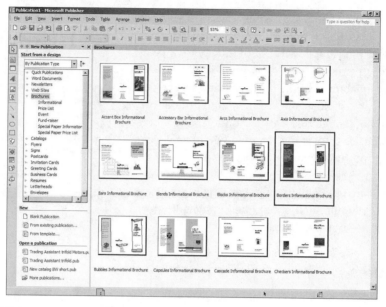

FIGURE 15.1
Publisher is a low-cost way to create advertising pieces.

Brochures should contain the following pieces of information:

★ What you do (sell people's stuff on eBay)

★ Your experience as a seller

★ How it works (customers bring in stuff or you visit them)

★ How long it takes to get paid

★ What it costs, who pays what, and when

★ What sells well on eBay, and any restrictions you have

★ How and when to contact you

Fact Sheets

Fact sheets are another great advertising tool. Besides being a great way to tell customers and prospects what service you provide and how much it will cost, you can use fact sheets to brag a little about your business. Rather than saying "We'll write a great auction description," consider saying "We'll use our combined 10-plus years of eBay experience to write a description that will get top dollar for your item."

Direct Mail

Direct mail, also known as junk mail, is an aging, relatively expensive but still effective way to reach your prospects. Direct mail pieces should always include a "call to action," which often includes a coupon. "Bring an item in by June 13th and we will [whatever]."

As a Trading Assistant you might want to broadly target everyone within 10 miles of your operation just to let them know that you sell for people on eBay. Or if you are a specialized Trading Assistant you might want to target all the owners of used SCUBA gear, or mom and pop camera stores that might not be selling used gear on eBay. A business-to-business direct mail campaign might include offers to "try liquidating an item for free any day this month," and so on.

Once you are established you can keep in touch with your customers via direct mail, or even opt-in email ads as well. Tell them "Thanks for your business." Or "Look how much we just got for a snowboard. Do you have one in your garage you would like to turn into cash?"

Traditional letters stuffed in envelopes are expensive ways to use direct mail. Postcards are almost certainly cheaper, and usually just as effective, especially if you use color postcards. The post office has a series of post card direct mail services. Get started at www.usps.com/directmail/welcome.htm. Figure 15.2 shows the welcome you will get.

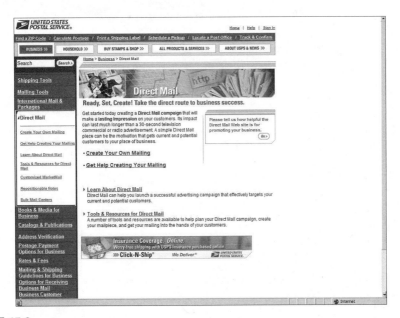

FIGURE 15.2
The U.S. post office provides some handy, albeit expensive, direct mail tools.

There are a slew of competing postcard printing and mailing services, some local, others national in scope. A few places to check on the Net include

- ★ www.iprint.com
- ★ www.ImageMediaPrint.com
- ★ www.modernpostcard.com
- ★ www.SmallBusinessPrinting.com

Note

Besides postcards, the post office provides templates for brochures and letters. It also has a variety of free instructional materials, booklets, and samples designed especially for small businesses. Check out its Small Business School at www.usps.com/smallbusinessschool.

PennySaver and Similar Mailings

Another direct mail option is the PennySaver and its clones. These broadly mailed collections of ads, coupons, and inserts always find their way immediately into my recycling bin, but many PowerSellers tell me they work effectively for them, particularly if coupons are included in the mailings.

You have numerous options when making a media buy of this type, perhaps the most important of which is territory. Be sure you work closely with your sales rep to focus on just the neighborhoods you want to reach. By the way, prices are often negotiable, so don't take the first quote as gospel. Figure 15.3 shows the national PennySaver web site. Use it to find your local sales rep.

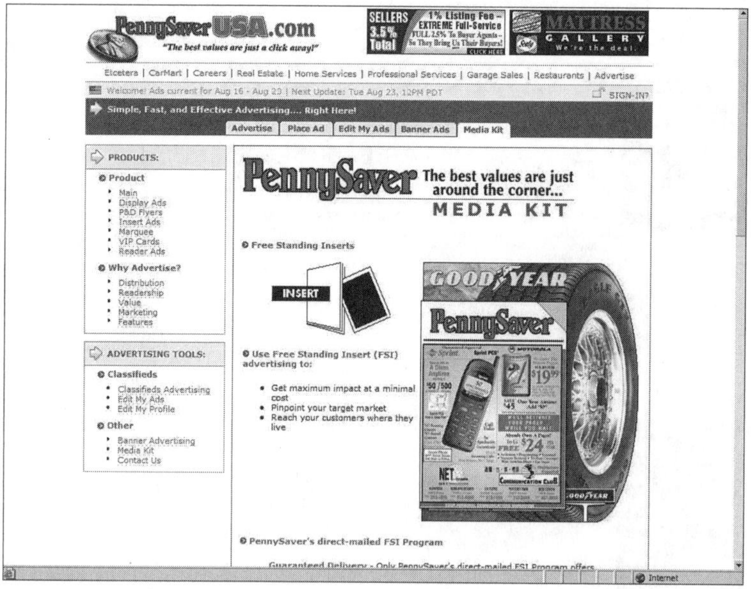

FIGURE 15.3

The PennySaver web site.

Newspaper Ads

Local newspaper advertising can be quite effective if you can afford it, and if the newspapers will let you do it. Display ads are best, of course, and a small ad that runs every week is probably going to be more effective than a one-time full-page splash that blows a gaping hole in your budget. If you are trolling for specialized stuff to resell such as collectibles, consider making regional or even national print advertising purchasers from folks like the ones illustrated in Figure 15.4.

Tip

No PennySaver in your neighborhood? I bet there's something similar. Look in your mailbox or wastebasket. Chances are somebody's mailing you ad packs like these. Give them a try.

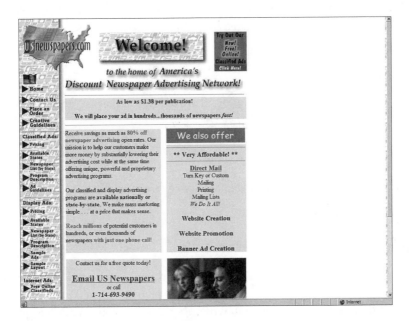

FIGURE 15.4
Discount advertising networks can place regional or national buys on your behalf.

They make bulk purchases of ad space and then resell it often for less than you could get it on your own. The good ones also take care of placement details, deadlines, and so on. Examples of consolidators like these can be found at

★ www.le-services.com

★ www.naps.cc

★ www.national-classifieds.com

★ www.nationwideclassifieds.com/usrpa

★ www.usnewspapers.com

Phonebooks

Phonebook display ads make the most sense if the local book has a specific category for eBay sellers. If yours doesn't the next best thing is to advertise in the consignment store section, or better yet skip the display ads altogether and stick with a listing in the white pages.

Speaking of the white pages, do not use the word "eBay" as part of your phonebook listing. eBay is not in the phonebook because eBay doesn't want to be bombarded by calls, especially from grumpy people. So when angry folks call directory assistance looking for eBay they are liable to find you instead:

"Directory assistance..."

"The number for eBay, please?"

"Sorry, no eBay. I do show a listing for "Sell Your Stuff on eBay" though. Would you like that number?"

"Sure."

A moment later you are getting an angry phone call, and it's not even regarding one of your auctions! Worst of all, you can talk for several minutes before figuring out the call is not about your auction.

Radio and Television

Especially in smaller markets, radio and television can be powerful, affordable advertising weapons. Check out your cable company's plans for reaching selected special-interest groups. It will even help you write, shoot, and produce your ads. Investigate radio spots, particularly on oldies and talk stations. Ask about becoming a guest on talk shows. Ask if the station has plans where you can be highlighted by the same radio host all the time.

If your ads will be rotated, as opposed to scheduled at a specific time, be sure you understand what this means. You don't want the bulk of your spots aired when nobody's paying attention, so it might make sense to pay a little more for guaranteed placement timeslots.

TRADE SHOWS AND EVENTS

Trade shows and local events are great ways to meet potential customers. Business expos in your town are worth at least visiting with a fistful of business-related brochures, and if the price is right you might want to consider having a booth there. The same advice goes for your local strawberry festival, or rodeo, or my favorite in my town, "Big Hat Days." Honest.

INTERNET ADVERTISING

Internet advertising takes a number of forms besides spam these days. You will probably want to use a combination of things including link trades, keyword buys, your own web site to funnel folks to your eBay items, and more. The following sections discuss some specific suggestions.

Trading Assistant Directory

Be sure your Trading Assistant directory page is up to date and effective. We discussed this earlier in the book. It should include your location, hours, specialties, pricing, and important terms and conditions.

Related Web Sites

Perhaps the most effective approach for many PowerSellers will be to target specific online communities, especially if you are selling (or trying to buy) specialized items. Where does your target audience hang out on the Internet? Google your fingers numb. Make notes. Trade links.

If there is no good place to hang out, create one. I developed a site called www.ChildhoodRadios.com visited by collectors of mid-century electronics. It has a message board, research material, and of course, links to my eBay auctions and store.

By the way, purchases made in your eBay store that come from "off-eBay" sites like this are billed at a discounted rate. Which is to say, if you direct visitors of a non-eBay site to your eBay store you will be billed less for purchases they make in the eBay store.

Keyword Advertising

eBay keyword advertising purchases are a fairly new concept, but well worth trying. The main site for this new adMarketplace feature can be reached at https://ebay.admarketplace.net.

The eBay keywords program gives you a way to place advertisements for your eBay Store or auctions at the top of eBay search listings. They appear as though in text boxes or banner ads. Figure 15.5 shows some examples.

FIGURE 15.5
Keyword ads at the top of a search screen.

Notice that even though I searched for iPod I got ads for football fantasy games and PC repair services. The keywords need not be directly related to what people are searching for. You can decide, for example, that iPod seekers love to pay fantasy football and have PCs that need to be fixed, and therefore pay to target them when they search for iPods.

adMarketplace is a pay-per-click system. The prices you pay to have your ad plopped on the top of peoples' search pages are determined by, what else? Prices are set by an auction.

You decide how much you are willing to pay per-click-per-keyword, and see what your competitors are currently bidding for the same keywords. You specify the maximum cost-per-click (CPC) you are willing to pay any time a user clicks on your ad. The ad is then ranked and rotated relative to what the maximum CPC bid is for others in the system. The higher your CPC bid, the higher your ad is ranked in the ad rotation for that keyword, and the higher the likelihood that your ad will be shown first to an eBay user. The ads are served to eBay users in response to a keyword search that contains one of your keywords or keyword phrases selected for your ad.

YOUR EBAY STORE CAN GENERATE SEARCH HITS

This is such an important concept that I am repeating it here. Google, Froogle, and similar search engines do not index eBay auctions because auctions don't last long enough for searchers to find them, and indexing them would result in billions of dead links. Most search engines, especially Froogle, index eBay store pages. So, a well-run store containing items that stick around for a while can get you a nice placement on search engines, virtually for free. Check out Figure 15.6 for an example.

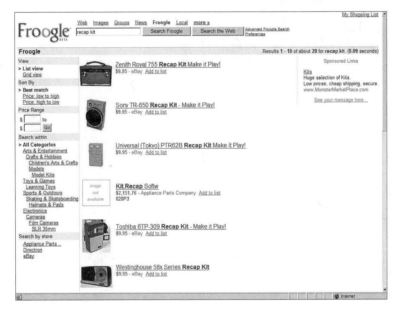

FIGURE 15.6

Store listings are indexed by search engines and can bring traffic to your auctions.

A Froogle search for "recap kits" fills the screen with items from my eBay store, and little else. The cost for this placement? My monthly store fee and a miniscule amount to list the items. After viewing my store listing, visitors will likely see my other stuff too, including active auctions.

YOUR ABOUT ME PAGE

Don't forget that your About Me should be an advertisement too. It should brag about your experience, reputation, special interests, and more. It can also show feedback if you like, and perhaps most important of all it's the only place on eBay you are permitted to place links leading away from eBay to a competing selling site, like your own e-commerce web site. Figure 15.7 shows my About Me page.

FIGURE 15.7
Your About Me page can advertise other sites as well as your eBay items.

NON-TRADITIONAL ADVERTISING

Non-traditional advertising can work well, or it can cheapen your image, so consider it but use it wisely. In the sections that follow are some examples.

Handbills

Twice I have been handed small pieces of paper advertising Trading Assistants, once by a guy on a skateboard and once by a young woman in a bikini. Handbills do work for local advertising, but they can also cause a mess and can harm your reputation.

I know one PowerSeller who plastered a whole parking lot with fliers. He paid kids to stick one under each of hundreds of cars' windshield wipers. Wind blew them off of the cars and onto the parking lot pavement. Then it rained. The cleanup was a nightmare, and expensive. His landlord charged him for the costs involved, which considerably exceeded the income from the campaign. If you use handbills make sure there are trash cans nearby. Then be sure to clean up after the folks who don't use them.

Car Wraps

Car wraps are the latest rage. There are dozens of companies that specialize in plastering advertising all over vehicles, turning them into movable signs. Everywhere you drive and park people will see your message. Some towns and landlords have regulations regarding how long, how often, and where you can park vehicles thus adorned, so you might first want to be sure you are not painting yourself into a corner by wrapping your car or delivery van.

Inflatables and Other Gimmicks

Want to launch a tethered balloon over your location? Feel like dressing up in a gorilla suit and waving an arrow in the direction of your store? Give it a try; just be sure it's legal in your town and not in violation of your lease.

MEASURING SUCCESS

No matter how you advertise, keep track of how it works. If you use coupons, code them. For web referrals, check your traffic statistics. Ask people how they heard about you. Live and learn.

CO-OP ADVERTISING REIMBURSEMENTS FROM EBAY

eBay will help offset certain advertising expenses you incur as a PowerSeller. This is described in more detail in Chapter 29, "eBay as a Partner," but the important information to take away here is be sure your ads meet eBay's co-op requirements, and get the necessary approvals. Learn more at www.ebaycoopads.com.

MAKE A ROUGH PLAN

Take some time to rough out a six-month advertising plan and budget. Kick it around with your associates and advisors.

> **Note**
>
> eBay is constantly tweaking its co-op advertising reimbursement policies. For example, with very little warning in September 2005 it stopped paying for eBay Store advertising. Be sure you check with the eBay co-op ad folks before spending a lot of money creating ads for which you hope to get co-op funds.

Element	Notes (When, Where, etc.)	Budget Amount
Signs		
Brochures		
Newspaper advertising		
Other print ads		
Local radio/TV		
Web-based ads		
Direct mail		
Handouts		
Sponsorships		
Free promo items		
Tradeshows		
Separate web site		
Keyword advertising		
Nontraditional (car wrap, and so on)		

GETTING DOWN TO BUSINESS

in this Part

In this Chapter

* **The Level Playing Field Dilemma**
* **What Sells Best on eBay**
* **But Will It Work?**
* **That Crazy Community of Ours**

Bug-a-boo

with and without D. D. T.
kills all 9 major pests

● Spray those pests away for good — with Bug-a-boo! This super-insect spray, with and without D.D.T.—far exceeds U. S. Government standards for an AA Grade insecticide. Even kills roaches and moth larvae!

Yet Bug-a-boo won't harm humans, won't damage home furnishings, when used as directed. And it's pine-scented—and so pleasant to use.

For long-lasting protection from pests, you may prefer the new Bug-a-boo with 3% D.D.T. It contains Bug-a-boo's time-tested, insect-killing ingredients, plus all the D.D.T. that's required for effective residual deposit, and the full amount considered justified for home uses.

Caution: Use Bug-a-boo with D.D.T. carefully, according to the directions.

TRIUMPHANT BURLEIGH returns from a tour of feats the champion by a fluke, marries his girl, retires to

KILLS
FLIES · ANTS
MOTHS · ROACHES
MOSQUITOES
BEDBUGS
SILVERFISH

CHAPTER 16

WHAT TO SELL

What you sell is at the heart of your eBay business, of course. If you are a Trading Assistant or run a Trading Post you'll be selling things that other folks find for you. "Pure" PowerSellers sell their own items from an inventory they purchase themselves.

This chapter looks at some "deciding what to sell" strategies for both types of sellers. The next chapter, "Getting Great Stuff to Sell," explores ways to find what you have decided to sell.

THE LEVEL PLAYING FIELD DILEMMA

When eBay was founded one of its key goals was to "level the playing field" so that ordinary buyers and sellers could find each other and the items they wanted at reasonable prices. And in the beginning, the playing fields, especially in the antiques and collectibles worlds, were anything but level. A few people knew a lot about specialized subjects, could quickly spot treasures in yard sales and flea markets, and then make a killing buying low and selling high.

I admit it. Back in 1999 I often found bargain radios at flea market and yard sales, dusted them off, and sold them to other collectors on eBay for a healthy profit. Over time the field leveled considerably. We collectors all started trading with each other on eBay, which meant there were usually multiple, similar items available all the time. This tended to lower prices a bit because we all soon realized that if we didn't win the one we were looking at today there would likely be another next week; perhaps even a nicer one.

And then the flea market and yard sale folks discovered eBay. Soon their prices were pretty close to market, even in thrift shops. Yup. They do their homework now too. (The next time you are in a thrift store look through the back door when it swings open. I bet you'll see a computer hooked up back there!)

This is probably all good in the long run. We get to find the things we want at reasonable, community-defined prices. It puts some extra pressure on sellers, however. Profit margins are thinner, and we need to work harder and smarter now than before.

It also means that you are much less likely to be able to buy things on eBay to resell on eBay at a profit. But it's not impossible.

WHAT SELLS BEST ON EBAY

At the risk of oversimplifying, the things that sell best on eBay seem to fall into four broad categories:

★ Deeply discounted commodity items

★ Hard to find and collectible items

★ Trendy items

★ Items with value added to them by a third party

A quick tour of eBay will confirm this. Jewelry often sells for considerably less on eBay than it does in retail stores, and often at or below wholesale prices.

There are many PowerSellers offering factory refurbished "like new" consumer items at prices that are likely less than your local retailer pays the factory for the identical item in brand new condition. Hard-to-find items, such as industrial machine parts, rare antiques, and collectibles do well too.

Trendy items—everything from this week's hot running shoes to the latest, skinniest cell phones—can be great sellers on eBay, particularly if demand is outstripping supply at the moment. The trick to selling trendy items, of course, is to know when to get in and out. Yesterday's hot item is tomorrow's distressed merchandise.

Perhaps the most intriguing eBay segment is what I call the value-added niche. Let me give you a couple of examples.

My color printer uses a disposable drum as part of its imaging system. After printing a predetermined number of pages the printer intentionally "blows" a tiny fuse in the drum, disabling it and requiring me to buy a new drum, even though the old drum is still capable of printing thousands more pages.

An enterprising eBay seller offers replacement fuse kits with the necessary instructions for resurrecting the drum. He pays perhaps a dime for the fuse and a nickel for the photocopied documentation he provides, and then charges more than $20 for the kit. He also makes money on shipping.

This is an example of taking an inexpensive commodity item (the fuse), adding value in the form of instructions, and making a killing. The problem, of course, is that now that he has taught me the replacement fuse trick, next time I'll just buy a fuse, and certainly not from him.

But there are variations on this theme that can earn you loyal customers. For example, I sell a series of radio restoration parts and instruction kits to help collectors get vintage radios playing. Each kit is for a specific, popular radio model. The kits are different for each model, and reasonably priced. It's also much quicker for collectors to buy my kits than to shop for the individual parts, which come from all over the country. I have even started investing in tooling to remanufacture popular replacement parts and restoration tools that have not been made by manufacturers for decades.

Priced properly and aimed at the right audiences, value-added products like these can be both profitable and fun. This works well in such fields as car and motorcycle repair, boating, vintage electric fans, model railroading, and so on.

Craft and hobby markets are another place where value-added can work. There are scrapbook kits, rug hooking kits, rubber stamp kits, computer upgrade kits, photography accessory kits, and so on.

Performing restorations is another way to add value. Some vintage poster sellers add value by shipping items in acid-free materials that can help preserve the items for years.

Look around you. What do you know and love? Can you package some commodity items along with instructions, and perhaps some hard-to-find embellishments? What can you provide that other sellers can't?

Specialize or Generalize?

If you are a "Pure" PowerSeller or Trading Assistant you can decide to specialize. You can pick a product category, or group of similar categories, and strive to be the best at selling there. Another quick tour of eBay will turn up dozens of examples of this. There are power camera sellers and shoe sellers and shipping supply sellers and movie memorabilia sellers, and on and on it goes.

The advantage to this approach is that by focusing on a single area of interest you get to know more than the average seller about the topic, and hopefully develop both strong supplier relationships and loyal repeat buyers.

You can often develop efficient systems and workflows around specialized inventory as well. For example, if you decide to sell only DVDs, your shipping process can be simple. You'll have one or two types of shipping envelopes, probably only use the post office as your carrier, have a nice uniform set of storage racks, and so on.

You need not sell nearly identical items in a single eBay category to specialize, either. One of the biggest clothing PowerSellers on eBay has contracts with suppliers who literally dump heaps of new clothing at the seller's warehouse. Here folks sort, check in, photograph, inventory, list, and ship a nearly unimaginable flow of men's, women's, and children's clothes. Each piece is unique, but because the PowerSeller specializes in clothing categories, it is easy to run a homogenous, efficient, profitable operation.

Selling What You Know and Love

The other cool thing about specializing is that you get to sell things you love and appreciate. Just be sure that you aren't more collector than seller at heart. If you go into business intending to make a profit by selling things you need to be able to let go of them. I know a guy who has more than a dozen used Oreck vacuum cleaners he can't part with. Honest.

Note

If you are a collector and are willing to part with things you take in, PowerSelling is a great way to build your collection while constantly trading up.

Seasonal Items

Seasonal selling can be rewarding, but tricky, especially if you sell items that go out of style each year. Calendars come to mind. Good luck trying to sell last year's calendar.

But if items are evergreen—Christmas decorations, for example—and if you have the room to store unsold inventory and don't mind tying up some of your cash that way, seasonal selling can be a nice supplement to your year-round endeavors. eBay provides a merchandising calendar to help you plan your sales. It also tells you about eBay's promotional plans for each season. Figure 16.1 gives you a glimpse of this. Visit Seller Central to see the real thing.

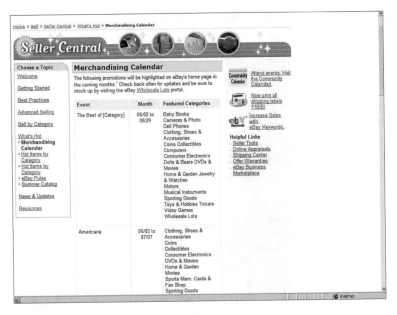

FIGURE 16.1
Part of eBay's Merchandising Calendar.

BUT WILL IT WORK?

It's fine to decide to only sell things that interest you, but can you make enough money doing that? And if so, what can you do to squeak out some higher prices? Let's dig a little deeper.

Can You Get Enough to Sell?

Dust off those goals you wrote back in Chapter 1, "Ten Keys to Success." Make sure you can get enough of what you want to sell to reach your objectives. Hand-cranked Victrolas might be your passion, but can you find enough of them to sell at a profit and meet your income objectives?

Perhaps you need to widen your scope a bit. Maybe it's early players and recordings you need to sell. Maybe you'll need to sell parts too, or restoration kits. Sometimes combining marginally workable, related niches can get you where you want to go.

Minimum Selling Price

I'll not harp on this topic again in this chapter, but I do want to remind you that what you sell affects your average selling price, and do consider this when picking an area of specialization and running your "what-if" numbers. Low average selling prices increase labor and other costs.

What Margins Do You Need?

Besides ending auction prices, you need to determine what profit margin you need on each item in order to survive. This is probably best determined with the aid of a spreadsheet and an accountant or other mentor who has insight into your business, but it will likely need to be in the 30% plus neighborhood for starters. Perhaps higher, much higher.

Dollars-per-cubic-foot

One of the first things that attracted me to collecting transistor pocket radios, and eventually selling them, was that they didn't take up much room. And since many of them are quite valuable, you can pack a lot of value into a small space. Items like these that have a high price-to-size ratio are perfect for garage sellers and anyone interested in simplifying his shipping chores.

Examples of small, valuable eBay items abound. Cameras, collectible fountain pens, jewelry, watches, personal electronics, are just to name a few.

Accessorizing

Another strategy used by PowerSellers is to improve profitability by packaging popular, deeply discounted items with more profitable accessories. Digital camera PowerSellers are experts at this. Because popular cameras are deeply discounted off of list price, many PowerSellers bundle them with accessories—memory cards, tripods, carrying cases, and so on. It's hard for bidders to calculate the true value of the individual accessories, particularly if their descriptions are vague, and it is often convenient and fun to have everything you need arrive in one shipment. So buyers will often pay more for a bundle than they would if they purchased individual pieces.

And as a seller, you stand a better chance of making profitable sales at higher average selling prices. Do be sure you don't go overboard with this. Inflated packages can turn off potential bidders. You might also want to consider running auctions selling only the main item (the camera, or whatever) at a higher price than you used to calculate the package price. This will give buyers a choice.

Up-selling

Up-selling is as old as commerce itself, I suppose. You buy a car; they try to sell you an extended warranty. Buy a burger, and you'll most likely hear "Would you like the meal instead?" Buy the meal and you know what comes next. "Supersize that?"

When picking things to sell on eBay, explore the possibilities of up-selling. Find related items—accessories, how-to videos, and so on. Open an eBay store (see Chapter 12, "eBay Stores"), use eBay's cross promotion features (see Figure 16.2), and mention related items in your listing. If you are selling poker chip sets maybe you should also sell poker instruction books, paintings of dogs playing cards…you get the idea.

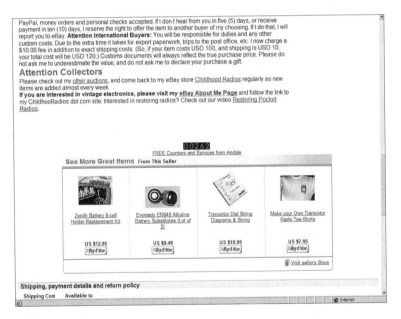

FIGURE 16.2
Use eBay's cross promotional tools to up-sell.

Trend Chasing

If you are interested in the risky—but exciting and potentially profitable—business of trying to spot and sell around trends, eBay offers some data that can at least tell you what's happening at the moment. This is no guarantee, obviously, that by the time you gather your baggage and attempt to hop on the train it will even still be in the station. Figure 16.3 shows part of the What's Hot feature.

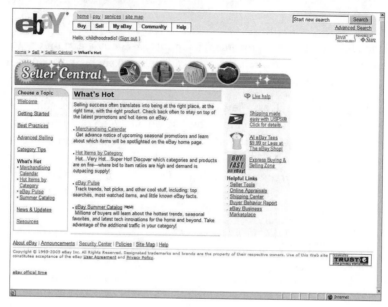

FIGURE 16.3
What's Hot?

You should check out eBay's Pulse pages too, also reached through Seller Central (see Figure 16.4) .

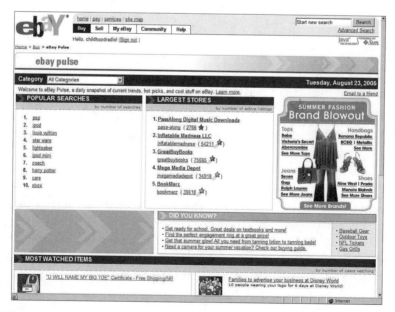

FIGURE 16.4
eBay's Pulse.

Mystery Sales and Other Gimmicks

There's another interesting trend developing as I write this. Sellers are taking gimmick sales to a whole new level. They are auctioning a chance to name their toes, or asking folks to bid on a sealed box without knowing the contents. For now at least, many of these auctions draw great traffic, and often appear on the What's Hot list. Whether this trend continues, and whether eBay will continue to permit such auctions to be run, remains to be seen.

THAT CRAZY COMMUNITY OF OURS

I just took a breather and decided to check out a handful of the 756 of eBay's "Weird Stuff" category pages available today as I write this. Holy cow. Here's just a sampling:

★ Area 51 Alien Skull

★ Weird Al Yankovic's Celebrity Doormat

★ Instant Sea Monkeys (simply add water)

★ Gothic Gargoyle Snow Globe

★ Chrome Skull License Plate Bolts (with choice of red or green eyes)

★ The Can Of Mystery (an unlabeled food can found in seller's cupboard)

★ Screaming Cat in a Bag (battery operated)

★ Fake Winning Lotto Scratchers —"The Best Joke In The World" (Yeah, I bet)

★ Royal King Tomato Happy Face ("Rare Act Of God")

★ Giraffe Novelty Party Hat (the hat is of a giraffe, not for a giraffe)

★ "Jesus Loves You Everyone Else Thinks Your A Tosser" T-shirt

★ Scolopendra Morsitans, 8-inch Giant Poison Centipede (framed)

★ Mini Replica Of an Outhouse (a nice one at that!)

★ FREAK OF NATURE Siamese pumpkins awesome (uh huh)

★ Cute College Girl Will Write You a Thank You Note Only $4.00

★ Super Cool Unique Bottle Cap Monkey (made with 200 bottle caps!)

★ Gag Stapler (press it and get an electric shock!)

★ **Most Potent** FART SPRAY Stink Bomb

Okay. That's enough fun for now. Let's get back to business. It's time to learn when to say "No!"

In this Chapter

TRIUMPHANT BURLEIGH returns from a tour of fix
feats the champion by a fluke, marries his girl, retires to t

Bug-a-boo

with and without D.D.T.

kills all 9

major pests

● Spray those pests away for good — with Bug-a-boo! This super-insect spray, with and without D.D.T.—far exceeds U. S. Government standards for an AΔ Grade insecticide. Even kills roaches and moth larvae!

Yet Bug-a-boo won't harm humans, won't damage home furnishings, when used as directed. And it's pine-scented—and so pleasant to use.

For long-lasting protection from pests, you may want Bug-a-boo with 3% D.D.T. It contains Bug-a-boo's tested, insect-killing ingredients, plus the D.D.T. that's required for effective residual deposit, and the full amount considered justified for home uses.

Caution: Use Bug-a-boo with D.D.T. carefully, according to the directions.

KILLS
FLIES · ANTS
MOTHS · ROACHES
MOSQUITOES
BEDBUGS
SILVERFISH

CHAPTER 17

GETTING GREAT STUFF TO SELL

It's everyone's dream. Find a pile of wonderful merchandise, buy it for pennies a pound, list it all on eBay, get rich, and move to a Maui beachfront home. It is certainly still possible to do that but you will have much more competition now than back when eBay started. Sometimes the best place to look for bargains is where things don't belong. Let's start with the obvious sources, and then get clever.

DIRECT FROM THE MANUFACTURER

If you can make an exclusive arrangement with a manufacturer, ideally one located near you, for their distressed merchandise—returns, end of season leftover stock, items used for catalog shoots, and so on—these can be profitable items to sell on eBay. You might create a Trading Assistant relationship with the manufacturer, or you might pay cash for the stuff, haul it off, and warehouse and sell it yourself. In the long run you are probably going to make more money by purchasing and owning the items if you can keep the costs low. This obviously requires cash and a cheap way to transport and store your inventory.

Some merchandise categories "spoil" quickly. Nothing loses value as fast as last year's cell phone or last week's basketball shoes. Buy low. Check current prices on eBay before committing to a price, and then sell the stuff as quickly as you can without flooding the category.

Small, valuable items are the best targets, of course. Jewelry, personal electronics, even high-end clothing should work.

LOCAL RETAIL STORES

Similar to working with manufacturers, you can explore arrangements with local retailers, particularly independently owned stores or small, local chains. As mentioned in the previous section, run the numbers with them, and consider purchasing deeply discounted inventory if you think that will work better for you.

LOCAL CAR DEALERS

Chances are your local car dealer has "oddball" cars that don't move quickly enough, such as Volvo stick shift station wagons, convertibles in the dead of winter up north, or highly modified cars. Consider developing a car program where you do the listings for a flat fee and the dealer does the actual selling, paperwork, and so on. You won't even need a car dealer's license in most states if you do this. Just don't expect to get 20% or 30% of the car's selling price. Instead, be sure you recover your eBay fees and labor costs come rain or shine, plus maybe an additional $50 or $100 if the car sells.

Note

If you are going to act as a Trading Assistant, the manufacturer needs to understand the financial realities. Things sell pretty cheaply on eBay, and you will be taking your percentage. They might be just as happy to get a predictable amount of cash upfront and have you haul it away.

WHOLESALE LOTS WAREHOUSES

You have driven by them. You see them advertised on television at midnight. They are wholesalers of "deeply discounted" merchandise offering stuff you can supposedly buy and resell profitably on eBay.

It is very difficult to make money using these as your sources. First, if you see the ads so do thousands of other eBay PowerSellers. Next, because these are middlemen (middlepersons?) the stuff comes to you marked up once already. Check on eBay. Chances are the same stuff is selling for about the wholesale warehouse asking price, maybe even less.

There's also a good chance the house you are buying from is also competing with you on eBay. Finally, be leery of anything with a shelf life—batteries, fire extinguishers, all manner of spoiled things find their way into these warehouses.

LOCAL AUCTIONS

It is still possible to go to local auctions and estate sales, but it is time-consuming, and you need to know what you are looking at, know how much it is really worth (on eBay), and then you must win, pay for, and get items back to your place without damaging them. People do this every week. Just don't assume you are going to steal much. You will likely be bidding against other PowerSellers in the audience, of course, but you will also run into people who don't need to make a profit reselling things. They want these items because they want to own them. This can drive prices up past wholesale in a hurry.

I recently saw an upcoming auction advertised more than 100 miles away. There was some vintage, high-end stereo gear I was interested in, but I wanted to know more about its condition before spending the time driving both ways and standing in the sun.

The auctioneer described the items to me over the phone, without being terribly reassuring. He asked if I would like to make a proxy offer on the phone, or perhaps come to the auction. I offered a reasonable amount for untested items in questionable physical condition. The auctioneer laughed. "Don't even bother. I collect this stuff too. There's no way I'd let it go for that little. I'd buy it myself first!" Hmmm. Note to self: Get a job in an auction house.

Still, it is worthwhile to get on auctioneers' mailing lists. Go once in a while. Do your homework. Be prepared. Be brave. Take a shot. It will be fun, if nothing else.

Many auction houses will send email notifications, and electronic catalogs if you request them. Use Google to find local auctioneers (see Figure 17.1), or visit a local antique consignment store, pick up one of those free directories you'll find in the front of the store, and flip to the Auctions section. There should be plenty of local contact information there.

FIGURE 17.1

Make friends with your local auctioneer.

STORAGE COMPANY AUCTIONS

Here's another hit-or-miss but fun possibility. Folks who run those private storage locations auction off the contents of entire storage lockers when customers don't pay their rent. The auctions are advertised several weeks ahead in local papers, and some places have online calendars and email notification options. The big chains seem to have auctions virtually every week somewhere in town.

You will generally only be allowed to peek inside, which is often not very helpful. (If you are nice to the location manager s/he might have a better idea of the contents to share with you.) You will be expected to pay for and move the entire contents pretty quickly. (Although I bet you could rent the locker and leave it there if you choose.)

One last caveat. The owner can swoop in at the last minute and, probably with the help of his mom or girlfriend, pay the bill and rescue his stuff only moments before the auction starts. I told you it could be fun.

Tip

Local law enforcement sells confiscated goods, unclaimed property, old crime fighting gear, and who knows what all? Once only traditional auctions were used, but now the stuff's finding its way online. Check out the local scene. You could get lucky.

EBAY'S WHOLESALE LOTS CATEGORIES

Many of eBay's popular categories have third-level subcategories called "wholesale lots." Sometimes, but by no means always, you can buy multiple items in a lot, and then resell them individually on eBay for a profit. This usually works best if you add some value—better packaging, instructions, accessories, and so on.

Examples of categories with wholesale lots subcategories include Jewelry, Collectibles, and Home & Garden. Figure 17.2 gives you an idea of some of the things sold in lots.

Note

Some sellers list their own lots in categories without wholesale lot subcategories. Search for the word "lot" in titles. Things tend to sell for lower prices in lots, so it might be possible to make some money buying things this way if there is not too much junk included. Don't forget to factor shipping into your acquisition costs!

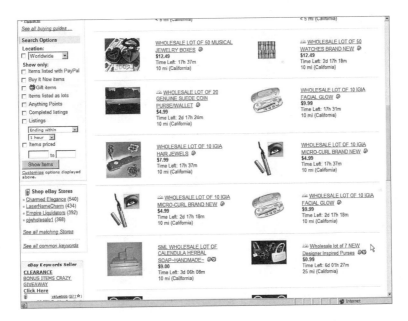

FIGURE 17.2

A sampling of lot sales.

EBAY'S NEW RESELLER MARKETPLACE

In about April 2005 eBay launched a new service for PowerSellers only. It's called the Reseller Marketplace. You need to log into the PowerSeller neighborhood to even see it. (So much for the level playing field.) Figure 17.3 shows the Marketplace.

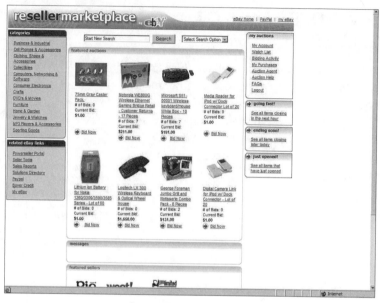

FIGURE 17.3

The New PowerSellers' Reseller Marketplace.

It's basically an "off eBay" auction site, supposedly stocked by manufacturers wanting to give PowerSellers a direct shot at closeouts. Figure 17.4 shows a typical lot listing screen.

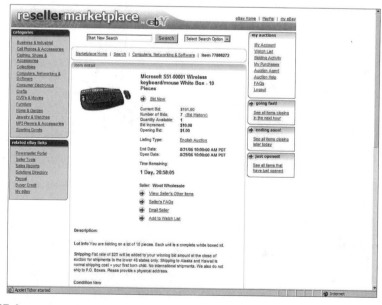

FIGURE 17.4

A typical Marketplace auction item.

HIDING IN PLAIN SIGHT

Sometimes the good stuff hides right there in plain sight. I wish I still had the auction photo. I was browsing with the search term "Vintage" I think, and right there in the middle of a pile of stuff the seller actually described as "some old '50s junk" was a $100 radio. The auction started at $0.99, and because even the seller thought it was all junk I ended up being the only bidder, and won at the starting bid amount. I asked the seller to toss out all the junk but the radio, which she did. Keep your eyes open.

WITH A LITTLE HELP FROM YOUR FRIENDS

I have a friend who buys and sells trains, many of them on eBay. Whenever I go garage selling I look for trains for him. He looks for radios for me. We haven't found much for each other yet, but you never know.

DIRECT SOLICITATION

Don't be afraid to go looking for items. I rent some display cases in a collectibles consignments shop. On one of them I've placed the sign advertising my Trading Assistant services. You can see it in Figure 17.5. The sign on another case simply says "I Pay Cash Vintage Electronics," and has photos of the stuff I am interested in purchasing.

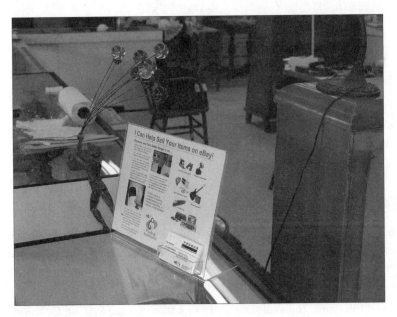

FIGURE 17.5
Let people know you want things to buy.

Direct mail can work too. Use a postcard program to reach out to potential sources. Do you specialize in beads? Send a postcard to 500 bead shops. Maybe one or two of them are getting ready to close or trim their inventory.

WANT IT NOW

Clever eBay PowerSellers are using the new "Want It Now" feature to troll for wholesale lots. Figure 17.6 shows an example of this.

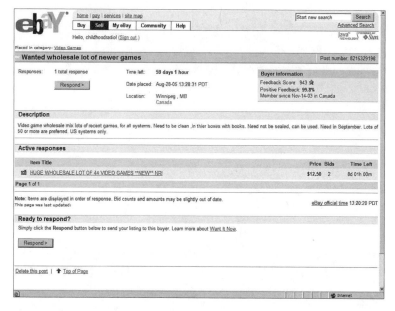

FIGURE 17.6.
The Want It Now feature.

This is a little-known eBay feature, but it is catching on and costs nothing to try. Sometimes we get ahead by trying things others don't. This could be one of those times!

SPREAD THE WORD

Having an eBay selling business with nothing to sell is like being all dressed up with no place to go. When you are the busiest selling and shipping is when you should also be the busiest looking for new merchandise. You are running two businesses actually—one acquiring and another selling. Here are some more tips and reminders:

★ Spread the word. Tell everyone you meet that you are looking for things to sell on eBay. Network, network, network.

★ Local businesses and manufacturers are great sources for steady streams of merchandise.

★ Repeat sources (local stores, regular customers, and so on) save time. Cultivate them.

★ Live auctions, while fun, can require considerable time and travel. Do your homework before heading out.

★ Get in the habit of looking for items to sell, whenever you are out and about. See that RV with the for sale sign on it? Write down the phone number. Perhaps you can sell it on eBay for the owner. Going out of business sign? Walk in and ask for the owner. "Sold" sign on a house? Ask if they need help emptying the garage.

★ Call local realtors and offer to help sellers clear the clutter before putting houses on the market.

★ Read the classifieds. When you see items worthy of eBay call the owner and offer to "potentially sell it for more" by reaching a wider audience online.

In this Chapter

★ **Customer Service for Buyers**

★ **Additional Customer Service Tasks for Trading Assistants**

★ **Use the Telephone**

★ **Creating Your Own Customer Service Policies**

TRIUMPHANT BURLEIGH returns from a tour of feats the champion by a fluke, marries his girl, retires to

CHAPTER 18

CUSTOMER SERVICE

The customer service that you and your associates provide will determine how your business will be judged and remembered. Repeat business is the cornerstone of any successful venture, and it always comes as a result of consistent, competent, friendly customer service.

If you are a PowerSeller offering your own items on eBay your bidders and buyers are your only customers and will be the focus of your customer service. Trading Assistants and Trading Posts have a second group of customers, folks bringing things to sell. Let's look at some tricks and best practices for both groups separately.

CUSTOMER SERVICE FOR BUYERS

Customer service for buyers and potential bidders starts while your auctions are still running. It is very important to your reputation and to building your business. The following sections describe some specifics of customer service that you will need to pay particular attention to.

Put the policy or "best practices" in writing. It will make you think things through. Refer to it, even if you are working solo. Be sure employees read, understand, and adhere to it.

During the Auction

Care for the items being sold so that they will be as described when you ship them. Scratches, dings, and missing parts are a common source of winner dissatisfaction and negative feedback. Pay attention to these details.

Monitor active auctions and answer questions quickly and politely, even if the questions are dumb or the answers can be found right in the listing. Post the answers to general questions publicly so that all potential bidders can see them.

Point out any important new facts you notice or learn about the item after launching an auction by adding to the description. Once there are bids on an item, and near the end of an auction, you cannot change the description. You can, however, append descriptions as shown in Figure 18.1.

FIGURE 18.1

Use the Add to Description link to append descriptions in active auctions.

Be sure it is easy for bidders to know how much they will be paying for shipping and handling before they bid. Use a shipping calculator populated with all the options bidders might be interested in using. Do reality checks immediately after you launch items by testing the shipping calculator's results. Something's wrong in Figure 18.2. Perhaps the weight used to set up the calculator was too high. Typos like this can kill bids.

Boilerplate Email Responses

During auctions you will get emails from prospective bidders wondering if they can pick items up locally if they win, or if you will ship internationally even though your listing says you won't. You can develop boilerplate responses to these common requests. For example, local pickup is obviously an option for Trading Assistants with storefronts. If you work at home you might not want the bother or the risk.

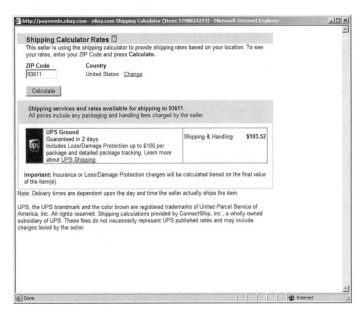

FIGURE 18.2

Test the results of your shipping calculator.

If you will permit winners to pick up their items locally you should craft a boilerplate email that answers that question and anticipates the next questions. Here's a sample:

"Yes, winning bidders are always welcome to pick up items at our location. We are at [address, intersections and landmarks]. Our hours of operation are [days and hours]. We accept [these] payment methods, but not [cash, or whatever]."

If winners will be paying state and local sales taxes remind them. If you charge a local pickup fee remind them. Close with a telephone number they can use if they still have questions.

Personalized Email and Phone Responses

Keep an eye on email at the end of auctions. When winners have trouble paying you, or "checking out" if you use a third-party auction management tool, jump on these problems ASAP. Offer to help winners manually check out by taking information over the phone if necessary. Do be sure you confirm the authenticity of the caller, and be very wary about ever shipping to addresses that you are not able to confirm through eBay, PayPal, or your merchant bank.

Shipping and Post-Sale Communication

Ship everything as promised, and as quickly as promised, using the shipping service and insurance options selected by the winner.

Always send an email when an item ships, with tracking information if it is available. Many third-party auction management systems do this automatically, as do the programs provided by UPS and stamps.com. eBay's new Selling Manager Pro now makes it pretty painless for us to send them manually, as shown in Figure 18.3. You can customize these shipping messages to your own taste.

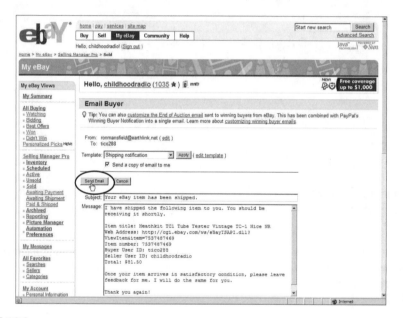

FIGURE 18.3

eBay makes it easy to send "item shipped" emails.

Leave feedback religiously. Whether you leave it before the buyer posts feedback for you is your choice (and explored in greater detail in Chapter 28, "Feedback"), but in any case, don't put off feedback chores. They are an important part of customer service.

> **Tip**
>
> Some sellers also enclose a thank you card or unexpected surprise—a pen with the seller's logo, perhaps, or a small piece of candy. If it's something the winner might use every day the gift might remind her to keep an eye on your new auctions—nothing too big or heavy.

ADDITIONAL CUSTOMER SERVICE TASKS FOR TRADING ASSISTANTS

If you are a Trading Assistant you have much more customer service to perform because you also must communicate with the folks bringing you their stuff to sell. Customer service starts before the auction begins.

Pre-sale Questions

Sellers, particularly first-time sellers, will have many, many questions. They will come to you on foot, by phone, via email, and after awhile, in your sleep. Here are the common queries:

★ How does it work?

★ What do you guys do?

★ How long will it take?

★ How much will it cost?

★ What if my item doesn't sell?

★ How much will it likely sell for?

★ What if it sells for too little money?

★ Can we use a reserve?

★ Can I keep it at home while the auction is running?

★ When will I get my check?

A carefully crafted response to the first question might answer most of the rest, and can be accomplished in one breath, if you do it right. I call it my "elevator speech" because it can be done in the time it takes for an elevator ride. Here's a suggested script.

"Simply, we sell your stuff on eBay and send you a check. We start by doing some research, and if it looks like similar items are selling for at least [your minimum] on eBay we will take some professional-looking photos, write a great description, run the auction, collect the money, ship the item to its new owner, and mail you a check.

From the time you drop off your item until you get a check is about [your number of] weeks. Sometimes a little longer.

We charge [your percentage] which includes [your details]. So if an item sells for $100.00 you will get about [what they get].

We carefully store the items here during the auction since we want to be able to answer any bidders' questions that might come up, and so that you don't need to make a second trip. This also speeds up shipping, and gets you your check sooner.

Let's take a look at that first item of yours and see what things like that are selling for on eBay these days."

Alternatively, instead of jumping right into item research, discussed in Chapter 19, "Research," you might want to gather the customers' contact information at this point so that you can do follow-up marketing even if they don't leave anything with you. Some folks think this is a bit pushy. I am in that camp myself.

The only two questions ignored in the elevator speech are the thorny ones, and they don't always come up, so there is no sense answering them unless asked. You do need a canned response, however, and it will vary with your policy on starting prices and reserves. So determine what you want to say when faced with questions about reserves and high starting prices, and then practice for the inevitable. Refer to Chapter 10, "Pricing Strategies," for more information.

Once the Auction Begins

Customers love to watch their own auctions, and it's a great idea to send them an email with a link to their items so they can watch the progress. Remind them in the email that much of the bidding will take place in the last few moments or even seconds of the auction, and encourage them not to panic.

Some will panic. Rehearse your response to the occasional "I want my auction stopped now!" phone call or visit. Have a policy. When it does happen, show them how many people are "watching" the auction, and explain how that works. Try to find examples of similar items that started as low as theirs and finished satisfactorily. This handholding is a necessary part of a Trading Assistant's customer service role.

Painful as it can be, once in a while you might want to stop an auction if the item is valuable and attracting absolutely no attention while your customer looks on wringing his hands.

Once in a while a customer will object to the way you have photographed or displayed the item. You will need to decide if this is serious enough to cause you to kill and relist the item, or simply append it, or just reassure the customer that all will be fine.

Note

By the way, if you host your own photos it's easy to replace them even while the auction is running. That's not the case if you use eBay's or most other third-party image hosting services.

When the Auction Ends

At auction's end most Trading Assistants send "congratulations" emails to their customers. Some auction management software packages will do this for you, but it might be something you will need to do manually. If that's the case, develop a boilerplate email into which you can plug a link to the finished auction, and perhaps drop the price into the email's subject line.

The end of the auction is not the end of your customer service duties, however; you now need to do all the buyer's-side service mentioned at the beginning of the chapter.

If the Auctions End Badly

If something goes wrong with an auction—the item doesn't sell or the winner fails to pay—you need to be right on top of the problem. If the winner hasn't paid, proactively find out why not.

If the item failed to get any bids, start whatever wheels in motion that you and the seller have prearranged. If the item is to be donated to a charity, put it in the pile. If you have agreed to relist the item, perhaps at a lower price, get that ball rolling. If the seller has instructed you to return the item, send a "come and get it" email. Follow up with a phone call or two, if that's what it takes.

USE THE TELEPHONE

You will get a surprising number of phone calls. There will be voicemails left at all hours, especially if you put your phone number in your listings as many PowerSellers do. When working out of your home be sure you have a way to turn off the bell at night.

Voicemail boxes will fill to overflowing given half a chance, so retrieving messages should be a high-priority customer service task. If you are running a store assign someone the responsibility to answer and respond to voicemail promptly.

Have a standard, polite, professional way to answer the phone. If you have employees, listen to how they treat people on the phone and in person.

CREATING YOUR OWN CUSTOMER SERVICE POLICIES

Take a few moments to rough out a customer service policy that seems right for your business. Here are a few topic headings to get your juices flowing. What are the things that are likely to strengthen your relationships to your customers?

★ What's an acceptable delay when answering email and voicemail?

★ How long will you wait for winners to pay, and how will you remind them?

★ When do you issue feedback—when you're paid? When the buyer posts feedback?

★ How soon after payment should items be shipped?

★ What's your policy on discounts for combined item shipments?

★ What's your policy on bidders with low/shaky feedback?

★ If you are a Trading Assistant how soon after an auction closes will you pay customers?

★ How can you assure that customers get an accurate, consistent answer to the "How does it work" question?

★ Which employees should do what in your store when people are waiting in line?

★ Should you interrupt counter conversations when the phone rings?

★ Are employees trained to jump to the aid of folks struggling with items as they come and go?

★ How will you handle unclaimed, unsold items?

G'BYE

In this Chapter

Bug-a-boo

with and without D. D. T.

kills all 9 major pests

● Spray those pests away for good — with Bug-a-boo! This super-insect spray, with and without D.D.T.—far exceeds U. S. Government standards for an AA Grade insecticide. Even kills roaches and moth larvae!

Yet Bug-a-boo won't harm humans, won't damage home furnishings, when used as directed. And it's pine-scented—and so pleasant to use.

For long-lasting protection from pests, you may prefer the new Bug-a-boo with 3% D.D.T. It contains Bug-a-boo's time-tested, insect-killing ingredients, plus all the D.D.T. that's required for effective residual deposit, and the full amount considered justified for home uses.

Caution: Use Bug-a-boo with D.D.T. carefully, according to the directions.

TRIUMPHANT BURLEIGH returns from a tour of feats the champion by a fluke, marries his girl, retires

KILLS
FLIES · ANTS
MOTHS · ROACHES
MOSQUITOES
BEDBUGS
SILVERFISH

CHAPTER 19

RESEARCH

There are several reasons to do research. It can help you determine the value of items, and it can help educate you and your associates.

Even experienced PowerSellers have been caught off-guard by oddball items that look like trash. I remember choking back a laugh when a customer once handed me a broken, raggedy-looking copy of a Stradivarius violin. It looked like it had been run over by a truck. The bridge was detached; the case was a wreck. It wasn't even full-sized. It was a student model.

Just to be polite, and because it was a slow day, and perhaps because the customer was nice, I did my usual eBay and ándale research, and came up with nothing. Then I Googled "Stradivarius violin reproductions." Whoa. People collect these things! We started it at 10 bucks, auctioned it off for about $450, and the bidding was intense.

So the two primary reasons to research are to make the yes/no decision, and to learn what's important about specialty items. Research can also be a whole lot of fun, educational, and addicting.

ONLINE RESEARCH TOOLS AND TECHNIQUES

The yes/no decision on everyday items can often be made by searching eBay's recently completed items. You get a snapshot of the last 30 days or so. With any luck you will have half a dozen items or more to compare. Figure 19.1 shows the results of a search for a reasonably common collectible radio.

You need to be logged into eBay using your eBay ID to do these searches, and you must click the little Completed Listings box at the left of the search page.

I like to sort the results by price. It's pretty cool how eBay even takes the currency conversion rates into account when sorting by price, as you can see in Figure 19.1.

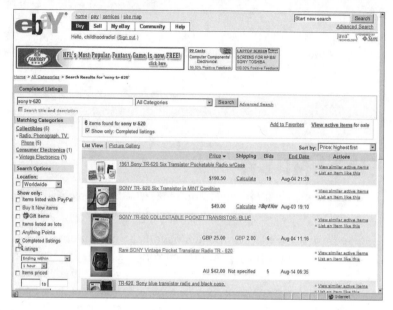

FIGURE 19.1

A typical eBay completed items search.

If my purpose was to see whether a similar radio was worth selling for a customer, my work would be done at this point. It looks like Sony TR-620 radios, especially nice ones with accessories, are worth selling. At this point I could dig a little deeper to see such things as what the starting prices were, which category was used, and what made one worth almost $200 and the next most valuable less than $50.

Which brings up an interesting point about research: This exercise really can't tell you why the second radio is only worth $50 because it might be worth much more. Look carefully at Figure 19.1 again. That second highest auction ($49) ended with a Buy it Now winner. Had it been a true auction the price might have been higher, though probably not $190 because the second radio did not have all the accessories offered with the first.

But the point is this: Besides looking at the condition of similar items when doing research, explore the context of the various auctions. Were the listings well written? Are the photos comparable? Was the correct category used in each case? Was the starting price too high?

The other thing to watch out for when using eBay's competed item search feature, and any other auction research tool, is this: Just because an item is

displayed does not mean it sold. If the reserve was too high or the starting price absurd, it will still be there, but don't let that fool you. You want to compare successfully completed, sold items.

Speaking of third-party research tools, let's look at my current favorite, Terapeak.

TERAPEAK

Years younger than the granddaddy of all eBay research tools, ándale's PriceFinder, Terapeak, a paid subscription service, claims to go farther back in time when gathering auction results. Figure 19.2 seems to bear that out.

FIGURE 19.2
The same search using Terapeak.

Terapeak found more radios than the eBay search (eight as opposed to six), and even found one worth more than $200. It also shows some other interesting numbers without needing to dig. The starting price is displayed, along with the number of bids and so on, all nicely formatted.

Like most other third-party research tools, Terapeak displays totals and averages with its searches. These can be very misleading. Here's an example:

> **Note**
>
> Terapeak's searches all start with a look at only one day. You need to click to display longer times—a week, month, and so on.

Suppose you want to search for a Motorola Razr cell phone. Take a look at the results in Figure 19.3.

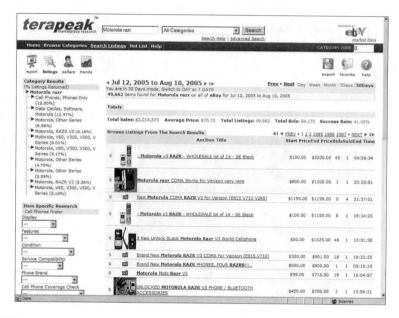

FIGURE 19.3

What's wrong? How can the average price of such an expensive phone be $70.70?

What's going on here? How can the average price of what should be a $200 phone as I write this be only $70.70? The answer is complex. First, I did a keyword (title) search so Terapeak picked up every historical auction containing the words "Motorola Razr." This includes batteries, headsets, and other accessories, which all get averaged together.

Narrowing the search to only things listed in the Phone category (12% of the total hits, by the way), gets us much closer, as you can see in Figure 19.4.

That's much better, but not perfect. Some of the listings were for lots of phones, and so this skews things too. Then there are used phones and new phones. Some sellers accidentally or intentionally miscategorize batteries and other accessories so that they will show up while shoppers are in the phone category browsing. Others sell the phones for $10 if you sign up for a long-service commitment outside of eBay. This all messes with the totals, quantities, and therefore the averages.

Your best bet is to always look for a few comparable items and check them out thoroughly rather than trusting averages.

FIGURE 19.4
Getting closer; now the results show just the phones.

OTHER RESEARCH TOOLS

Not surprisingly, the Internet is full of helpful research information, particularly about collectibles. Here are just a few of my favorite sites; I'll put links to these and others on my web site (www.RonMansfield.com).

The Collector's Information Bureau

This site offers research reports, price guides, manufacturers' links, and much more. Figure 19.5 shows its home page (www.collectorsinfo.org).

The PBS Antiques Roadshow and FYI Sites

This site offers information and links about appraisers, antiques, and more. The related FYI site has many helpful tips and tricks for antique hunting, appraisal, fake spotting, and more (www.pbs.org/wgbh/pages/roadshow/).

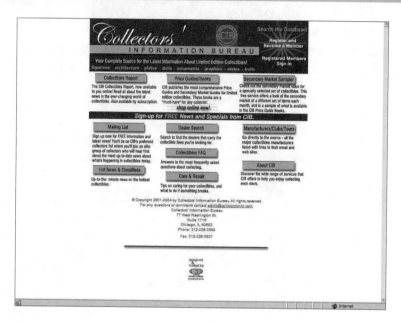

FIGURE 19.5

The Collector's Information Bureau home page.

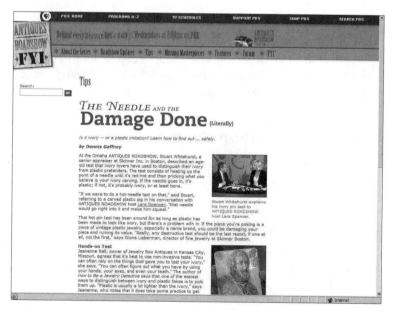

FIGURE 19.6

The Antiques Roadshow site.

The Antique Web

The Antique Web is run by a consortium of collectors, dealers, writers, auctioneers, show promoters, and trade leaders. Their site has many informative articles on such diverse topics as spotting fakes, flea market dos and don'ts, Scrimshaw, and so on (www.antiqueweb.com).

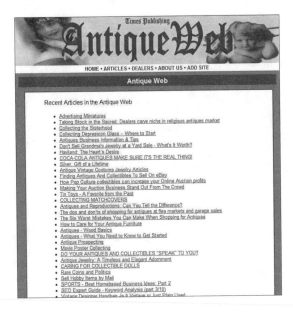

FIGURE 19.7
A small portion of the Antique Web article list.

Building Your Own Reference Library

If you are interested in collecting a real reference library of your own with bindings that crack and page corners you can turn down, check out this web site that seems to know about every book ever written. It's called idealocom (http://books.idealo.com). Figure 19.8 shows part of the collectors' book index.

Community Resources

Don't overlook the local library, the collectors' sections of your favorite bookstores, and antique malls. You will bump into friendly, knowledgeable

Tip

Speaking of knowledge banks, when hiring employees, look for people with interests and passions. And you franchisees—share among yourselves out there!

people often willing to share their years of experience if not for free, perhaps for the price of a cup of coffee.

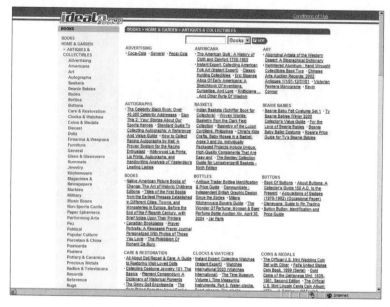

FIGURE 19.8
Part of idealocom's collectors' book index.

RESEARCH DO'S AND DON'TS

I've boiled down everything we discussed in this chapter to a brief list of do's and don'ts. You might want to create your own list (or copy this one) and keep it as a handy reminder when you begin to research new items.

★ Be sure you compare like items. Age, condition, completeness, color, and many other factors affect price.

★ Beware of averages. Many items are miscategorized or not relevant.

★ Don't be fooled by Buy It Now results. Sometimes BIN sellers underprice.

★ Consider paying for third-party tools such as ándale or Terapeak.

★ Doing Yes/No, "take it or leave it" research should be quick, perhaps no more than a minute per item when you get good at it.

★ Do additional research when writing descriptions for important valuable items. Don't forget Google and specialty sites.

★ Consider building a reference library for categories of items you sell frequently.

★ When hiring, look for knowledgeable people to add to your staff.

In this Chapter

★ It's Junk

★ It's Beyond Your Shipping Capabilities

★ It's on eBay's Prohibited List

★ It's On Your (or Your Franchisor's) Prohibited List

★ You Question Its Authenticity

★ You Think You'll Be "VeROed"

★ It Appears to Be Stolen

★ You Have Safety Concerns

★ To Sell or Not To Sell?

TRIUMPHANT BURLEIGH returns from a tour of [...] feats the champion by a fluke, marries his girl, retires to [...]

Spray those pests away for good — with Bug-a-boo! This super-insect spray, with and without D.D.T.—far exceeds U. S. Government standards for an AA Grade insecticide. Even kills roaches and moth larvae!

Yet Bug-a-boo won't harm humans, won't damage home furnishings, when used as directed. And it's pine-scented—and so pleasant to use.

For long-lasting protection from pests, you may prefer the new Bug-a-boo with 3% D.D.T. It contains Bug-a-boo's time-tested, insect-killing ingredients, plus all the D.D.T. that's required for effective residual deposit, and the full amount considered justified for home uses.

Caution: Use Bug-a-boo with D.D.T. carefully, according to the directions.

Bug-a-boo

with and without D.D.T.

kills all

major pests

KILLS

FLIES · ANTS

MOTHS · ROACHES

MOSQUITOES

BEDBUGS

SILVERFISH

CHAPTER 20

WHEN TO SAY NO

One of the great things about being your own boss is that you get to call all the shots. That's also the downside. One of the hardest things to do is turn away business. And if someone brings you something to sell, or you spot an irresistible deal on things you can resell at a profit it can be very difficult to say no. Sometimes you should.

IT'S JUNK

How many times must I say it? If it's junk, it's junk. Set your price limit and stick to it. My favorite junk story concerns a delightful woman who brought in a box of old shoes. There was something from each of her seven family members in that carton. The shoes were pricing out at about five bucks a pair as I did the research. Our minimum was $30.

"Couldn't we just sell them altogether as a lot?" She wondered?

I guess we could have, and with any luck we would find a bunch of bidders competing with each other to get one pair of men's 10s, and a girl's 6, and a boy's 7.... You get the idea. A big pile of junk is still a pile of junk.

IT'S BEYOND YOUR SHIPPING CAPABILITIES

One of the most frustrating things about eBay is how often a large item's buyer and seller are on opposite sides of the country. This is a big country, but even so we can move just about anything given the time, tools, and money.

There are eBayers successfully selling and shipping furniture, machinery, and other big stuff every day. The trick is they are set up to do it properly. They are able to build their own crates, or have contracted with a good local crating and freight forwarding company. You can do this too, but until you get those ducks lined up be very careful about selling things that UPS, USPS, Fed Ex, and DHL can't ship.

IT'S ON EBAY'S PROHIBITED LIST

To keep the eBay community a safe and politically correct place, eBay prohibits the sale of some items and restricts the sale of others. Deciding what gets on the list must be a fascinating and sometimes frustrating job. I once heard a Trust and Safety employee describe the lengthy evolution of eBay's "no used underwear" policy. I'll not go into detail here, but it was side-splittingly funny and a little sad all at once.

eBay publishes the list and it gets updated regularly. The quickest way to find the list is to search for "prohibited items overview" on eBay's Help search page.

Note

If you sell the same things over and over you'll not need to visit the Prohibited and Restricted list very often. But because Trading Assistants sell such diverse things for so many people, it's easy to slip up unless you get in the habit of checking. It's a good idea to bookmark the list and refer to it regularly. It changes.

Just because something is on the list does not mean you cannot sell it. It means that before you sell it you should do some additional research. Figure 20.1 shows the jumping-off point for your explorations.

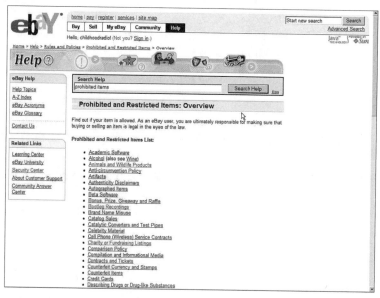

FIGURE 20.1

The eBay Prohibited and Restricted List.

When you find a general category or topic of interest you can learn more by following the links. For example, Figure 20.2 explains bootleg recordings. ("But dude. They said it wuz okay to record the kon-surt!")

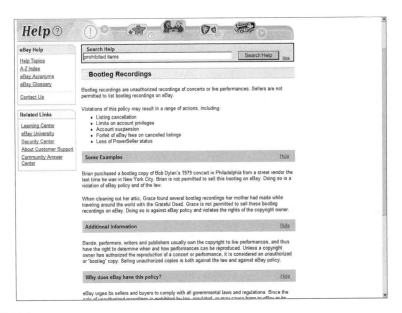

FIGURE 20.2
Gain additional clarity by following the links, grasshopper.

At the time this book was written eBay had policies in place for the items and topics shown in Table 20.1. (You can see an updated list at http://pages.ebay.com/help/sell/item_allowed.html.)

Prohibited	Questionable
Airline and Transit Related Items	Artifacts
Alcohol (also see Wine)	Autographed Items
Animals and Wildlife Products	Batteries
Catalog and URL Sales	Catalytic Converters and Test Pipes
Counterfeit Currency and Stamps	Charity or Fundraising Listings
Counterfeit Items	Contracts and Tickets
Credit Cards	Electronics Equipment
Drugs & Drug Paraphernalia	Event Tickets
Embargoed Goods and Prohibited Countries	Food

Prohibited	Questionable
Firearms	Freon
Fireworks	Hazardous Materials
Gift Cards	Imported & Emission Non-Compliant Vehicles
Government IDs and Licenses	International Trading - Buyers
Human Parts and Remains	International Trading - Sellers
Links	Manufacturers' Coupons
Lockpicking Devices	Mature Audiences
Lottery Tickets	Offensive Material
Mailing Lists and Personal Information	Pesticides
Multilevel Marketing, Pyramid, and Matrix Programs	Police-Related Items
Plants and Seeds	Pre-Sale Listings
Postage Meters	Slot Machines
Prescription Drugs and Devices	Used Airbags
Recalled Items	Used Clothing
Satellite and Cable TV Descramblers	Used Medical Devices
Stocks and Other Securities	Weapons & Knives
Stolen Property	Wine (also see Alcohol)
Surveillance Equipment	
Tobacco	**Potentially Infringing (copyright & trademark)**
Travel	Academic Software
Special	Anti-circumvention Policy
Real Estate	Authenticity Disclaimers
	Beta Software
	Bootleg Recordings
	Brand Name Misuse
	Celebrity Material
	Comparison Policy
	Contracts and Tickets

Prohibited	Questionable
	Downloadable Media
	Encouraging Infringement Policy
	Faces, Names, and Signatures
	Importation of Goods into the United States
	Misleading Titles
	Mod Chips, Game Enhancers, and Boot Discs
	Movie Prints
	OEM Software
	Recordable Media
	Replica and Counterfeit Items
	Promotional Items
	Unauthorized Copies

IT'S ON *YOUR* (OR YOUR FRANCHISOR'S) PROHIBITED LIST

Even if eBay thinks its okay to sell something, you might disagree. For example, many eBay buyers and sellers love exchanging vintage *Playboy* magazines, pinup calendars, and other nostalgic adult collectibles, much of it tame when compared to current primetime television viewing options, especially on cable. You might disagree, and you have every right to refuse to sell these items. But what if I told you a single copy of *Playboy* Volume 1 Number 4 recently sold for $310? Does that make it tougher to say no?

And you should be clear in your mind about why you find things or categories objectionable. For example, at about the same time that the magazine sold for over $300 an original Playboy bunny costume sold on eBay for $950. So if you object to the magazine would you still be inclined to sell the outfit? Is it the magazine's nudity you object to, or the whole Playboy notion and lifestyle?

I don't raise these issues to be argumentative. Customers will bring you things they value and love. Similar items are probably already selling on eBay. It will be helpful for you, and your staff, if you have one, to not only establish guidelines, but also understand the underlying principles so that you can generalize and be as consistent as possible, which is not always easy.

Even if you like *Playboy* magazines your franchisor might not. Ask about company policies so that you don't cross the line and unintentionally degrade the brand or violate your contract.

YOU QUESTION ITS AUTHENTICITY

This is another tough one. If you are uncertain about an item's authenticity, you should not sell it. In fact, if you know it is a fake and you sell it, you are violating eBay's policies, and your auction might be taken down. Do this too often, and you will be suspended, perhaps indefinitely.

> # Note
>
> Write down your prohibited items policy, perhaps even jotting down a few words about "why" you won't take certain items. Some Trading Assistants print copies of their policy to hand to customers with questions.

The guidelines couldn't be any clearer on this one. Here's the direct quote from eBay:

> "Counterfeits, unauthorized replicas, unauthorized items (such as counterfeit watches, handbags, or other accessories) or unauthorized copies (such as copies of software programs, video games, music albums, movies, television programs, or photographs) are not permitted on eBay. Unauthorized copies include (but are not limited to) copies that are pirated, duplicated, backed-up or bootlegged. It is illegal to sell unauthorized copies of media.
>
> Guideline: If the product you are selling bears the name or logo of a company, but it wasn't made or endorsed by that company, don't list it on eBay.
>
> Sellers may not disclaim knowledge of, or responsibility for, the authenticity or legality of the items offered in their listings. Sellers should take steps to ensure that their items are authentic before listing them on eBay. If a seller cannot verify the authenticity of an item, the seller is not permitted to list it."

And no, it's not okay to say in your description, "We are not sure if this is authentic or not." That is also a violation.

Some frequently counterfeited items include the following:

★ Autographed items, especially sports collectibles

★ Name-brand handbags, shoes, and other designer items

★ Name-brand sunglasses

★ Replacement parts (even for airplanes!)

★ Music and videos

★ Software

★ Antiques

* ★ Stamps

* ★ Pottery

* ★ Jewelry and gemstones

* ★ Paintings, lithographs, and so on

* ★ Metal signs

YOU THINK YOU'LL BE "VEROED"

Another reason to say "No" is if you think VeRO members will complain to eBay about you. "Ver-who?" *VeRO* stands for *Verified Rights Ownership*. It's designed to protect the intellectual property rights of manufacturers, artists, and others. Examples of protected property include trademarks, music performances, and so on. VeRO also extends to product logos, specifications, web-based product information, photos, and more.

It works like this. Manufacturers and other "rights owners" join the program. Then they look for violators, report them to eBay, and eBay terminates the offending auctions and can suspend the seller either temporarily or into perpetuity. Want some examples?

You list a Prada handbag, turn on your computer the next morning, and find it terminated. You list a high-end stereo receiver and copy information from the manufacturers' web site, and then paste it into your auction description. Poof. Auction pulled. You visit the Nike site and see a great photo of the exact same new-in-the-box Nike shoes you plan to sell. You copy the photo and use it for your auction. These all qualify as VeRO violations.

Yes, eBay looks at auctions for violations such as these, but it's the VeRO members who do most of the sleuthing and complaining. And when they complain, eBay usually acts without a lot of communication with sellers. For example, the only thing a VeRO member needs to do is claim that they have "a good faith belief that the merchandise you are offering for sale is counterfeit or otherwise infringes their trademarks and thus is in violation of the law."

To see a list of VeRO members, read their various policies, and get contact information for many of them, visit http://pages.ebay.com/help/community/vero-aboutme.html.

What does this mean to you as a seller? Lots of people sell Prada shoes and Kate Spade handbags on eBay without a problem. Others sell known authentic items and have them taken down regularly. The risk is yours. Some PowerSellers have decided it's not worth the risk. What you don't want to do is become a "repeat offender" in the eyes of eBay Trust and Safety. This can put an end to your career as a PowerSeller.

IT APPEARS TO BE STOLEN

A customer walks in with a nice watch. Something doesn't seem right. He tells you two different stories about it. He has trouble making eye contact. He cringes when you ask for his drivers' license number and asks if that's really necessary. Or someone arrives with a car stereo, or maybe a whole box filled with car stereos. The wires are cut short, and scratches around the edges and case make you think they might have been, umm, uninstalled in a hurry.

You are handed a nice power tool but the serial number has been filed off.

A woman walks in with bags full of guy stuff—gadgets, watches, an expensive bike. "He's cheating on me," she gloats. "And he is gonna pay. I want to sell these things."

In the case of the betrayed girlfriend it's a pretty easy call. You hand her the stuff and say that because it does not belong to her, which she told you, you can't sell it.

The car stereo scenario and tool scenarios get a little iffier. Perhaps your customer works for a car stereo aftermarket store and is the rightful owner of the old gear. In this situation I would be inclined to suggest that you either say no, or offer to try to sell one item as a test; get the seller's name, address, driver's license, and so on. After the seller leaves, contact local law enforcement and describe your encounter and the item you have in your possession. Disclose the serial number if there is one. See what, if anything, they suggest.

YOU HAVE SAFETY CONCERNS

Another reason to say no is concern for your safety or the safety of others. You don't want to accept items that you cannot safely store or ship. It is also against eBay policy to sell "recalled" items. I don't know of any PowerSeller who has the time to do an extensive recall search for every item brought in, but if someone asked me to sell a truckload of "discontinued" baby cribs or car seats, I might spend a minute or two Googling the model number.

TO SELL OR NOT TO SELL?

Here are all my suggestions for what not to sell and how to decide whether or not to sell, summed up in one convenient list—refer to it often!

★ No junk! (ever!)

★ If you don't know how to ship, it don't sell it.

★ Check eBay's Prohibited and Questionable lists often (they change).

★ If you are a franchisee be sure you know the company's policies.

★ Post your list of unacceptable items.

★ Train new employees.

★ It's illegal to sell counterfeits, even if you disclose their real source.

★ Check the VeRO list, and consider avoiding those items to simplify your life.

★ It's against the law to sell stolen goods or items not owned by your customers.

★ Don't take items that are unsafe to store, use, or ship.

In this Chapter

TRIUMPHANT BURLEIGH returns from a tour of feats the champion by a fluke, marries his girl, retires to

CHAPTER 21

CHECK-IN AND RECORDKEEPING

It doesn't matter if you are reselling your own items as a standalone PowerSeller or are dealing with items you are selling for someone else as a Trading Assistant. You need to get the items into your "system" and keep accurate records.

WHAT RECORDS SHOULD YOU KEEP?

You want to know what you have in your inventory both for production and insurance purposes. If the items are yours, your accountant and various taxing agencies will want to know when you purchased them, how much they cost, and perhaps what value, if any, you have added to them (restoration, repackaging, and so on).

If you are selling commodity items, such as new electronics or office supplies, you will want to know what's in your inventory so that you can monitor how quickly it is "turning," and which things sell best.

If you are acting as a Trading Assistant you need to keep a close eye on the items owned by your customers. Are they getting listed quickly enough? Did they sell? What condition were they in when they arrived? Did you damage them, or were they like that when they came in? Have the unsold items been re-listed, returned to the owner, or donated as you agreed?

At a minimum, you need to know when you acquired each inventory item, who the owner is, costs if the items are yours, and where each item is to be stored. If you are acting as a Trading Assistant you also need to record the details of your agreement with the items' owners.

Item Information

You want enough detail about items to keep track of them while they are in your possession and to begin writing auction titles and descriptions. If items are traveling through your system together as a "lot" (12 hats in one auction, for example), you need to know that, too. At a minimum, you should record the following:

★ Date the items came into your possession

★ Source of the items (owner of the items if not you)

★ Cost of the items if you own them

★ Description of the items, any accessories, and so on

★ Condition of the items

★ What to do if the item does not sell (relist, return, donate)

★ Where they are stored (bin number, warehouse area, and so on)

Customer Information

If you are acting as a Trading Assistant or running a Trading Post you need additional details regarding the owner of the items, the agreements you have reached regarding starting prices, reserves, costs, and percentage paid by the customer, where to send the check, and perhaps more. At a minimum you need to know

★ Customer's full name

★ Customer's company or organization name, if any

★ Customer's address

★ Customer's phone and email address

★ Customer's drivers license, passport, or other government ID number, and perhaps even a fingerprint if required by local law

★ Financial arrangements (your fees, costs customer pays, and so on)

★ Auction specifics (how long, starting prices, reserves, and so on)

★ Unsold item handling agreements (return to owner, donate, or relist)

★ Where checks will be sent (home, company, charity)

Additionally, you might want to collect some marketing data about each customer—how did they hear about you? Which coupon(s) did they bring to you? Have they opted-in to your email or direct mail campaigns?

MANUAL OR AUTOMATED?

In a garage operation you might be able to keep track of things using paper records, but as the business grows this will be a frustrating, inefficient way to work. Imagine for a moment running only 100 auctions per month. That's 1,200 auction file folders. Moreover, customers and accountants are going to want their questions answered quickly, and you will not have the time to go rummaging through file folders, especially when there are thousands of them.

If you are not acting as a Trading Assistant you can probably automate the entire process using eBay's listing tools, perhaps integrated with QuickBooks (see Chapter 9, "Software"). But if you are a Trading Assistant and throw customer payment checks into the equation, you are going to need to either pick from a very small selection of off-the-shelf packages designed for Trading Assistants (see Chapter 9) or develop your own software.

As anyone who as ever developed software can tell you, it is a long, expensive, frustrating process, and a task you should undertake by yourself only reluctantly, and only after ruling out all other options.

Another alternative is to hook up with a franchisor that has developed software tools and recordkeeping procedures already.

DISCUSSIONS AT CHECK-IN

If you are a Trading Assistant, and especially if you run a Trading Post, you will be spending time speaking with customers when they bring you items to sell. This can be the most delightful part of the job, or the most frustrating. It can also be the most profitable part of your operation or a huge money pit, especially if you pay employees to chat with customers. Here are some of the things you can potentially learn from customers, at least sometimes:

★ Details (maker, model, features, size, pattern name)

★ Approximate age of the item

★ Its origin

★ What's included and missing (instructions, accessories, and so on)

★ Historical significance, if any

★ Flaws

★ Background information about the category, era, and so on

The challenge is to be friendly, professional, and thorough without rushing the customer or taking too long. Many customers, especially retired ones, love to talk. They will be bringing you things that will remind them of their past, and they will want to talk about that. Some of this reminiscing will be fascinating, and it will be tempting to get drawn into, and perhaps even enjoy an impromptu history lesson. Other times you will be thinking, "Come on, come on, come on, lady!"

There are situations where it makes sense to have dialogues with customers about their items, even prolonged discussions. Watch the *Antique Roadshow* on PBS. Frequently, those hosts draw out details about items that add value to them, and vouch for their authenticity.

It makes sense for you to explore the heritage of a beautiful Tiffany lamp, but probably not an MP3 player unless, of course, it was owned by Madonna's road manager and has a great story to go with it.

So, get in the habit of quickly sizing up your customers. Scan the piles of treasures folks bring to you, and triage them. Start with the most promising items. and then do some research (see Chapter 19, "Research"). Keep control of the conversation and the pace of the research as best you can.

Make three quick piles—yes, no, and dig a little deeper. Remember that at check-in you really want to determine only two things: Do you want to list this item, and is there anything this customer knows that you should know before s/he leaves?

HOW YOU SAY "NO" IS IMPORTANT, TOO

You, and your staff, if you have one, will need to find polite ways to say "No, thanks." Unless it's something obvious like an item you have a policy against taking, the main reason to say no will probably be lack of value (which is a nice way of saying the customer has brought in junk).

> **Tip**
>
> Don't forget to carefully tag and store items so that they can be tracked as they make their way through your operation. Your tracking system can be as simple as a consignment tag purchased online or at an office supply store or as fancy as a computer-generated bar code label that gets scanned as the item moves from workstation to workstation. The important thing is that you identify each item and all of its accessories, and move them into the system without damaging or losing anything.

I think the best approach is to do some research on a representative item or two and say "Sir, these are really nice shirts, but it looks like, at the moment, people on eBay are only paying about two dollars apiece for similar items. It would be a shame to see you let them go for so little. Why don't you hang onto these, and let's see what else you brought?"

Which is not to say you should jump to conclusions. A typical 45 RPM record when sold in a lot might fetch $0.15 to $0.50 or less on eBay. Recently a single 45, Roy Orbison's, *The Teen Kings,* the Je-wel (or Jewel) label, sold for $368.

You won't always know what's in those dusty piles. Sometimes the owners can give you clues. If they are avid collectors and the pile looks specialized, there is likely at least some valuable stuff in there.

You won't get it right every time, but you will eventually develop a sixth sense. If you are a smart, active PowerSeller you will also develop a research library, a collection of links to favorite Internet specialty sites, and perhaps the phone numbers and email addresses of experts.

NEGOTIATING STARTING PRICES, RESERVES, AND FEES

Settling on starting prices is perhaps the trickiest part of a Trading Assistant's "negotiations" with customers, especially first-time customers who have little eBay experience. It's pretty scary to list an item with a starting price of $0.99 hoping that it will grow to $600 or $1,000 or more, though we have all seen it happen in our experience as PowerSellers.

When we are selling our own items it's a little easier to take that risk than it is when we are listing things for customers. I always encourage customers to start as low as they can comfortably go, and then try to help them see how it works. For this purpose I keep a three-ring binder containing sample auctions that I started low. Most of the examples ended high, as you would expect. A few tanked, and you want to show an example or two of this just to make the point. eBay is not foolproof, and as PowerSellers we are not perfect. Stuff happens.

My personal rule of thumb is to never start an item at more than one-third of the expected ending price, and lower if at all possible. I have one exception to this rule that I have learned (and relearned) the hard way. When listing really obscure items of high value, but with a very small following, start the item at a price you will be comfortable taking if only one person bids.

You know my position on using reserves. If you use them, explain the consequences to the seller, and consider having a way to recover your costs if the items do not sell because of the reserve.

If you have a written fee structure there won't be much need to negotiate your fees unless the items in front of you are so valuable and so exciting that you don't want to see them being sold by anyone but you. For large, very promising lots, estate sales, business inventories, and so forth you can, of course, discuss discounts or fee waivers.

Be sure you put these things in writing, and if the discounts are only for a particular batch of items, make sure the customer understands that the old fee rules will be used for subsequent "everyday" auctions.

TERMS AND CONDITIONS

Terms and Conditions (T&Cs) should be preprinted on the paperwork your computer spits out and added as boilerplate to manual forms, if that's what you use for checking in items. Unfortunately, you will need to develop these forms by yourself because office supply stores don't usually stock consignment store forms, never mind forms with appropriate Terms and Conditions for eBay Trading Assistants.

The exact wording of Terms and Conditions will vary, and you should consult with your insurance company and an attorney familiar with local law when developing yours. In general, at a minimum your T&Cs should document the fact that

★ The customer stipulates that the items being sold are his or hers to sell legally

★ The customer understands the type of relationship you have

★ The customer understands that there is no backing out if an auction ends with at least one successful bidder

★ The customer owns the goods during the auction

★ The customer is responsible for any insurance before, during, and after the auction, if that's the case (ask your insurance company)

★ The customer has not misrepresented the items

Beyond that you will need a thousand words, all in the context of your state and local regulations, dealing with consequential damage waivers, the survival of the contract if parts are invalid, and so on. You really should have professional help developing your Terms and Conditions page. Explain your business to a lawyer with experience in the field of retail consignment and you should be on the right track.

SIGNED ITEM RECEIPT

Always have the customer sign a document specifying what was left in your care, and attesting to the fact that the customer understands the terms and conditions. Ideally, the signature should be on the page carrying the T&Cs.

"WHAT HAPPENS NEXT?" INFORMATION

Customers, especially new ones, want to know what will happen next, and about when it will start happening. You can go over this verbally with them, or have it print out on the customer's receipt, or perhaps, as some PowerSellers do, develop a little "welcome" package that answers all the questions, shows them how to follow their auctions, and so on. Regardless of how you do it, make sure the customer knows what to expect so that you won't get a slew of panicky phone calls or emails. You won't have time for that. Taking stuff in is just the beginning.

CUSTOMER PAPERWORK

After you have decided which items you will be listing the customer should walk away with paperwork specifying at least the following:

★ What items are being left with you

★ Their condition, accessories, and so on

★ The agreed-upon starting prices and reserves, if any

★ The planned length of the auction(s)

★ Fees and costs to be paid by the customer

★ Estimated starting date of auctions

★ Approximate anticipated date customer will be paid

★ Method of payment, and where payment will be sent

★ A copy of their signed receipt

★ A printed "what happens next?" reminder

★ Your other terms and conditions (the "fine print")

In this Chapter

TRIUMPHANT BURLEIGH returns from a tour of feats the champion by a fluke, marries his girl, retires t

Bug-a-boo

with and without D. D. T.

kills all 9

major pests

● Spray those pests away for good — with Bug-a-boo! This super-insect spray, with and without D.D.T.—far exceeds U. S. Government standards for an AA Grade insecticide. Even kills roaches and moth larvae!

Yet Bug-a-boo won't harm humans, won't damage home furnishings, when used as directed. And it's pine-scented—and so pleasant to use.

For long-lasting protection from pests, you may prefer the new Bug-a-boo with 3% D.D.T. It contains Bug-a-boo's time-tested, insect-killing ingredients, plus all the D.D.T. that's required for effective residual deposit, and the full amount considered justified for home uses.

Caution: Use Bug-a-boo with D.D.T. carefully, according to the directions.

KILLS
FLIES · ANTS
MOTHS · ROACHES
MOSQUITOES
BEDBUGS
SILVERFISH

CHAPTER 22

MANAGING WORKFLOW

I promise. I am not about to go "MBA" on you here. But this is an important topic, and whether you develop a formal written workflow plan or just keep workflow efficiencies in the back of your mind as you develop and grow your business, be it a solo venture, or bristling with employees, workflow is a key ingredient to profitability.

I once took a college course from a Zen-like professor who taught us early printing techniques—lithography, hand-set typography, and so on. The first time I ever thought about workflow was watching him demonstrate how to clean a printing press.

He attacked the project with a plan. He had just the right number of the perfect rags for the job and a place to put them when they were dirty. He folded them each "just so," making it possible to use the maximum cleaning capacity of each folded surface without getting his hands dirty. He had several specialized cleaning tools and solvents. He moved from one specific part of the press to the next in a well-reasoned ballet, knowing when to speed up, where to slow down, and why. He seemed to love the one task that we students disliked the most. And he could do it in about half the time that it took us.

Regardless of the size of your PowerSeller operation, the more efficient and well–thought-out your workflow, the more profitable and happy you are likely to be. In eBay selling, time really is money.

The objective is to launch, sell, and ship as many items as possible with the lowest possible labor cost. The key factors you need to get your arms around to improve workflow are the following:

★ The necessary tasks (check-in, photography, listing, and so on)

★ The players: Who will do each task?

★ The required order of completion and dependencies (you can't ship until an item is paid for, for example)

★ Potential bottlenecks and remedies

★ Standards and limitations (how many photos can you take in a day, for example)

★ Goals

WHAT IT TAKES TO SELL AN ITEM

Let's take a look at these factors and see how they affect each other. It's a little sobering when you make a list of everything that needs to be done as a PowerSeller. Failing to realize that it all needs doing or, worse yet, failing to do any one of these things in a timely fashion, can ruin your business. At a minimum you must

★ Research, check in, and move items to temporary storage

★ Move items to the photography area and photograph them

★ Possibly edit the photos (crop, color correct, resize, and so on)

★ Move items to the listing area; write titles and listings

★ Move items to the "on-auction" storage area

★ Launch auctions, initiate store sales, update inventory counts, and so on

★ Monitor auctions and other sales; answer questions

★ Monitor payments and solve after-sale problems

★ Locate and move sold, paid-for items to shipping area

★ Pack and ship

★ Leave feedback

In a typical garage operation this might all be done by one or two people, and moving items from one workstation to another might be as simple as handing them to each other. In a large operation you might need to wrangle multiple warehouses, pallets, forklifts, and delivery trucks.

Even a 1,600 square foot Trading Post has some materials that present handling challenges, because the workstations are usually widespread and the storage requirements are considerable. (It takes quite a few shelves filled with other peoples' stuff to make an operation profitable.) For example, Figure 22.1 shows just a portion of a typical Trading Post storage area.

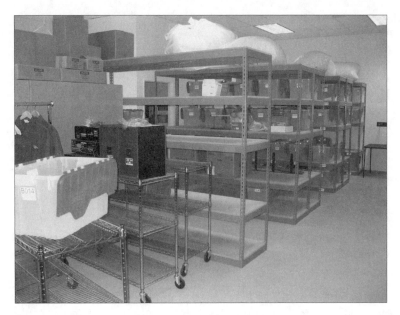

FIGURE 22.1

Part of a Trading Post storage area.

Notice the rolling carts with the wheels in the foreground of Figure 22.1. These carts can be a handy way to move your work-in-progress from station to station. For example, you could load a cart with new items during check-in, and then move it to photography, and then on to the listing station, without bringing items in and out of the shelving storage area. This only works, by the way, if your whole operation can process items quickly and smoothly.

MANAGEMENT TASKS AND COMMUNICATIONS

Besides moving items from place to place in your location there are other "nonproduction" tasks that someone will need to perform. For example, someone will need to obtain items to sell (through marketing, garage sale scrounging, wholesale contracting, and so on). Someone will need to answer the phone and emails, do the bookkeeping, banking, supply shopping, housekeeping...the list goes on.

In a solo operation these tasks all fall to the production person as well, and can lead to interruptions and inefficiencies that need to be minimized. This is perhaps the best argument for employing at least one part-time helper even in a new PowerSeller business. If you can't do that consider making Friday or Saturday item acquisition day, Monday listing day, Wednesday shipping day, and so on.

THE PLAYERS

Whether you have two or two hundred workers the objective is the same. You need to make certain they each know what they are expected to do, and how to do every part of their jobs correctly and efficiently. They must also learn how to work together (see Chapter 32, "Finding and Keeping Great Help).

Caution

By the way, buyers hate waiting nearly a week for items to ship, so as tempting as the notion of having a single shipping day each week might sound, it's probably not a good long-term solution. You will be better off hiring a part-time shipping person instead.

As any rowing team can tell you, it's not enough to have all the seats filled in the boat. In order to win everybody needs to know what to do and when to do it. And they all must want to win.

An important part of workflow is teaching employees how things should work, and why. Then you need to be sure it all happens.

ORDER AND DEPENDENCIES

In any process there are dependencies. You can't launch an auction until the photos have been taken and perhaps edited, for example. This makes photography a pretty high priority. If you work alone, consider taking and editing batches of photos for multiple items before sitting down to write titles and descriptions. This is usually more efficient than taking photos for one item, and then editing them, and then writing the description, and so on.

If you employ separate workers for photography and listing, consider having the photographer start early in the day to create an inventory of photos for the lister to use when s/he comes in to write and launch the day's listings.

You can't ship until payments have been made and cleared. You can't ship until the delivery truck comes. And, if you take things to a delivery drop-off point you can't ship after the drop-off point closes. So, whereas someone needs to be monitoring and coaxing along payments in the morning, perhaps the shipping person need not arrive until noon, and then take items to the drop-off point on the way home at four, or whenever.

This will obviously vary with the size of your operation and local realities, but you get my point. Look at the dependencies, and do everything in your power to avoid having people sitting on their hands waiting for each other. Or, better yet, cross-train them to pitch in when bottlenecks do occur.

BOTTLENECKS AND REMEDIES

No matter how carefully you plan there will be days when things grind to a halt. You will have too many photos to take, or some really challenging items to pack and ship, or a flood of new customers with questions to ask and items to research.

If your bottlenecks are rare, and random, you can overcome them by working a few extra hours or by cross-training employees so that they can pitch in to get things done. In fact, in a Trading Post it's essential to have employees cross-trained because the environment is so often unpredictable and customer-service driven.

But if you see the same problems cropping up routinely—never getting everything shipped out on Monday, the lister constantly waiting for photographs, and so on—you need to find out why and solve these problems permanently. Sometimes it's as easy as adjusting schedules or adding an employee. Training can often help. Ask your co-workers for suggestions. What do they think would be the most effective solution?

Look at the facility, too. Are there simple tools that could help? Is the layout as efficient as it should be? Are your systems slowing you down?

LAYOUT

The right layout can contribute to efficient workflow. You want to move things short distances, with a minimum of physical effort, and not very often. You don't want to be tripping over items at any stage of the process (see Figure 22.2).

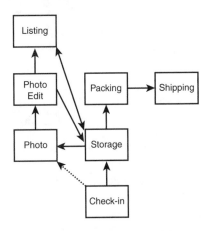

FIGURE 22.2
Storage is central to most PowerSeller operations.

In a typical operation one of two things happens to items once you check them in. Either they go to storage or directly to the photo station for photography. Once they have been shot, they either go to storage or to the lister (or if you work alone, the area where you do your listings), so that items can be inspected, weighed, and described.

The photo images need to be delivered to, or at least be made available to, the computer where listing is done by either downloading them directly from the camera or by saving them after they are edited, cropped, and so forth.

While the auction runs the items need to be back in storage where, unless you need to pull them out to answer bidders' questions, they remain until they move to the packing table, and eventually to your loading dock, rolling cart, or panel truck.

Obviously, the storage area is pretty central to your operation regardless of whether you work in a garage or a citywide network of stores. This is why it is a good idea to have storage onsite whenever possible. Remote storage locations are usually inefficient in a PowerSeller operation. You might also want the storage area to be in the middle of, or at least adjacent to, the photographer, lister, and shipping workstations.

Shelves should be numbered and designed to hold a minimum of three-weeks' worth of inventory, probably more. You want most manageable items stored in bins on shelves, but you will need floor and wall space for any large items you plan to list—skis, bikes, and so on.

If you will be selling clothing, and have sufficient room, get at least three rolling garment racks, one for recently checked-in items, one for items waiting to be photographed and listed, and one for items that have already been listed.

SETTING GOALS AND STANDARDS

Although not every item you list will require the same amount of time and effort, it's a good idea to develop standards, or time expectations for the various tasks performed as a PowerSeller. You can do this from the bottom up or the top down. For example, the top-down approach might start with you asking "How many items do I want to list each day?" Is it 10? Is it 20? Then you can break this down further—10 minutes to shoot and edit photos, 15 minutes to list and launch, and so on.

After setting what seem to be reasonable goals, do some time testing. Get out the stopwatch. Take notes. See if your standards are realistic. And remember, things that go quickly while working by yourself quietly in the basement or garage might take longer as you add employees, walk-in customers, an expanding volume of email and phone interruptions, and so on. Being a sole PowerSeller is one thing. Running a bustling operation can be quite different.

At any rate, once you have established standards, or at least goals, see what happens. How close are you getting? What's taking longer than expected? Is there something about the workflow or the tools you use that can improve things?

PLANNING FOR GROWTH

Out of more than a hundred PowerSellers I have met only one who wished he had leased less floor space rather than more. And in truth, what this fellow needed was more stuff, not less space. If you do your marketing well you will be amazed one day at how much stuff comes in. People would like you to sell their big items for them, and if you are geared up properly this can be great business. Even veteran PowerSellers will bring you things to sell if you can handle the big stuff efficiently.

Given the choice between a space that's a little too big or a little too small, opt for too big. You'll grow into it.

TIPS AND TRICKS

★ Think about workflow every day. When you say to yourself, "Gosh I hate doing this," see if there is a better way, or if it's possible to eliminate the step entirely.

★ Work in batches, particularly if a task requires setup and teardown.

★ Install pegs, cubbies, and drawers for tools and props.

Tip

Don't forget to purge! Some percentage of your stuff won't sell through, and if you are a Trading Assistant you need to get that stuff either back to its rightful owner or into the hands of a charity. Tripping over unsold, off-auction junk will negatively affect your productivity. If you are selling your own inventory, and some of it fails to move satisfactorily, price it to sell or donate it.

★ Label work areas, storage areas, and carts so that it's easy to put things where they belong.

★ Put things where they belong.

★ Get an opinion from others. Do you ever say to yourself, "There must be a better way"? There probably is.

★ Put someone in charge, even if more than one person does the same task.

★ Set standards, and review your results frequently. Are things better or worse than you expect? Why?

★ Toss things that get in the way. Pallets, used boxes, and last month's magazines are all clutter, and probably hinder efficient workflow.

In this Chapter

★ **Take the Right Pictures**

★ **Take Enough Pictures**

★ **Make Photos Inviting**

★ **Illustrate Scale**

★ **Think About the Gallery Shot**

★ **Don't Mislead**

★ **Use Props to Set the Stage**

★ **Include Nameplates and Serial Numbers**

★ **Ten Quick Photography Tricks**

TRIUMPHANT BURLEIGH returns from a tour of fi... feats the champion by a fluke, marries his girl, retires to f...

PHOTOGRAPHY

Good auction photos let bidders get as close as possible to the items they are considering without actually touching them. Photos need to be accurate, flattering, and tell the whole story. Great pictures will increase ending prices and improve your return rate and feedback. Back in Chapter 8, "Computers, Office Equipment, and More," you looked at the hardware you need to make great photos—a contemporary digital camera, tripod, soft lighting, and a seamless background. Now let's look at what you need to do with those items.

TAKE THE RIGHT PICTURES

When deciding which pictures to take, imagine that you are about to describe the item to someone over the telephone. What features would the person want to know about—color, size, what's on the top, bottom, and sides? Is there a maker's mark or other detail that would help the interested party come to some conclusion about the item's value? Are there any flaws? Does it come with accessories? Packaging? Instructions?

TAKE ENOUGH PICTURES

A simple, inexpensive item might only require a picture or two to tell the story. A car or motor home might require 30 or more to do the job right. If you don't take enough pictures, you will get more phone calls and email inquiries, or worse yet, fewer bids.

The average $50 item probably deserves between four and eight photos. But sometimes the story can be told with one. Figure 23.1 shows a single photo that was used as the only photo in a successful auction. It also served as the Gallery shot. The photo shows the controls, the mounting screw hole, the cable, connectors, and instructions. You even get a sense of the size of the device by comparing it to an adult hand.

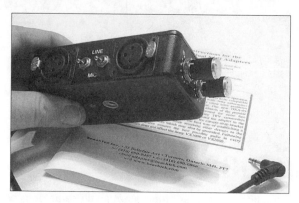

FIGURE 23.1
Sometimes one photo can tell the whole story.

MAKE PHOTOS INVITING

Sometimes, simply changing the angle of a shot can make the items seem more interesting and inviting. Consider the almost straight-on photo in Figure 23.2 with the angled from above shot in Figure 23.3. They are both photos of similar items.

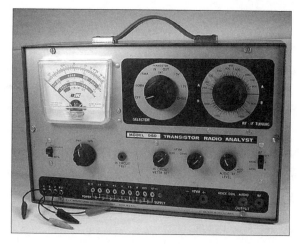

FIGURE 23.2
A boring straight-on photo.

FIGURE 23.3
A similar item shot from above and at an angle.

Neither photo will ever hang in the Guggenheim Museum, but the angled photo is more appealing; and shooting from that angle solved a nasty glare problem near the top left of the item.

ILLUSTRATE SCALE

Sometimes it's difficult to judge the size of something by looking at a photo. Some things—collectible baskets, for example—come in such a wide range of sizes that, unless you put some scale reference in the shot, there is no way of telling how big or small an item is.

Some of the strangest things can be misconstrued this way. I once sold a child's baby stroller on eBay. It was a toy that a toddler would put a doll in and push around the nursery. This stroller was perhaps 24" tall. We took a bunch of photos of the empty carriage and wrote a poor description that did not contain dimensions. A local woman called on the phone to ask if she could see the carriage before she bid. I heard a baby crying in the background. "You aren't thinking of buying the stroller to push that new baby of yours around in are you?" She was. I saved her the trip. But imagine. What if the woman had lived across the country, or across the ocean, and won the item?

Figure 23.4 shows a great example of illustrating scale in a photo.

FIGURE 23.4

Show scale in at least one shot.

THINK ABOUT THE GALLERY SHOT

When taking photos you also want to keep the Gallery shot in mind. It's a shot that tells the whole story, but in one bold, easy-to read, close-up image. This is simple if you are selling a watch or a shirt or a car, but it gets trickier if you are listing a lot of small items. A wide shot of the whole collection will turn to mush when eBay reduces it to Gallery size.

Figure 23.4 shows one solution to the problem. Take a close-up of a representative item with the remainder of the lot as a backdrop. It says, "Here's one of many." Then you will want to follow up with establishing shots of the entire lot, and perhaps some additional close-ups of other important details. For example, Figures 23.5 and 23.6 show the entire lot of crystals depicted in Figure 23.4. Figure 23.5 is an overview of the entire collection in its wooden case; Figure 23.6 shows the collection with the case closed.

FIGURE 23.5
An overview of the collection in its case.

FIGURE 23.6
The collection with the case latched shut.

DON'T MISLEAD

Never intentionally hide flaws or damage. For example, the photo in Figure 23.7 shows a great-looking vintage radio. But when you take the radio out of the case it is obvious that it has suffered sun damage over the years (see Figure 23.8). It's important to include both photos and point out the damage in the description.

FIGURE 23.7

The radio looks great in its leather case.

FIGURE 23.8

But there is sun damage to the grill, visible in this photo.

USE PROPS TO SET THE STAGE

Props can be helpful, particularly when photographing small items such as jewelry. For example, Figure 23.9 shows a prop that comes in handy for shooting watches and bracelets.

There are similar low-cost holders for earrings, necklaces, and rings. You can also employ simple found objects such as rocks or twigs or metal blocks as props. Figure 23.10 shows an example of this. (Be sure folks understand that they won't be getting the prop if it looks like it has any value.)

Tip

Consider purchasing male and female mannequins if you plan to sell clothing. All of these props can be found on eBay. Search eBay category 1079 for mannequins and 67697 for most earring, necklace, and similar props. Froogle is another good source.

FIGURE 23.9
Use props to help showcase small items.

FIGURE 23.10
Even a rock can help tell the story.

INCLUDE NAMEPLATES AND SERIAL NUMBERS

Collectors are often interested in nameplates and serial number photos. It's a good idea to include them. Figure 23.11 shows an example.

FIGURE 23.11

Photograph serial number plates, especially on collectibles.

TEN QUICK PHOTOGRAPHY TRICKS

Here are 10 factors that can make you and your staff better, more efficient photographers.

1. Minimize Editing Time

Shoot tight photographs so that you won't need to spend time cropping them. Use a clean background and get in close enough to fill the camera viewfinder with the image whenever possible. Keep items out of the shot if they will not be included in the auction.

2. Consider Download Speed

When preparing photos for auction your want the final size to be no more than 800 pixels wide, or perhaps as few as 400 to 600 pixels wide. This offers enough detail for most items, reduces the file size, and makes screen-drawing speeds tolerable even for eBayers using dial-up connections.

3. Shoot Big, Reduce Only Once

Even though your final auction photos need to be around 800 pixels wide or smaller, you should shoot at a relatively high resolution (perhaps as large as 3264 pixels or more wide); then, after doing any necessary cropping or color correcting, resize the image to its final auction size. Try to resize and compress images only once if possible, to minimize quality loss.

4. Remember, It's Not Art—It's Product Photography

Photography can be fun. It's tempting to labor at getting just the right lighting, angle, and mood for each item you auction, but resist the temptation. Budget a reasonable amount of time to shoot and edit each series of photos for a single item, ideally 10 minutes or less, and then keep an eye on the clock. Obviously you will want to spend more time on complex, valuable items, less on simple, inexpensive ones.

5. Use a Tripod

People really resist this advice, but it is sound just the same. Use a tripod whenever possible. Your photos will come out much sharper and you will need to reshoot far less often. There is no substitute for a rock-steady camera, no matter how good today's in-camera stabilization and software sharpening features are.

6. Batch Similar Items

If you have a lot of clothes to shoot, set up the mannequin and lights once and shoot them one after the other in a batch. The same is true of tiny items that require close-up photography and props. It will save you setup and teardown time.

7. Cut the Cord

As tempting as it might be to use an AC adapter to power your camera, I recommend that you buy two rechargeable batteries (or sets of batteries) and an external charger so that you can shoot using one set of batteries while recharging the second. Working with the camera plugged in can be a tripping hazard, particularly when used with a tripod. I have seen more than one camera destroyed when someone tripped on the power cord, sending the camera to the floor.

8. Read the Bloody Manual, and Then Experiment

Your camera came with a thick manual, probably containing instructions printed in six languages. Pick a language, and at least skim the whole thing. Cameras work differently. Some, for example, make the best close-ups if you zoom out to the wide angle position first. Others have "close-up modes."

Start by seeing what the manufacturer has designed for you and how to use the features; then experiment, and practice on your own before things get busy. Take notes, too. Train your staff if you have one.

9. Avoid Extraneous Light

Light comes in different colors. Outdoor light, at least in the afternoon, is fairly blue compared with incandescent light. Overhead fluorescents usually emit greenish light. Your camera and photo editing software will try to deal with this, but if you have light pouring in from three sources—the window, overhead fluorescents, and your photo lights—the results will be disappointing. One corner of the photo might be blue, the other green, and so on.

Try to shield your subject from all but the photography lights. Take out those overhead tubes. Locate the photo area away from windows, if possible. If not, find a way to block the outside light with curtains, moveable walls, and so on. Sometimes light domes and cubes such as the ones discussed in Chapter 8 can help you control light too.

10. Organize Your Image Library

If you sell 10 items a day and take 8 pictures of each item you will be shooting and managing nearly 1,800 to 2,500 images a month! At a minimum, you should create dated, daily folders on your hard disk to organize the images. Get in the habit of deleting or at least archiving old images once a month or quarterly.

If you sell commodity items over and over again, keep those images organized and readily at hand as well.

TRIUMPHANT BURLEIGH returns from a tour of fi... feats the champion by a fluke, marries his girl, retires to...

G'BYE

In this Chapter

★ **The Objectives**

★ **The Title**

★ **Abbreviations**

★ **Misspellings**

★ **The Description**

★ **Text Sells!**

Bug-a-boo

with and without D.D.T.

kills all 9 major pests

● Spray those pests away for good — with Bug-a-boo! This super-insect spray, with and without D.D.T.—far exceeds U. S. Government standards for an AA Grade insecticide. Even kills roaches and moth larvae!

Yet Bug-a-boo won't harm humans, won't damage home furnishings, when used as directed. And it's pine-scented—and so pleasant to use.

For long-lasting protection from pests, you may prefer the new Bug-a-boo with 3% D.D.T. It contains Bug-a-boo's time-tested, insect-killing ingredients, plus all the D.D.T. that's required for effective residual deposit, and the full amount considered justified for home uses.

Caution: Use Bug-a-boo with D.D.T. carefully, according to the directions.

KILLS

FLIES · ANTS

MOTHS · ROACHES

MOSQUITOES

BEDBUGS

SILVERFISH

THE SUPER INSECT SPRAY

Bug-a-boo
WITH QUICK-ACTING TOXIC INGREDIENTS

THE SUPER INSECT SPRAY

Bug-a-boo
Plus 3% D.D.T.

CHAPTER 24

WRITING GREAT TITLES AND DESCRIPTIONS

Titles are the signposts pointing to your listings, and descriptions are the equivalent of your sales staff. You want both titles and descriptions to work as hard as possible for you. Because most eBay users start shopping by searching titles, and because titles can be only 55 characters long, yours need to be carefully crafted. Once drawn in by a great title, readers want to know why they should buy your item instead of someone else's. They need you to "hold" the item in your hand and tell them about it.

THE OBJECTIVES

Selling on eBay is a competition. There can be literally millions of other items besides yours that bidders will be tempted to buy instead. Every other seller of a similar item is a competitor. You want to win! Here are the key goals your listings need to accomplish:

★ Reach the right audience

★ Make browsers stop, read, and bid

★ Make bidders want yours the most of any

★ Answer questions so you don't have to

★ Accurately represent items to minimize returns

★ Get browsers and bidders interested in you as a seller

★ Cross-promote your other auctions

THE TITLE

Most eBay buyers begin their quest with a title search. A large percentage of the time they will switch to browsing a category, or searching both titles and descriptions, so a messed-up title isn't the end of the world, but the wrong title will reduce the number of eyeballs seeing your auction, and almost certainly will lower the ending price. You need to squeeze all the possible mileage out of your titles.

You can use up to 55 characters (including spaces) in an eBay auction title, and you should try to use all 55 characters without looking goofy. So forget "L@@K!" and "WOW!" and "YIKES WHAT A DEAL..." You want to use those precious 55 characters to write words buyers will search for; and if you have a few characters left over use them to draw searchers in. Look at the following five title examples for the same item:

★ Old Camera

★ Minolta Camera

★ Vintage Minolta Camera

★ Vintage Minolta SRT-101 SLR Camera

★ VINTAGE MINOLTA SRT-101 35MM SLR CAMERA ZOOM TESTED NR!

Do you know how many old cameras there are on eBay? I just did a search for "old camera" and got 22,336 hits this afternoon. What are the odds of somebody finding your camera if you list it that way?

Searching for "Minolta camera" turns up an equally unmanageable 10,536 hits. Although these first two titles are aimed at your audience, they are so broad as to be useless. Faced with 10,000 listings a searcher is either going to use additional search words to narrow the results (vintage, or 35mm, or SLR, perhaps), or search by a model number he knows.

The phrase "Vintage Minolta Camera" uncovered 430 listings, many of them not for cameras, but now the searcher is at least getting warm, and will likely switch to Gallery Picture view and flip through to find the first instance of something he likes— a Minolta SRT-101, perhaps. So you would likely be lost by using the first two titles, but in the running with the third and subsequent expanded titles.

A search for "Minolta SRT-101" turned up 128 matching cameras and accessories. If someone is looking for an SRT-101 they would almost certainly find yours if you used this title.

Some of the other words in the title are there to draw searchers in. "Tested" makes them want to know if it works, and how well. Zoom tells them there is a lens, and maybe a nice one. We'll discuss abbreviation in the next section.

ABBREVIATIONS

Abbreviations abound in titles, and there are three in our sample title—35mm, SLR, and NR. Abbreviations can very useful, but can also be tricky.

Some abbreviations, like *NR* for *No Reserve*, are widely known by the eBay community. Other abbreviations, such as *SLR* (*Single Lens Reflex*), will only be known by people with technical knowledge of the category. Usually abbreviations do not help narrow searches, but sometimes they can. "35mm," a film format abbreviation, is something some shoppers search for.

Don't fill your titles so full of abbreviations that they read like NASA astronauts' training manuals. And make sure that your target buyers, at least some of them, will recognize and be drawn in by the abbreviations.

Some common abbreviations are listed in Table 24.1.

TABLE 24.1 Common eBay Listing Abbreviations

Abbreviation	Meaning
NR	No Reserve
NIB	New in Box
NWT	New With Tags
NOS	New Old Stock
G, or GD	Good Condition
LDT	Limited Edition
MIB	Mint in Box
MITB	Mint in the Box
MIMB	Mint in Mint Box

There is a great web site devoted to auction abbreviations, among other things. It's run by Times Publishing and is called Antique Web. A portion of the abbreviations page is shown in Figure 24.1. Visit www.antiqueweb.com or www.RonMansfield. com/links.htm for a direct link to the abbreviations page.

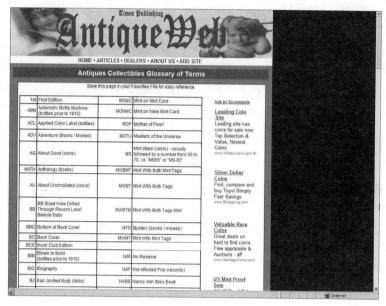

FIGURE 24.1
A list of commonly used abbreviations on the web.

The **TOP 10** Title Do's and Don'ts

10. Consider including misspellings, but include the proper spelling too.

9. Don't use apostrophes (write mens, not men's).

8. Consider repeating yourself with small variations in some categories, i.e. Men Man.

7. Avoid the words "prohibited," "banned," "illegal," "outlawed," or any other descriptor that might bring into question the legality of an item by either governmental or eBay standards.

6. Use all 55 characters if possible.

5. Use brand names (and artists names), but only the specific name of the maker. For example, writing "Timex Watch, Not a Rolex" is against eBay policy, and considered to be *keyword spamming*.

4. What words would *you* use to search? Include them.

3. Consider using ALL CAPS to stand out, and subtitles in crowded categories even though title searches do not examine subtitles.

2. Research auctions (active and closed) for similar items. What do their titles say?

1. Tell them exactly what it is (camera, necktie, and so on).

MISSPELLINGS

Misspellings are commonplace on eBay, and there is much folklore about bargains to be had by searching for common misspellings. The theory is that items with misspelled titles have fewer hits.

As a seller you can turn this on its head. Simply include common misspellings in your titles and descriptions, but be sure to spell the item correctly as well. Because after all, if sellers misspell things, shoppers probably can't spell either, right? And because there are more shoppers than sellers, people who can't spell will find your auctions if you include popular misspellings.

Because there is a web site devoted to every oddball thing on the planet, you'd expect at least one

Tip

Some sellers put misspellings in their descriptions and change the font to the same color as the background so that searches hit the misspellings but readers don't see them.

site devoted to misspellings, and you won't be disappointed. My current favorite is www.bargaintoolbox.com. You start by entering a correctly spelled word. In Figure 24.2 I've typed "transistor."

Bargintoolbox then looks for auctions containing misspellings and rounds them up for you to explore. Notice in Figure 24.3 that the seller of the GE radio appears to have intentionally added a misspelling of the word transistor to his title. In addition to the correct spelling he has entered "Transitor" to gather up spelling-challenged shoppers, I suppose.

Using this tool, take a look at auctions in your favorite categories. Do misspellings work? Maybe. Give them a try.

Another site worth checking out is SearchSpell.com, designed to help web developers get traffic to their sites by including misspellings in meta tags used by search engines. This site can give you ideas of which misspellings to include in your listings and titles as well.

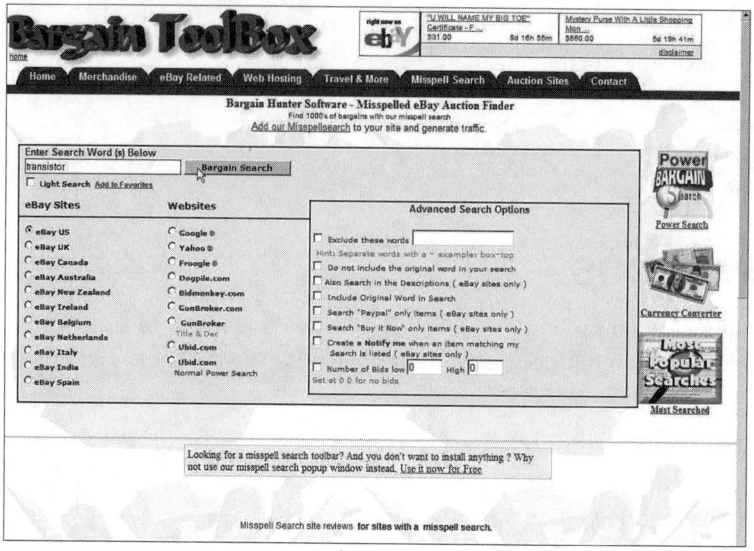

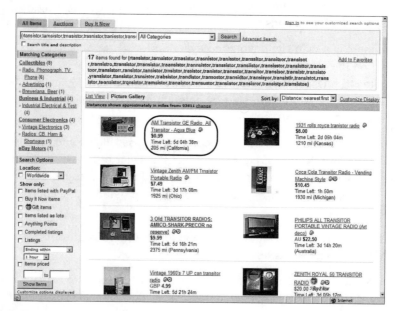

FIGURE 24.2

Bargaintoolbox.com has a misspelling tool worth exploring.

FIGURE 24.3

Bargaintoolbox shows you eBay auctions containing misspellings.

THE DESCRIPTION

A good description needs to do the same things as the title, only in more detail. Begin with the basics. Repeat the title at the beginning of your description. Name the brand and model number; describe the color, condition, and size; and list any accessories. Is there a warranty? Tell us.

The description is also the place where you can point out details, reassure bidders, and promote yourself as well as your other auctions. Let's look at some of those opportunities.

What's Unique?

Use the description to point out why your item is better or more interesting than the rest. Does it have an interesting backstory? Tell it briefly. For example:

"The owner of this canteen says he had it with him when he landed on Normandy Beach during the 1944 invasion. He clams that dent you can see in the photos is from a deflected bullet, and that the canteen saved his life."

Do you offer a better than average warranty or return policy? Brag about it in your description. Is the item more complete than most or in unusually good condition? Let browsers know. Point things out even if they seem obvious to you in the photos.

Reassure Buyers About You as the Seller

If you are an expert, or have above average knowledge of an item you are listing, it's perfectly legitimate to brag, or at least allude to your expertise. For example:

"When I was in college in the sixties I sold stereo equipment at a high-end electronics store. These vintage ElectroVoice EV4s were my favorite speakers back then, and they still make the hair on my neck stand up when I hear them today."

Make Buyers Imagine Owning It

Flip open a Sharper Image catalog. These folks write great ad copy, and that's what you are doing here in your auction description. Notice how they draw readers in and make them imagine owning the product. You can use this technique too. For example:

"Your collector friends will be envious when they flip this over and see the serial number. Imagine owning one of the first (whatevers) made!"

Cross-Promote

Mention your other auctions and your store if you have one. If the item is one of many from an estate sale, mention that too. Savvy shoppers will automatically check to see what else you found on the estate, and will likely bookmark you as a favorite seller to watch for later listings from the estate.

Build Customer Confidence

Tear down the roadblocks. Sound nicer and easier to do business with than the rest. For example, here's what I say in all of my auctions:

> *"You Are Gonna Love it, Guaranteed! First, check out my store description and feedback. Still not sure? Your purchase is guaranteed to be as described in this listing. If you disagree after holding it in your hands, simply notify me within five (5) days of receiving it, and pay only the return postage and insurance for a prompt refund. The item must arrive here in the condition it left and security marks, if any, will be verified."*

Point Out the Flaws

Nothing's perfect, especially if you sell used items, so don't pretend they are if they aren't. You can often put flaws in perspective to do damage control, but be honest, and when in doubt, err on the conservative. Here's an example:

> *"As you can see from the first photo this will look fantastic on your shelf, and you will want to feature it in your collection. There is a scratch on the bottom (see the second photo), so while this is not a mint item, it is darn close to it."*

If you test an item, tell readers what you tested, what you didn't test, what worked, and what this means regarding returns.

One last tip: Don't say that you can't swear to about an item's authenticity. This is against eBay policy.

TEXT SELLS!

Here's a quick rundown of the tips you learned in this chapter to help you write top-notch titles and descriptions that help you sell:

★ Titles draw buyers to your auctions. You have only 55 characters to catch their attention. Don't waste them.

★ Be specific in your title. Use brand names and model numbers.

★ Make titles and descriptions interesting and engaging, but accurate.

★ Look at the titles and descriptions of successful competitive auctions. What worked for those sellers?

★ Don't copy and paste other peoples' auctions or web content.

★ If you abbreviate, make sure people will understand.

★ Consider placing misspellings in descriptions and perhaps even in titles. But always include correct spellings in titles at least once.

★ Be reassuring. Tell bidders why they should want your item the most.

★ Cross-promote your store and other listings in every auction!

In this Chapter

CHAPTER 25

LISTING ITEMS

Your photos are done and it's time to get those items listed and sold. Chances are if you are reading this book you have sold a lot of items on eBay already, so I'll not take you step-by-step through the process of launching a listing on eBay. If you were a beginner, you'd be reading the *Absolute Beginner's Guide to eBay*, right?

Instead, I'd like to point out what I think are some best practices and pitfalls—choices you should and shouldn't make when listing. Where you make these choices, and how the screens look when you make them, will vary with the listing software you use, but in the end you will be choosing eBay options.

TYPE OF AUCTION

When listing multiple similar items it's often a good idea to run a few as auctions, others as fixed priced items (Buy it Now), and park some more in your store, long-term. Even if you don't have multiple identical items you can mix things up a bit for added effect. For example, when I sell a collectible radio on auction that uses an oddball battery I make sure that I have some of those batteries in my store, and also as current, short Buy-it-Now "auctions."

Also, as you can see in Figure 25.1, if you are using eBay's Selling Manager Pro you can quickly launch a new instance of an existing inventory item right from within eBay's top-level Sell page.

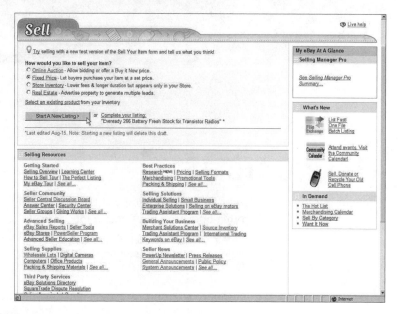

FIGURE 25.1
Pick the type(s) of auction you want. Mix it up if you can.

GET HELP PICKING CATEGORIES

If you always sell in the same handful of categories you know their numbers by heart. But if you are unfamiliar with an item or a category, eBay's Keyword search feature, shown in Figures 25.2 and 25.3, can be a big help. For example, suppose someone brings you an old Heathkit tube tester from the '60s. Type in the keywords "Heathkit tube tester," and maybe the model number if you know it, and then click Search. You'll get results similar to those in Figure 25.3.

eBay proposes at least one category, and often several. It shows up to the top 10 categories chosen by people selling items containing the keywords you entered, Heathkit tube tester in this example.

I picked an intentionally obscure example here to illustrate a point. There can be a number of good choices for your listing, at least three in this case. This might be an item that would profit from listing in multiple categories, perhaps the first and third ones shown in the list in Figure 25.3.

Note

Even if you use a third-party listing tool such as ándale or your franchisor's proprietary system you can use this category search tool. Simply open a browser window and pretend to use it to sell an item on eBay, stopping at the search category step. Leave the browser window open in the background and search multiple items with it as needed.

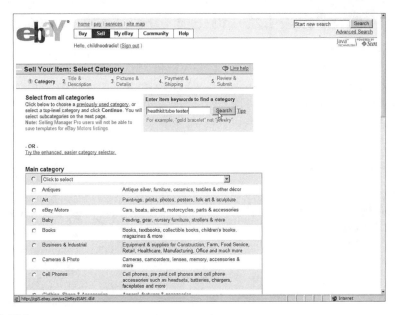

FIGURE 25.2

eBay's category keyword search can help find the right categories.

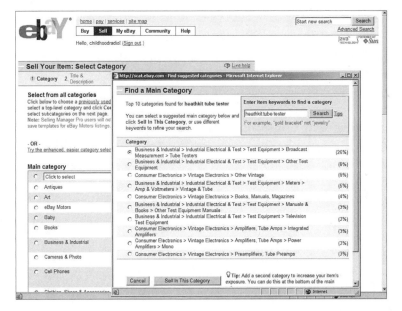

FIGURE 25.3

Results of a category keyword search for Heathkit tube tester.

USE ITEM SPECIFICS WHEN OFFERED

Many categories offer "item specifics," which are simply multiple-choice questions that you answer about items when you list them. Savvy buyers narrow down their searches by doing item-specific searches. For example, if you list a laptop eBay will ask you to specify the brand, processor type, speed, RAM, drive size, screen size, and so on. It's worth the extra effort.

PICK STORE CATEGORIES

If you are a PowerSeller you need a store (see Chapter 12, "eBay Stores"). When listing items, specify at least one, and ideally two, store categories for every item you list, as shown in Figure 25.4. Auctions always show up in store view when people visit. And people do visit stores, and while there they browse by category within stores. This is especially important if you have lots of listings active at any one time.

Tip

When selling identical items, consider mixing up the durations. Try some 3-day auctions as well as the traditional 7-days. Start some 10-day auctions on Thursdays. This gets you eyeballs on two weekends.

FIGURE 25.4

Always pick store categories for auction items.

SCHEDULE FOR YOUR AUDIENCE

If you plan to sell mostly in the U.S., launch (and therefore end) auctions between 9:00 a.m. Pacific time and 9:00 or 10:00 p.m. on the East Coast. Business items should probably start and end Monday through Friday, while collectibles, hobby, and consumer items can do slightly better on weekends, but not dramatically so. If your items are primarily of interest to international buyers (or folks in Hawaii, perhaps), aim at those time zones instead.

All of that notwithstanding, ending times will become less critical as more and more buyers use sniping tools to bid for items automatically at any time of the day or night.

Using eBay's scheduling feature costs money. Many third-party listing tools such as ándale do scheduling without incurring eBay fees by keeping your listings out of eBay's system until the desig-nated time. If you are launching hundreds or thou-sands of auctions this can be a money saver.

USE YOUR OWN PICTURE SERVER OR SERVICE

> # Tip
>
> When launching similar things of interest to a partic-ular buyer (10 separate Indy car models for example), schedule the items about 15 minutes apart so that buyers can bid on and win multiple items from you in a leisurely fashion.

The new eBay Picture Services are pretty cool, but if you host a lot of auctions it can get costly. To have more control over your photos, host them off of eBay, and tell eBay that you are hosting externally by checking the box shown in Figure 25.5. This will assure that the little camera icon will appear in certain search lists and elsewhere.

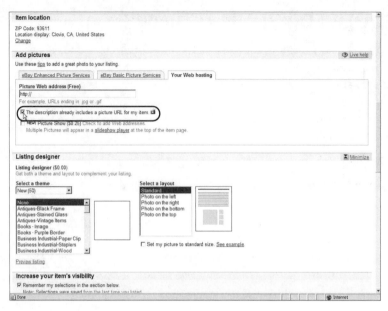

FIGURE 25.5
If you host pictures yourself, click the box to tell eBay.

REMEMBER TO SPECIFY GALLERY PHOTO ADDRESSES

When hosting your own photos and using Gallery photos, two things I recommend, don't forget to specify the location (web address) of the photo you want to use as the Gallery shot. This is shown in Figure 25.6.

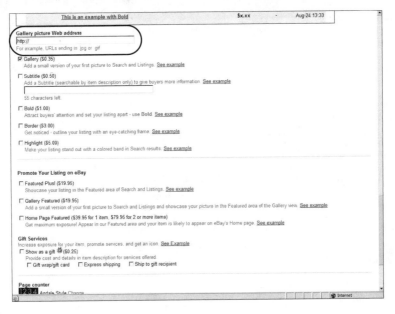

FIGURE 25.6

Don't forget to specify a web address for your Gallery photo.

SPECIFY THE RIGHT PAYMENT OPTIONS FOR EACH AUCTION

As you can see from Figure 25.7, PayPal and eBay now offer a broader range of payment options than they used to, and you can specify your own merchant bank for credit cards if you like. It is possible to specify different payment options for specific items. For example, you might want to require immediate payment on certain items and not others.

Buyer financing on expensive items is a popular and powerful option, worth considering if you sell big-ticket items.

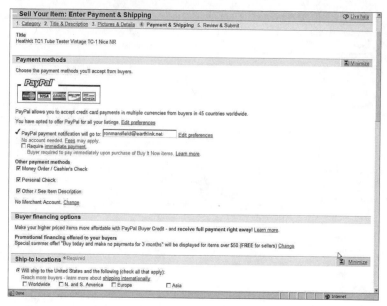

FIGURE 25.7
PayPal and easy payment options can be different for each auction.

CHOOSE SHIPPING LOCATIONS CAREFULLY

Although welcoming international bidders can increase bids and improve final auction prices, the additional work and headaches involved might not be worth it on lower-priced items. As shown in Figure 25.7, it is possible to selectively permit international shipping on an auction-by-auction basis. Consider doing this.

> **Note**
>
> In order for restricted international shipping to be truly effective, you must also restrict international *bidding* in your Buyer Requirements settings as described later in this chapter.

SHIPPING OPTIONS AND COSTS ARE IMPORTANT

Nothing can sour an auction quicker than excessive shipping fees, and your definition of excessive might differ from the eBay community's. Be sure you offer at least one low-cost option (UPS Ground, Parcel Post, Media Rate, and so on), as shown in Figure 25.8.

FIGURE 25.8
Pick shipping options carefully and on an item-by-item basis.

Don't offer rates that are impossible with the items you intend to ship. For example, Media Rate can only be used for items such as books, magazines, videos, and software. You cannot use it for a package of books-on-tape that includes a tape player, for example, or a software package that comes with a joystick.

Certain flammable and other items can't be shipped by air, so don't offer those choices when listing such items. Check your carriers' lists of acceptable items. Examples include gasoline, kerosene, and other flammable liquids, matches, flares, and items containing them. For example, if you sell a used chainsaw, be sure the tank is empty and fume-free.

GET THE WEIGHT RIGHT

When listing items you need to specify the size and weight of the item in order for the shipping calculator in your listings to accurately estimate the costs. Shipping calculators are only as accurate as your input. Remember that you need to add the weight of the shipping carton and packing materials (bubble wrap, peanuts, and so on) to the weight of the item to get the weight right.

Some PowerSellers simply "add a few pounds" to the weight of the item, hoping to guess the right final weight. Others like to box items up and weigh them, and then put the actual weight in the listing.

I don't like either approach. Guessing will get you in trouble many ways. Boxing items before they sell is a pain. Besides the fact that boxed items take more space than naked ones, bidders often have questions that will necessitate looking at, and therefore unpacking, your items.

I prefer to use a spreadsheet to estimate the final size and weight of the item, carton, and shipping material. It uses assumptions about the weight of various materials, cubic dimensions of the item, box, and padding, and it tells me if an item will be considered oversized by carriers (see Chapter 27, "Packing and Shipping," for more about this). The spreadsheet makes it possible to tell the auction shipping calculator accurate enough information to get the correct results almost always. Create your own, or visit my web site (www.RonMansfield.com) to get a free copy of mine.

Tip

Buyers love fixed-price shipping quotes—$7 to anywhere in the United States, that sort of thing. On some items it's entirely possible to do this. Give it a try.

OFFER COMBINED ITEM OPTIONS IF POSSIBLE

It is now easier than before for your customers to purchase and pay for multiple items, and you should probably enable these features if possible. Figure 25.9 shows many of the available options. You get to specify, for example, how much time a buyer has to continue shopping before the opportunity to combine is lost.

Figure 25.10 shows how you can also offer combined shipping discounts. The options are confusing and need to be examined carefully before committing to them.

Note

Some third-party listing and auction management tools don't support combined payments or shipments properly. Check with your auction management software vendor or franchisor before turning on these eBay features!

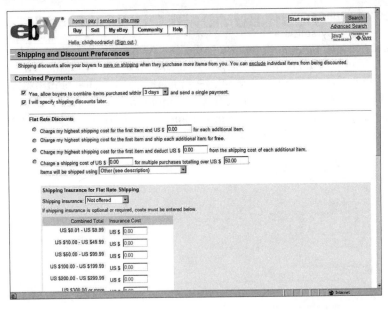

FIGURE 25.9
Consider offering shoppers a chance to pay for multiple purchases with one payment.

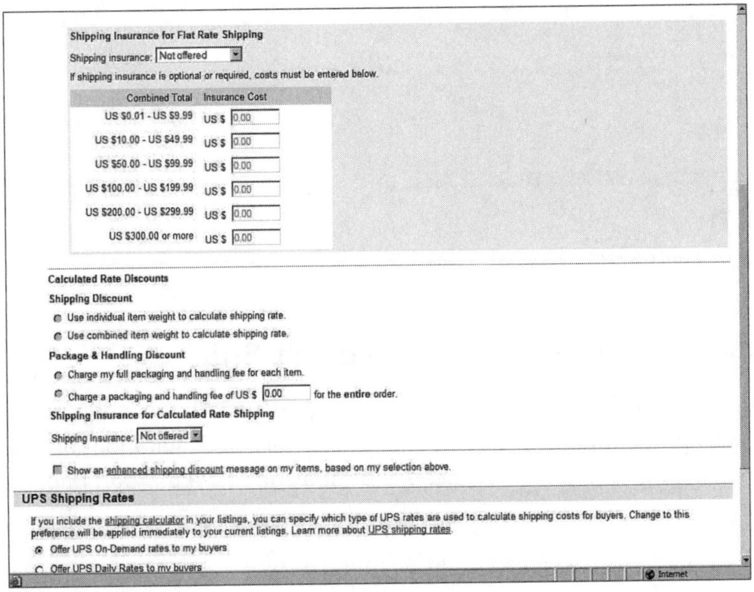

FIGURE 25.10
Be sure you understand the effects of combined shipping discounts before listing with them.

FINE-TUNE YOUR BUYER REQUIREMENTS

Sadly, there are folks out there who want to take advantage of us, and others who just like to mess around. In the early days, it was much easier for them to do just that. Over the past few years eBay and PayPal have put new seller controls in place that can help you specify minimum "Buyer Requirements." Figure 25.11 shows the options page. Putting checkmarks in the appropriate boxes blocks bids from those meeting the description. We'll examine these choices next.

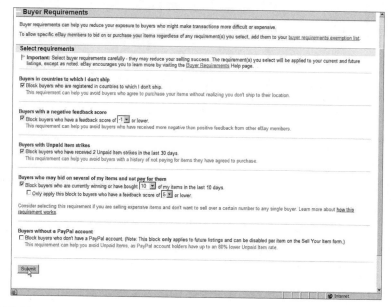

FIGURE 25.11
Choose your buyer requirements carefully.

Buyers In Countries to Which I Don't Ship

Unless you are always willing to ship anything you sell to any country in the world (a very bad idea, by the way), put a checkmark in this box! A number of "third world" countries, including Nigeria, are hotbeds of eBay and PayPal fraud rings.

For example, eBay warns that when selling a high-priced item you might receive emails from bidders in foreign countries (often in Africa) asking you to accept foreign cashier's checks as payment for their items. Some of the requests offer to "overpay" for an item, and ask you to wire the overpayment back to the buyer through services such as Western Union or MoneyGram. eBay urges all sellers to use extreme caution when accepting foreign cashier's checks for high-priced items because foreign checks may take weeks or months to clear and may be counterfeit. They may even appear to be from a U.S. bank but, upon closer inspection, include foreign country or city names. Never accept overpayments from buyers for items where the buyer is asking to be reimbursed for overpayment.

> **Note**
>
> A good source of information on international money order scams is http://www.state.gov/www/regions/africa/naffpub.pdf.

Buyers with a Negative Feedback Score

This option lets you block folks with bad feedback, and you get to say just how bad it can get. Check the box, and I say stick with the default of –1. There is no zero option, presumably because eBay wants to give brand new buyers the benefit of the doubt.

Buyers with Unpaid Item Strikes

I vote "Yes" here, too. Block them. Although this might cause you the occasional lost bid from some honest eBayer having trouble with checkout or arguing with some messed up seller, mostly folks with more than two unpaid items in the past 30 days spell trouble.

Buyers Who May Bid on Several of My Items and Not Pay for Them

"Huh?" You might say when first encountering this one. Why block really good bidders? This option is the result of some jerks who like to bid on things just to mess up a seller's auctions. They often bid obscenely high amounts for many or all of the items a seller has listed, thereby always winning, and then they fail to pay for any of them. The result is a sea of headaches for sellers and buyers alike.

> **Tip**
>
> Use the feature, but consider softening it with the second option, which takes feedback into account. It's not perfect by any means, but it's better than a sharp stick in the eye.

This was a big sport in late 2004 and early 2005, with chains of Trading Posts being the primary targets.

So eBay has instituted this admittedly imperfect but somewhat helpful tool. It's difficult for me to recommend using this to low-profile sellers, but because PowerSellers, and especially Trading Posts, strive to be high profile, you will be attracting attention—some small amount of it unwanted.

DOUBLE-CHECK YOUR LISTINGS

"Measure twice, cut once," as grandpa used to say. He was right. Always take a moment to look over your listings before launch, as shown in Figure 25.12, and then again immediately after they launch. Look with the assumption that something's wrong, and remember, there are many things that can only be changed before an item gets its first bid.

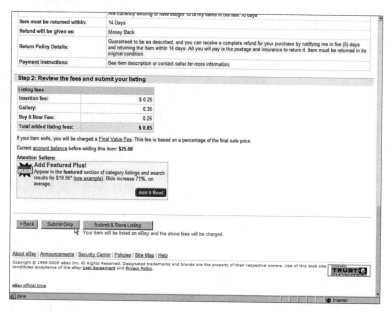

FIGURE 25.12

Review your auction carefully before submitting, and then review again when it's active.

CHAPTER 26

MANAGING CURRENT AUCTIONS

Once auctions are running they need to be tended. You should make sure they look right, answer prospective bidders' questions, keep out the riffraff, and, unless you are completely passionless, you'll be interested in knowing how the bidding's going. Here are some tips.

MODIFYING AUCTIONS

Right after you launch auctions it's a good idea to make sure your auctions look right on eBay. Are there typos? Do the pictures look good? Test the shipping calculator. Do the results make sense?

If your item has received no bids or purchases and does not end within the next 12 hours, you can revise anything in your listing except the selling format. For example, you can rewrite the description, but you can't change your auction to a fixed price listing.

Once a bid is received you can only add to the item description or add a second category, or add optional seller features to increase your item's visibility such as bold or featured.

If your listing has a bid, or ends within 12 hours, you can't add to your description or add a second category.

Table 26.1 shows a comprehensive list of things from eBay that you can and cannot do under a variety of circumstances.

Note

If you have employees, especially new hires, it is particularly important to check auctions either before (best) or immediately after they launch. You can change just about anything in an auction until the first bid is received or the auction is near ending.

Note

Recently eBay has also made it possible to lower your reserve price while the auction is running, even if your item has received bids.

TABLE 26.1 Listing of Restrictions to Changing Existing Listings

Auction-style Listing

Time Left Before the Listing Ends	Did the Listing Receive Bids?	What You Can Revise
More than 12 hours	No	Revise any information but not the format Remove the following optional features only: Buy It Now, eBay Picture Services, Reserve Price, 10-day listing Add optional features to increase your item's visibility (for example, bold) Add or change a Gallery picture
More than 12 hours	Yes	If your item has already received a bid/purchase or ends within 12 hours, you can only ★ Add to the item description or add a second category (exception: if your listing already has a bid/purchase *and* ends within 12 hours, you can't add to your description or add a second category) ★ Add optional seller features to increase your item's visibility
Less than 12 hours	No	Your changes should not affect the basic item description: ★ Change the category and add item specifics. ★ Add optional seller features to increase your item's visibility (for example, bold) ★ Add page view counters ★ Add or change a Gallery picture You can also add to the item description: ★ More details about the item ★ Previously unspecified item specifics ★ New payment methods and ship-to locations

Auction-style Listing

Time Left Before the Listing Ends	Did the Listing Receive Bids?	What You Can Revise
Less than 12 hours	Yes	Your changes should not affect the basic item description. You can ★ Add optional features to increase your item's visibility (for example, bold) ★ Add or change a Gallery picture

Fixed Price Listing

Time Left Before the Listing Ends	Has An Item from the Listing Been Sold?	What You Can Revise
More than 12 hours	No	Revise any information but not the format Remove optional features Add or change Gallery picture
More than 12 hours	Yes	Add to item description Add optional seller features to increase your item's listing visibility
Less than 12 hours	No	Add to item description Add item specifics and gift services
Less than 12 hours	Yes	Add optional seller features to increase your item's listing visibility

Store Inventory Listing

Time Left Before the Listing Ends	Has An Item from the Listing Been Sold?	What You Can Revise
Any time while listing is active	No	Revise any information but not the format Remove optional features Add or change Gallery picture
Any time while listing is active	Yes	Revise price, quantity, and store category Add or remove optional features Add to the description

Ad Format Real Estate Listing

Time Left Before the Listing Ends	Did the Listing Receive Bids?	What You Can Revise
More than 12 hours	No	Revise any information but not the format
More than 12 hours	Yes	Not applicable, as the ad format does not have bids
Less than 12 hours	No	You can edit any information but not the format You can change some item specifics but not the category
Less than 12 hours	Yes	Not applicable, as the ad format does not have bids

WATCHING BIDS AND WATCHERS

Tracking bids and watchers on your My eBay screen can be so much fun that it distracts you from the real work, but it is worth checking a few times each day to get a sense of what's selling and what's not.

Figure 26.1 shows a typical collection of auctions in various stages of their lives. Notice the high number of watchers verses the low number of bids for many items. Watchers frequently, but not always, become last-minute bidders. You can sometimes use high watcher counts to reassure nervous customers if you are a Trading Assistant or run a Trading Post.

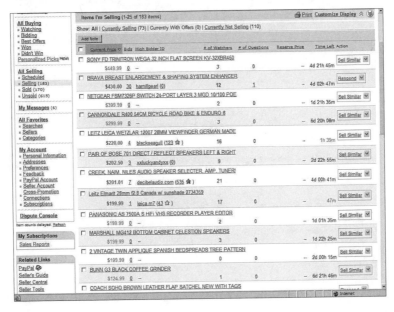

FIGURE 26.1

It's easy to keep an eye on bids and watchers from your My eBay screen.

ANSWERING QUESTIONS

You will receive questions via email from prospective bidders. If the questions come to you through eBay's "Ask Seller a Question" feature you will be able to post the questions and the answers at the bottom (and I do mean the bottom) of your auctions so that others can read them.

As you can see from Figure 26.2, the questions and answers are truncated in your listings so shoppers need to click links to read the full text. Not all will. Some won't even understand. For this reason put the "meat" of your answer in the first few sentences.

Figure 26.3 shows the complete text of the Q&A for the item in Figure 26.2.

Note

There is no law saying you must answer questions publicly. You can always reply in private. Publicly answer questions of general interest that will inform bidders and boost prices or clarify condition descriptions. Consider answering rude, provocative questions like "Why do you bozos charge so much for shipping? What a RIP!" privately, if at all.

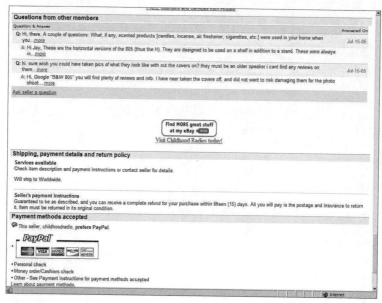

FIGURE 26.2

Questions and answers are at the bottom of the listing, and are truncated.

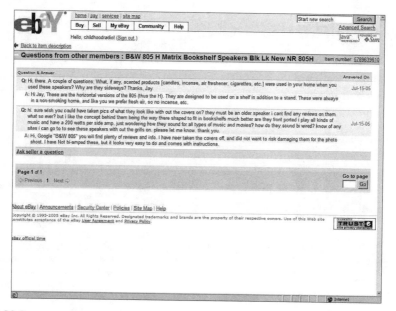

FIGURE 26.3

The complete text questions and answers can be opened through a link in the auction.

SPOTTING PROBLEM BIDDERS

If you followed my advice back in Chapter 25, "Listing Items," about setting safe buyer requirements, you should not have too many problems with malicious bidders, but you should still always be on the lookout for them. Some signs include unusually high bids for everyday items, lots of bids on an eclectic mix of things from your inventory by the same bidder, or bidders traveling around in pairs bidding on your items.

Bidders with low, unsavory feedback, and especially bidders who leave rude feedback, routinely need to be watched very carefully or blocked from bidding on your items.

Blocking Bidders

When you become alarmed enough by a bidder you should block that bidder immediately. Do this by choosing the Block or Pre-approve Certain Bidders link near the bottom of your my eBay page if you are a Selling Assistant Pro user, look for the equivalent link in the eBay site map. Either way, work your way to a page that looks like Figure 26.4. Enter the eBay IDs of bidders separated by commas, and don't forget to click the Submit button to save your work.

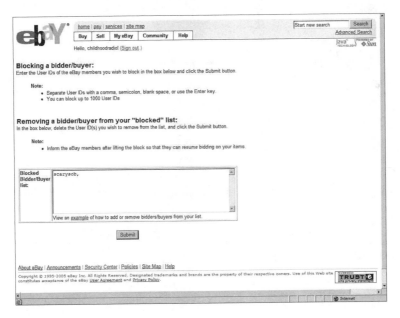

FIGURE 26.4

Blacklisting a scary bidder.

Canceling Bids and Ending Auctions Early

If you subscribe to Selling Manager Pro you can simply scroll down to the bottom of your My eBay page to find links for canceling bids and ending auctions early, as shown in Figure 26.5. Don't do this unless you absolutely must. It's annoying to bidders (and your customers if you are a Trading Assistant). Too many auction cancellations will draw eBay's Trust and Safety scrutiny as well.

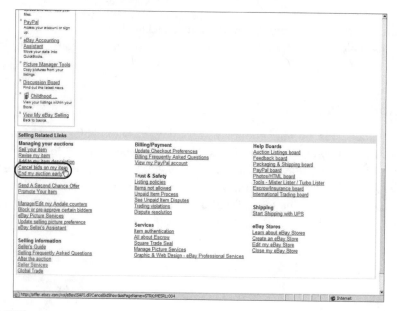

FIGURE 26.5
eBay's Selling Manager Pro makes it easy to cancel bids and end auctions early.

Harnessing Your Power

There's a lot to juggle as a PowerSeller, and it's tempting to let auctions run along on their own. If you have the time, your life can be made more pleasant in the long run if you

★ Check auctions right after they launch to make sure they look right.

★ Make any modifications before you get bids.

★ Keep an eye out for potentially troublesome bidders, and cancel their bids.

★ Immediately add potential troublemakers to your blocked bidders list.

★ Answer questions promptly, and in public when it helps the cause.

★ Answer rude questions too, but privately.

In this Chapter

TRIUMPHANT BURLEIGH returns from a tour of fixe feats the champion by a fluke, marries his girl, retires to th

CHAPTER 27

PACKING AND SHIPPING

Selling is only half the battle. You need to get items to winners promptly and undamaged. Because you are likely already a seller, I'll skip the basics and concentrate on some ways to save time, money, and aggravation.

GETTING HELP FROM CARRIERS

Shipping carriers love eBay PowerSellers. We make them a ton of money. Consider the U. S. Postal Service. At the 2005 eBay Live! conference, besides being the title sponsor of the event (which is to say, a really big spender), the post office had a booth where attendees could mail things home via Priority Mail at no cost!

The USPS has developed free Priority Mail boxes co-branded with the eBay logo. Figure 27.1 shows some of them. If you haven't seen these on your front porch yet, you will. Order your own by visiting http://ebaysupplies.usps.com/.

The post office also provides free shipping tape and other items directly. You can either order them from the post office site (www.usps.com) or through the co-branded USPS/eBay page. Find it at http://pages.ebay.com/usps/home.html. It's worth bookmarking. The page pulls together tracking, insurance, cost calculator, and other links in a way that is useful to PowerSellers. The information is all available elsewhere; this is just a nice organization of it, as you can see in Figure 27.2.

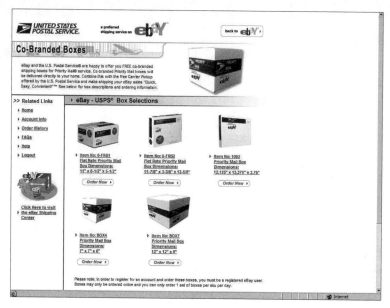

FIGURE 27.1

The USPS and eBay have joined hands to offer co-branded logo boxes.

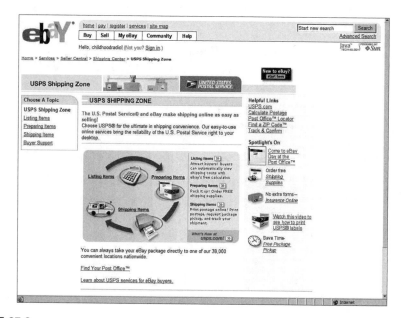

FIGURE 27.2

The eBay/USPS Shipping Zone.

Other carriers offer free supplies and advice, of course. For example, there's a UPS Shipping Zone on eBay as well (http://pages.ebay.com/ups/) shown in Figure 27.3. Again, you will find a handy collection of eBay-related links worthy of a bookmark.

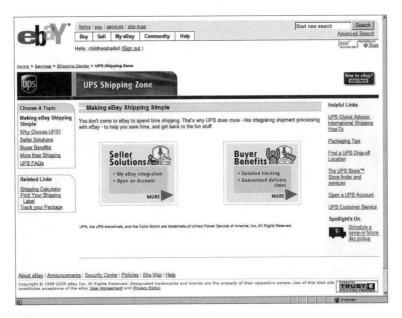

FIGURE 27.3
The eBay/UPS Shipping Zone.

Carriers will also help you become better packers and shippers. For example, your UPS representative can arrange for someone to come out to your facility and make suggestions about better packing and shipping techniques. The post office has regional teams designed to improve the interface between large volume shipping customers and the local post office.

You might also be surprised to see how helpful your local postmaster can be. If you haven't already done so, introduce yourself to the postmaster for your ZIP code. Tell her or him about your business. You might even be able to schedule automatic daily pickups if your volume warrants it. This will make it unnecessary for you to visit the USPS web site each day to schedule tomorrow's pickups. Ask about using the business drop-off door around back if your local postal facility has one. It might keep you out of those nasty lines, particularly around the holidays.

PACKING EVERYDAY ITEMS

You may already be an expert packer and shipper, but we can always learn a new trick or two. This section gives you some specific guidelines to follow and some tips to make sure your items arrive at their destination unharmed.

Everyday items need a minimum of 2" of effective padding on all sides. Bubble wrap is probably the best bet for most items, perhaps augmented with packing peanuts. Don't use peanuts by themselves, especially for small, heavy objects, because the items will tend to migrate through the peanuts and end up relatively unprotected at the bottom of the box over the course of the journey.

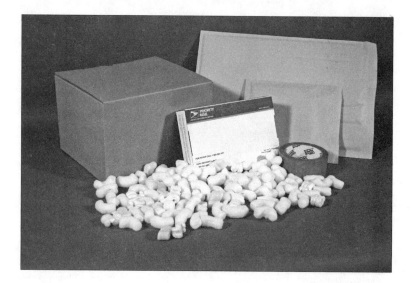

Kraft or newsprint might be a little cheaper to buy than bubble wrap, but these paper products weigh more than bubble, and often compress in transit, resulting in less protection for your item and "crushed box syndrome."

Never ship collectibles by simply slapping labels and postage on the original box. This devalues the item. Figure 27.4 shows a typical example of this rookie move that probably cut the value of the collectible item nearly in half. Always double-box collectible boxes.

Note

As an experienced seller you might have picked up best practices and shipping short-cuts over the years, but don't assume your employees, especially new hires, know what they are doing. Have beginners wait to seal box tops until you can inspect their work. Do this every day until you are sure they get it.

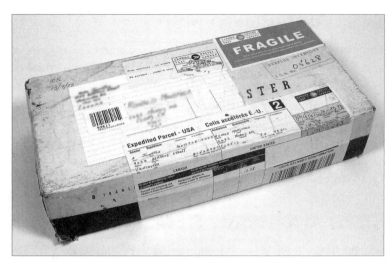

FIGURE 27.4
How to devalue a collectible.

PACKING FRAGILE ITEMS

Fragile items are an even bigger risk. If you ship a 50-piece china set and only two dishes break, that's not a 95% success rate, it's a 100% screw-up. Some Trading Assistants and Trading Posts actually refuse to sell certain fragile, difficult-to-ship items because they don't want the risk.

If you decide to ship fragile goods, make sure they are painstakingly packed, with a minimum of 4" of excellent padding around all sides.

I once asked my UPS driver, a tall fellow, what to expect as my packages make their way through his system. He held his arms straight out, parallel to the ground, holding an imaginary box, and pretended to let go. "Assume that's gonna happen a few times each day the thing's in transit," he advised. And he wasn't kidding.

Used specialized boxes for things like laptops, guitars, dishes, and so on. They can be purchased from uline.com and other box vendors.

Yes, you can insure items, but as you know if you have ever tried to collect, step one in any claim is to blame the shipper (you), and ask you to prove it should be otherwise. Shipping is always a gamble. The better the packing job, the better your odds.

SHIPPING VALUABLE ITEMS

Never ship valuable items to unconfirmed addresses, and be very leery of shipping to addresses that don't match billing addresses, even when buyers have pretty good feedback. Always require signatures for shipments where the addresses don't match. There are many fraud schemes that involve stolen payment information.

The best, albeit most expensive, way to ship valuable items is via U.S. Registered Mail, where items are signed for at every step of the way, even when moving within a post office.

Note

Consider requiring insurance on all expensive items. You'll need to remember to do this when originally listing the item.

OVERSIZED AND HEAVY ITEMS

Oversized and heavy items are a pain in the butt. This can actually be the good news for you if you figure out how to do it right because even experienced sellers will bring you the tough items to sell for them. Oversized items can, however, be a real profit killer if you are not careful.

The definition of oversized is different for different carriers, and even differs between service categories within the same shipping company. And there are limits to the size and weight of packages some carriers will accept.

For example, UPS has established specific weight and size limits for the packages that you send with all UPS services. The restrictions listed here only pertain to individual packages. There are no limits to the total weight of your shipment or the total number of packages in a shipment.

The specific limits are as follows:

★ Packages can be up to 150 lbs. (70kg)

★ Packages can be up to 165 inches (419cm) in length and girth combined

★ Packages can be up to 108 inches (270cm) in length

★ Packages that weigh more than 70 lbs. (31.5kg, 25kg within the EU) require a special heavy-package label

★ Oversize packages and packages with a large size-to-weight ratio require special pricing and dimensional weight calculations, described shortly

★ Packages that exceed UPS weight and size limits are subject to an Over Maximum Limits charge

Measuring Dimensional Size

FIGURE 27.5
Measuring box size.

To determine whether a package is oversized, you must measure the length and girth, and then combine the numbers to get a total. *Girth*, represented by number 1 in Figure 27.5, is the distance completely around your package or object at its widest point, perpendicular to the length. *Length*, represented by number 2 in Figure 27.5, is the longest side of your package or object.

Add the length plus girth together to get your total package size.

For example, if the length (2) was 10" and each side was 5", then the length + girth (1) would be 10" + 5" +5" + 5" +5", or 30".

Using this measuring technique, UPS and FedEx define oversized parcels as shown in Table 27.1.

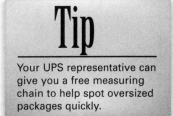

Your UPS representative can give you a free measuring chain to help spot oversized packages quickly.

TABLE 27.1   Oversized Package Definitions

Category	Size
Oversized 1	84"
Oversized 2	108"
Oversized 3	130"

Send Big Items on the Bus

Greyhound's PackageExpress (GPX) service is an often-overlooked option for large, heavy items. If you haven't already, check out http://www.shipgreyhound.com, and their FAQ link: http://www.shipgreyhound.com/faq. You need to take the items to the local Greyhound counter, and residential recipients will probably need to pick up items at their local Greyhound terminal counter, but delivery to business addresses is available in many markets.

Rather than turn this book into *Shipping to the Max* I'll not continue this exploration much further; but take away this: Bookmark the shipping cost calculators for the shippers you use, and before listing large or heavy items be certain that once boxed up the items will not be considered oversized by any of the shippers you offer in your listings. If they are oversized be sure your shipping charges account for this. If not, you will not charge buyers enough, but shipping companies will bill you, perhaps after the fact, when they discover that a package is oversized.

TO RECYCLE OR NOT?

I am a big fan of recycling, and there are times when it's a great idea to use recycled materials when shipping. But there are some considerations to think of, as follows:

★ Local retailers might be happy to give you their recycled peanuts and bubble wrap.

★ Make sure recycled materials don't smell, especially of tobacco.

★ Only reuse boxes that are clean and sturdy. Boxes often lose quite a bit of their original strength the first time they are used.

★ If boxes are marked "perishable" or "explosive" and so on, don't reuse them.

★ If you charge a lot for shipping and handling, never reuse supplies. Buyers will expect and deserve new materials.

PRINT YOUR OWN LABELS AND POSTAGE

This probably goes without saying, but to be a PowerSeller you need to print your own postage and labels. Never stand in line for stamps again, and never handwrite shipping labels. There are now almost too many ways to automate this task, especially now that eBay and PayPal have eliminated their fees for postage printing.

Together, eBay and PayPal make it easy for you to print shipping labels and pay for the shipping costs directly from your PayPal account. This all integrates seamlessly with the Selling Management tools as well. Figure 27.6 shows one of the steps.

There are other label printing services, obviously. Many users swear by stamps.com, for example. But for a growing number of PowerSellers the convenience of the new eBay/PayPal feature is compelling.

Ask for a Discount

As you grow, you might be able to negotiate shipping discounts with certain shipping carriers. You will need to be sending hundreds of packages each month, and the postal service is unable to discount, but once you get big enough, don't be afraid to approach most other carriers for a volume discount.

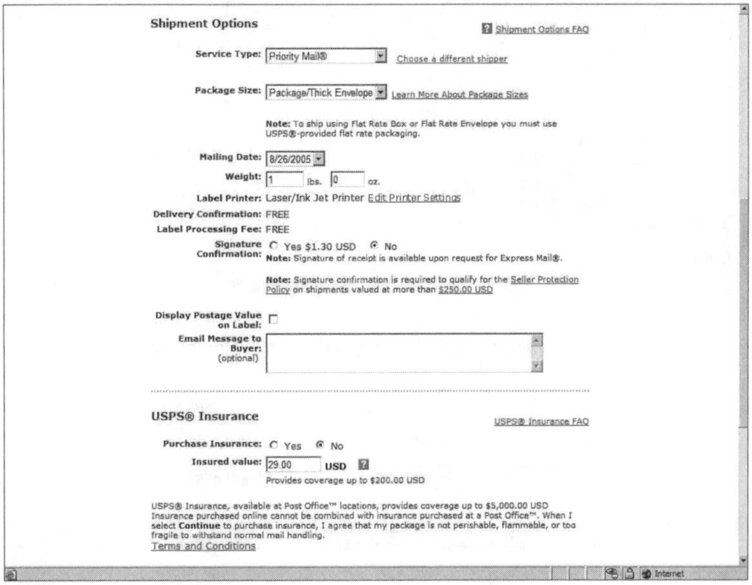

FIGURE 27.6
PayPal and eBay can automatically prefill shipping information, and then print labels if you like.

Use Stealth Mode Postage Printing

Stealth mode turns off the printing of the postage dollar amounts on USPS labels. Many PowerSellers like this feature, particularly if they mark up shipping costs. Most stamp and label printing programs have a way to enable stealth printing. Don't get carried away, though; buyers can weigh packages and check the post office shipping calculator too. Excessive shipping charges will earn you negative feedback.

A FINAL THOUGHT

Many folks find packing and shipping boring, or "dirt simple," and underestimate its importance. What a shame it is to go through the entire listing and auction process only to deliver landfill at the buyer's end. Pay attention to packing and shipping, especially if you have employees doing it for you. This is no place to cut corners.

In this Chapter

G'BYE

Bug-a-boo

with and without D.D.T.

kills all 9 major pests

TRIUMPHANT BURLEIGH returns from a tour of feats the champion by a fluke, marries his girl, retires to

● Spray those pests away for good — with Bug-a-boo! This super-insect spray, with and without D.D.T.—far exceeds U. S. Government standards for an AA Grade insecticide. Even kills roaches and moth larvae!

Yet Bug-a-boo won't harm humans, won't damage home furnishings, when used as directed. And it's pine-scented—and so pleasant to use.

For long-lasting protection from pests, you may prefer the new Bug-a-boo with 3% D.D.T. It contains Bug-a-boo's time-tested, insect-killing ingredients, plus all the D.D.T. that's required for effective residual deposit, and the full amount considered justified for home uses.

Caution: Use Bug-a-boo with D.D.T. carefully, according to the directions.

KILLS

FLIES · ANTS

MOTHS · ROACHES

MOSQUITOES

BEDBUGS

SILVERFISH

CHAPTER 28

FEEDBACK

Invented because eBay's founder Pierre Omidyar didn't have time to resolve the growing number of disputes among his burgeoning flock, feedback has reached pop-culture status. Everyone's talking about feedback, even Judge Judy. Feedback is a big part of every PowerSeller's "brand value," or at least it affects your perceived trustworthiness in the community.

THE FEEDBACK FORUM

World headquarters for feedback-related topics is eBay's Feedback Forum, a page worth bookmarking. Figure 28.1 shows ground zero. Reach it from your My eBay page.

FIGURE 28.1
The Feedback Forum.

PEOPLE CARE ABOUT FEEDBACK

Some eBayers are even more passionate about feedback than they are about "excessive" shipping costs, if that's possible. When you state in your auctions that you never leave feedback until you receive it, they will not buy from you. Wait too long to send feedback and you risk getting a negative or neutral feedback in return from some of these folks. They believe that leaving positive feedback is part of your job as a seller, and you have not completely satisfied them if you wait too long or fail to leave it.

I once put my store in "vacation mode" and then left the country for 10 days, having accidentally failed to leave feedback for a $25 item someone purchased. When I returned I had five emails from the buyer first requesting, and then demanding, positive feedback. The last email was in ALL CAPS.

The more items you sell, the more feedback you will handle, and some of it will be downright wacky. Fortunately, eBay has made some tweaks to the feedback program, and is a little more accommodating than usual when PowerSellers have unwarranted feedback grief.

NEW EBAY FEEDBACK POLICIES

Some new eBayers don't understand the importance of feedback and can be a little freewheeling with the Caps Lock key. As you learned in Chapter 26, "Managing Current Auctions," some rogues win things simply to leave negative feedback and ruin your reputation. To stop what seemed like a flood of negatives from newbies and buttheads, eBay recently initiated some helpful new policies and procedures designed to educate and moderate beginners. They also help correct damage done by malicious bidders. Here's a direct quote of eBay's announcement of those recent changes:

"Neutralizing feedback left by members who don't participate in issue resolution processes.

We believe that members unwilling to participate in processes designed to help resolve issues, such as the Unpaid Item process or the Item Not Received process, shouldn't be able to impact another member's reputation. After this change is implemented, if a member leaves feedback for a transaction and does not participate in these processes, eBay will neutralize their feedback. This means the rating (whether positive or negative) will not affect the recipient's feedback score. While the feedback comment itself will remain, it will include an administrative note from eBay indicating that the feedback doesn't count towards the member's total score.

Removing feedback from users who are indefinitely suspended within 90 days of registration.

We believe that members who are indefinitely suspended within 90 days of registering on eBay were never truly members of the Community, and so their feedback comments and ratings should not count. We will automatically remove feedback (positive, neutral, and negative) left by such users.

Requiring new members to complete a tutorial before leaving neutral or negative feedback.

This change will require all new users (members with a feedback score of less than 10) to complete a short tutorial before leaving neutral or negative feedback. We hope that the tutorial will educate new members about the feedback system as well as ensure that they are aware of the various communication tools available to them prior to leaving feedback for their trading partner.

Since we will now be addressing member nonparticipation within the eBay issue resolution system, we will align eBay-approved certified dispute resolution services' feedback withdrawal systems with eBay's and only accept mutual feedback withdrawal when both members agree to the withdrawal. This will take affect when we introduce the process for neutralizing feedback from members unwilling to participate in issue resolution processes.

THE "PILE ON" PROBLEM

Because you will get so much feedback as a PowerSeller you really need to keep an eye on any incoming negative feedback and jump on it right away. It might be tempting to just let negatives slide away to the back pages, which happens quickly if you do many transactions each day, but I advise against this strategy. People are usually reluctant to leave negative feedback. We all want to give each other the benefit of the doubt, and of course it's normal to fear retaliation. But the community can be emboldened by a couple of negatives, especially if you get them all at about the same time.

Suppose a buyer "negs you" (leaves negative feedback) for high shipping costs on multiple items and you ignore these multiple negative feedback postings. Another buyer, only slightly peeved at your markups, sees the multiple negs and instead of contacting you for a partial refund writes "Yeah, these guys are rip-off artists! Beware." The ball is rolling. More and more buyers will be looking at your charges with a closer eye, and will have what seems to them is community permission to join the complaining.

You need to at least reply to every negative and in cases where it is truly unwarranted you need to try to get it removed, time consuming as that can be.

SPOTTING TROUBLEMAKERS

Figure 28.2 shows a great third-party web site that can help you quickly find all the negative and neutral feedback left by and about eBayers. The site's URL is www.tool-haus.org.

This no-nonsense site lets you quickly see any eBayer's negative and neutral feedback. Be sure to check the "Left by" option to get a sense of what might happen if you do leave a negative. Not only is this a helpful tool at feedback time, you can use it if you are trying to decide whether or not to block a bidder during a live auction. (See Chapter 26 for more about blocking bidders.)

There are some other interesting features on this site also worth exploring, including the "mutual feedback" tool. Toolhaus is funded by donations. They have some other intriguing tools aimed at fraud, among other things. Great work gang, thanks!

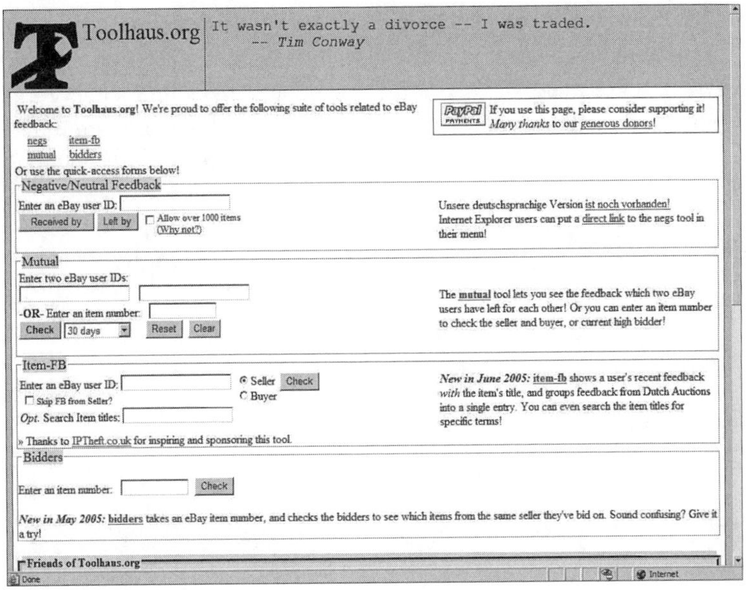

FIGURE 28.2
Toolhaus lets you quickly see negs and neutrals.

MANAGING FEEDBACK

Stable owners need to muck the place out. Pool owners need to scoop the leaves. PowerSellers need to manage their feedback. And just as with barns and pools, it's much easier to deal with feedback every day in an organized, professional fashion than it is to wait. Some buyers will go absolutely ballistic if you fail to leave them feedback.

Who's in Charge of Feedback at Your Place?

If you are working solo the feedback ball is in your court, but if you have employees, you need to designate someone as the feedback guru. If it's not you, the person in charge needs to understand your philosophy and have guidelines. You need a policy stating that any negs or neutrals received, or about to be given, need to be brought to your attention ASAP.

When to Leave Feedback

This is another hotly debated issue among PowerSellers. Some say you lose the "advantage" if you leave feedback first. On the other hand, if you are doing a good job, most feedback should be rosy, and as a busy PowerSeller you have better things to do than manually walk each individual feedback posting through the system. So, in my opinion, unless you sell just a few expensive, risky items every month (such as cars or high-end collectibles), you should automate feedback, and have it sent as soon as a buyer's payment has cleared. Fortunately, that's pretty easy to do now.

Automating Feedback

Third-party auction management tools, such as the ones provided by ándale, and franchise companies, will leave automatic feedback for you if you choose. Now, with eBay's Selling Manager Pro, eBay can do this for you as well.

In Selling Manager Pro you automate feedback by visiting the Automation page, shown in Figure 28.3.

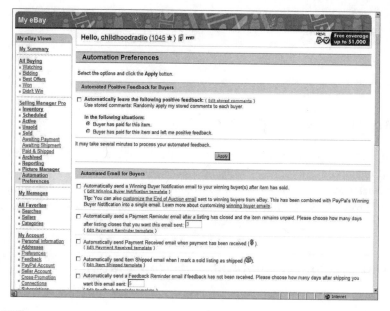

FIGURE 28.3

Automating feedback in Selling Manager Pro.

You get to pick whether feedback is automatically left for buyers when they have paid, or not until they have left positive feedback for you. The tool randomly chooses 1 of 10 comments you predefine. Obviously, these will all need to be generic and suggest that you are the seller. Figure 28.4 shows the screen used to set up feedback phrases and some examples.

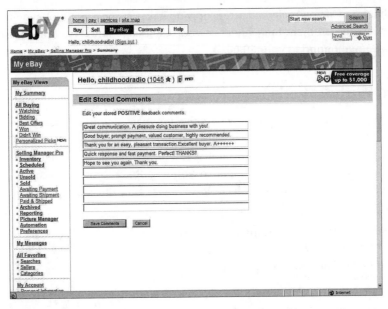

FIGURE 28.4

Creating feedback phrases in Selling Manager Pro.

You see the problem here, of course. You could unwittingly send positive feedback praising quick payment to a slug who took 10 days to cough up the dough. Moreover, there is also no way that I am aware of to turn off automatic feedback on an item-by-item basis. It's all or none.

Responding to Ugly Feedback

When you get unflattering, abusive feedback it's tempting to respond in kind. For example, suppose someone negs you like this: "SHIPPING WAS $8.85, CHRGD ME $17.35. Item NOT as DESCRIBED. Ripped OFF !!!"

> # Caution
>
> Selling Manager Pro can automatically remind buyers to leave feedback for you, though I advise against this. Some in the community consider "feedback begging" bad form. I agree.

The temptation might be to reply, "This idiot never used shipping calculator B4 bidding. And what's WRONG w/item anyway?"

A better approach might be to respond: "We want all of our buyers to be happy. Please contact us ASAP."

This doesn't mean you will necessarily make the guy happy, or even refund any shipping money. But it says to other readers "Maybe this seller isn't so bad after all." On the other hand, if you really did screw up, and it was a once-in-a-thousand thing, own up to it. Fix the problem then say so in your feedback reply. "We are very sorry. Our mistake. Have refunded your $9.00."

Mutual Withdrawals

You and your buyers can withdraw negative feedback if you manage to resolve your disagreements through a process called *mutual feedback withdrawal*. Once withdrawn, any positive, negative, or neutral rating associated with that feedback comment will no longer show or count in your feedback score. Which is to say the negative or neutral is removed from your *score*. But, the feedback *comment itself* remains.

This is why it's so important to resolve issues before those feedback and reply rants start flying. (It's better for your blood pressure and karma, too.)

Begin by contacting the other party directly. Email if you must, but offer to discuss the problem over the phone if the buyer is willing. Spend most of your time listening, and always say that you are sorry that the buyer is unhappy, because you are sorry, even if on a rare occasion the buyer really is an idiot. You want this problem fixed too because problems are very unproductive and therefore costly. Sorry? You bet you are sorry!

Ask open-ended questions such as, "What seems fair to you?" You might be amazed at how easily and cheaply you can resolve things this way. If you agree to a solution—refunding a portion of the shipping fees, let's say—do it pronto.

You then need to initiate a request for mutual withdrawal using the online form shown in Figure 28.5. (You can find the form in the Feedback Forum.)

After you and your buyer have agreed to withdraw feedback, eBay will adjust both you and your buyer's feedback scores. Depending on the type of feedback withdrawn, your scores could increase, decrease, or remain the same. eBay will add a note to the feedback comment, saying that the feedback was mutually withdrawn.

> **Note**
>
> Mutual feedback withdrawal differs from feedback removal by eBay, where the feedback and all comments are completely removed. eBay will only remove feedback if it violates its Feedback Removal and Abuse Policy.

> **Note**
>
> Remember, the feedback comments you leave for each other remain publicly posted, it's just the numbers that change, so if you want your side to be heard you should leave feedback, or reply as you see fit before completing the withdrawal process. You will no longer be able to leave feedback or replies for a transaction after the withdrawal process has been completed.

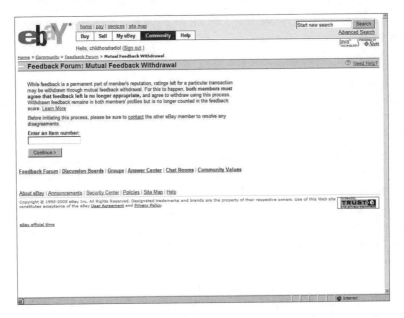

FIGURE 28.5
Starting the mutual feedback withdrawal process.

You may only request mutual feedback withdrawal once for every feedback left, and only if both you and the other person have already agreed to have the feedback removed in advance. You need to do this within 30 days of either person leaving feedback or within 90 days of the transaction end date, whichever is later.

Getting eBay to Withdraw Feedback

It is possible to ask eBay to remove feedback, and on occasion they might accommodate you. The feedback needs to violate their policy for your request to even be considered.

Quoting eBay, here are some activities that might cause eBay to consider withdrawing feedback:

★ eBay is provided with a valid court order finding that the disputed feedback is slanderous, libelous, defamatory, or otherwise illegal.

★ The feedback comment contains profane, vulgar, obscene, or racist language or adult material. Inflammatory language, such as "fraud, liar, cheater, scam artist, con man" etc., while strongly discouraged, will not be removed.

★ The feedback comment contains personal identifying information about another member, including real name, address, phone number, or e-mail address.

★ The feedback makes reference to an eBay, PayPal, or law enforcement organization investigation.

★ The feedback comment contains links or scripts.

★ Negative feedback intended for another member will be considered for removal only in situations where the member responsible for the mistaken posting informs eBay of the error and has already placed the same feedback for the correct member.

★ Feedback left by a person ineligible to participate in eBay transactions, according to Section 1 of the eBay User Agreement, at the time of the transaction or the time the feedback was left.

★ Feedback left by a member who provided eBay with false contact information and could not be contacted. In general, the transaction period is considered to be 90 days from the end of the listing or 30 days from the date the feedback was left, whichever was longer.

★ Feedback left by a member who bid on or purchased an item solely to have the opportunity to leave negative feedback for the seller, with no intention of completing the transaction.

As you can see, eBay understandably wants an issue to be pretty serious before getting involved, and you should respect that. If you think you have a valid, serious feedback issue and are a PowerSeller, I suggest you discuss it with your eBay PowerSeller representative to see if it is worth pursuing.

MEDIATION THROUGH SQUARETRADE

Another option is to use eBay's "preferred dispute resolution provider," SquareTrade, which can provide mediation services to regarding feedback disputes. Visit www.squaretrade.com to learn more.

In this Chapter

- ★ **Your PowerSeller Rep**
- ★ **PowerSellers' Site**
- ★ **Co-Op Ad Funds**
- ★ **Directories**
- ★ **The Announcement Board and Email Alerts**
- ★ **eBay Radio**
- ★ **Insurance Programs**
- ★ **Avoiding eBay's Wrath**

Bug-a-boo
with and without D.D.T.
kills all major pests

TRIUMPHANT BURLEIGH returns from a tour of fi feats the champion by a fluke, marries his girl, retires to

CHAPTER 29

EBAY AS A PARTNER

To help us succeed, eBay has put a lot of programs and team members in place to assist sellers. You should take advantage of them. And, as in any partnership, you have responsibilities to eBay as well. Let's take a look.

YOUR POWERSELLER REP

After you have reached silver PowerSeller status ($3,000 per month in sales), you can make toll free calls to a priority eBay support line. At $10,000 per month, which is not as hard as it sounds to achieve, gold sellers get assigned a real, live person who can be a big help. If you are Titanium seller, Pierre will come to your house every other Sunday to wash your cars. (Just kidding about that last one.)

PowerSeller representatives can help you clarify eBay policies, check into billing and other issues, and so on. They can even connect you with eBay insiders, but don't expect them to yell over the cubicle walls to Meg on your behalf. Most support folks are in Utah, not California, which explains the support line times being listed as Mountain. They are most likely going to give your contact information to the appropriate eBay employee rather than give you the employee's contact info.

If you have earned a PowerSeller rep, get to know him or her. Please realize that these are some pretty busy folks, and do your homework before bothering them with rookie questions. Save those calls and emails for important issues, and then arrive prepared and informed. You'll have a friend at eBay! (Right, Elizabeth?)

POWERSELLERS' SITE

There's an online home for PowerSellers, of course. Figure 29.1 shows its home page.

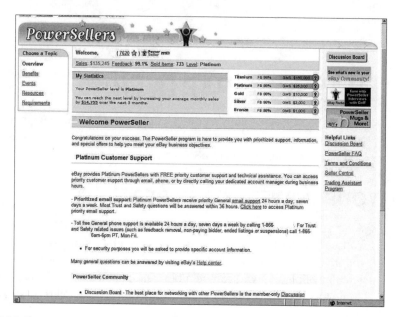

FIGURE 29.1

The PowerSellers' neighborhood.

You'll need to be a PowerSeller to log in here. It's a place to check the latest benefits, policies, event schedules, and more. Also notice that this page tells you what's required to graduate to the next PowerSeller level.

From the page shown in Figure 29.1 you can also jump to the PowerSellers' forum, shown in Figure 29.2. Here you will find tips, jokes, proclamations, and suggestions; you'll also find a little sniveling, lots of peers, and perhaps a few more new friends, which is, I think, what community is all about.

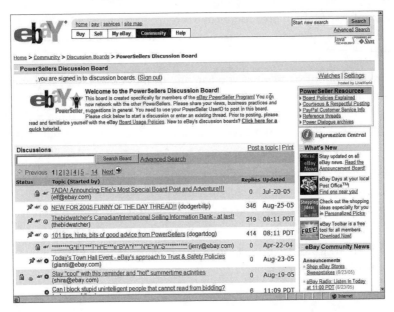

FIGURE 29.2
The PowerSellers' private forum.

CO-OP AD FUNDS

As I mentioned back in Chapter 15, "Advertising," if you are a PowerSeller and either operate an eBay Store or are a Trading Assistant, eBay will help offset certain advertising costs. eBay reimburses 25% of costs to a maximum of $8,000 per year. The amount you can receive varies with your PowerSeller level. At the time this book was written the maximums were as noted in Table 29.1.

TABLE 29.1 Maximum eBay Reimbursement

Power Seller Level	Maximum eBay Reimbursement per Quarter
Titanium	$8,000
Platinum	$3,000
Gold	$1,200
Silver	$800
Bronze	$500

You must follow stringent procedures to get reimbursements, which can take 45 days or more to arrive. Ads to be considered for co-op reimbursement must be pre-approved.

There are restrictions as to what you can and cannot do in the ads, such as specifications regarding how big the eBay logo and your eBay URL information must be, and so on. Not all media are approved. Not all types of ads are eligible. For example, ads for your eBay store are not covered any more. There are circulation criteria to be observed.

This is all pretty clearly spelled out in the Co-Op area of the PowerSellers' site, and there is contact information should you have additional questions. If you are advertising (and you should be), it makes a lot of sense to get eBay's help with at least some of the costs.

There is even a wizard designed to help you create qualifying print ads. Figure 29.3 shows one of the wizard screens.

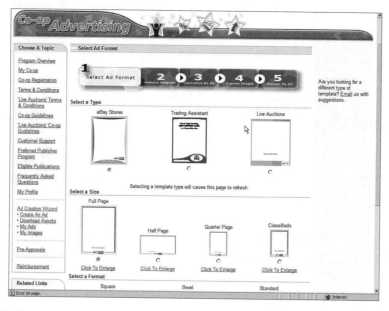

FIGURE 29.3
The Co-op Ad Creation Wizard at work.

DIRECTORIES

As mentioned elsewhere in this book, you should be sure you are accurately listed in eBay's Trading Assistant Directory. The best way to crawl there is by starting at http://pages.ebay.com/tahub/index.html or by going to the eBay home page and clicking thusly: Home, Services, Trading Assistants, Profiles.

THE ANNOUNCEMENT BOARD AND EMAIL ALERTS

Things change daily at eBay, and one great way to stay informed is to remember to visit the Announcement Board regularly. You can do this by clicking on Community in any eBay top header, and then on Groups, and then on Announcements. You should see something like what is shown in Figure 29.4.

> # Note
>
> If you find these announcements informative, simply join the group and you will be emailed announcements automatically.

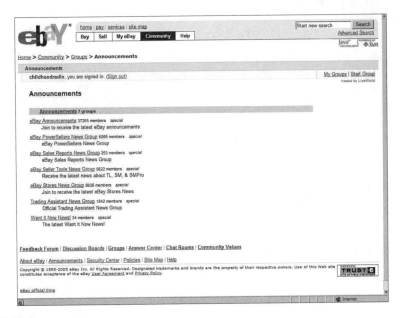

FIGURE 29.4
Keeping up with eBay's announcements.

EBAY RADIO

In conjunction with others, eBay produces audio training and promotional materials that it streams over the Internet in a variety of formats. Although these aren't radio broadcasts in the old school sense, they are called "eBay Radio" collectively. Figure 29.5 shows the home page for eBay Radio's web presence. Visit http://www.wsradio.com and either click the eBay Strategic Partner link or the eBay channel link. It is even possible to listen to these programs on certain cell phones. Visit http://mobile.streamos.com to learn more.

FIGURE 29.5
eBay produces Internet-delivered talk shows.

Although I have not done this yet, I am told we can put these shows on our iPods, enabling us to listen while on the go. They can be found in the iTunes podcast area.

INSURANCE PROGRAMS

PowerSellers have access to health and other insurance plans brokered by Marsh. As you can see from Figure 29.6, there are quite a few choices. Not all types of coverage are offered in every state, and just because a policy is offered to PowerSellers does not mean it's the best, or even appropriate for your situation. That said, it's worth getting quotes. It does seems to vary by location. PowerSeller insurance seems to be a better option in states with expensive insurance, but again, your mileage may vary.

> # Note
>
> An informal survey among my PowerSeller friends leads me to believe that there are times when these PowerSeller plans really do save money. Other times they are similar or more expensive than those from more "traditional" sources.

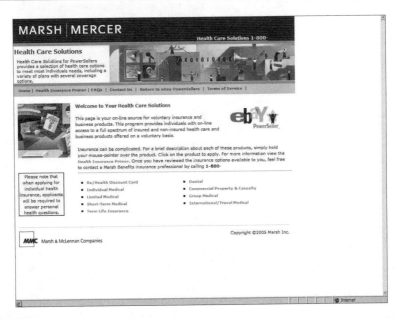

FIGURE 29.6
PowerSeller insurance options.

AVOIDING EBAY'S WRATH

Just because you are a PowerSeller does not mean you have much more clout than others where rules and regulations are concerned. This is especially true with such sensitive topics as shill bidding. Trust and safety will quickly shut your auctions down if it even looks like you or your employees or members of your household are bidding on your own auctions. Multiple shill bidding citations can and have gotten PowerSellers permanently shut down.

Understand eBay Policy

There is much to know about eBay's rules and regulations. You owe it to yourself to spend some time reading eBay's rules and regulations and bookmarking them for quick reference. A good place to start is the overview page you can access by choosing Home, Help, Rules and Policies, Rules for Sellers, Rules for Sellers Overview (see Figure 29.7).

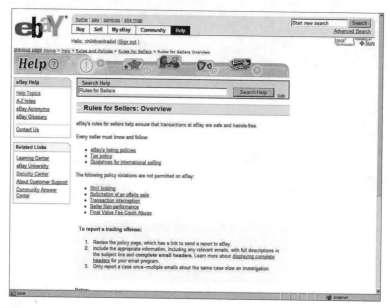

FIGURE 29.7

Brush up on eBay's rules and regulations.

Avoid Even the Appearance of Shill Bidding

Shill bidding is bidding that artificially increases an item's price or apparent desirability. eBay does not want you or your families or friends or employees "bidding up" the price of your auctions. Moreover, eBay's policy has recently changed to further restrict bidding by individuals with a level of access to the seller's item information not available to the general community.

Quoting eBay here, "Because family members, roommates, and employees of sellers have a level of access to item information which is not available to the general Community, they are not permitted to bid on items offered by the seller—even if their sole intent is to purchase the item."

There are circumstances where "insider purchases" are permitted, but I advise against them. Quoting eBay here again, "Family members, roommates, or employees may purchase items from a seller without violating this policy simply by using purchase options—such as Buy It Now—which do not involve bidding."

Making Suggestions

Although eBay is a very responsive company, and every one of the employees I have met listens carefully to users' concerns and suggestions, any company this size needs to be a little gun-shy about taking unsolicited brainstorms.

What they don't want is to hear a great idea from outside the company, implement it, and then get sued for "stealing" the idea. So they warn us that "any comments or materials you have submitted or may submit, including questions, technical or creative suggestions or ideas, are considered to be non-confidential and non-proprietary." Which is a lawyerly way of saying, "If you are not willing to watch us make money with your idea, please don't tell it to us." This is not unique to eBay. I know a television producer I can drive crazy by simply saying "Hey Eric. I have this great idea for a show." He'll literally cover his ears and glare at me.

You can make suggestions, as long as you agree to the ground rules. As you can see in Figure 29.8, there's even an eBay suggestion box.

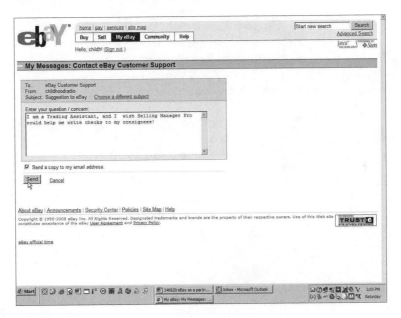

FIGURE 29.8

Make suggestions, but don't expect to own the results.

You can also suggest category changes this way. Reach the suggestion box from the eBay site map, or type all of this: http://pages.ebay.com/help/welcome/suggest.html and click on one of the links to reach the suggestion box.

In this Chapter

TRIUMPHANT BURLEIGH returns from a tour of fixed feats the champion by a fluke, marries his girl, retires to th

CHAPTER 30

PROBLEM RESOLUTION

Most of the time auctions progress pretty smoothly. But even if things go right 99% of the time, when you're running hundreds or thousands of auctions each month, the troublesome 1% can eat up a lot of your time and patience. This chapter presents you with some common problems and hints and tips for avoiding or resolving them.

NONPAYING BIDDERS

Every day people win auctions for which sellers don't get paid. It's probably the most frustrating part of PowerSelling. But before jumping to the conclusion that many buyers are scum, it's worth understanding that even earnest bidders sometimes have trouble paying. Here are some of the reasons why:

★ Checkout problems (an eBay issue, browser issue, buyer confusion)

★ Payment processing problems (payment was made but not cleared, for example)

★ The check's in the mail but you don't know it

★ Novice winner waiting for invoice

★ Spam blocker keeping you from communicating

★ The dog ran away, the iguana's sick, or the computer burned up

★ Buyer's remorse

Most of these problems are easy to overcome once you understand them. The rest need to be dealt with quickly so that you can move on to profitable business.

Checkout Problems

Although eBay is now a pretty reliable collection of technology, once in a while parts of it stop working or slow to a crawl. Sometimes winners try to check out and can't. Or they check out successfully but you don't get notified right away. In these rare cases simply waiting 24 hours and trying again is all it takes to fix the problem.

eBay's not the only culprit. If you are using third-party auction management tools from ándale or your franchisor's proprietary software, these intermediaries can cause frustrating problems.

It's complicated enough to get eBay, PayPal or your credit card company, and the buyer and seller all communicating reliably. Third-party programs that intercede can really mess things up. So if you are using a third-party auction management system, check with its maker to be sure you are using it right and that they are not having technical issues before accusing winners of not checking out or paying.

Browser compatibility and security setting issues can be problematic too. Foxfire and Macintosh users frequently report problems with certain checkout and payment processes. Sometimes just getting a buyer to try checking out with Internet Explorer on a Windows machine will clear things up.

If a winner complains that he is having trouble checking out, or if you see that someone, especially someone with great feedback, has not successfully checked out, contact the buyer to see if there are technical issues.

Payment Processing Problems

Winners having payment processing problems can also look like nonpaying bidders. Perhaps they have reached their PayPal or credit card limit, in which case they at least owe you an email of explanation with a planned payment date, or better still, the promise of a money order in the mail.

Sometimes the payment processing problem can be on your side of the transaction, however. For example, some credit card merchant bank systems automatically reset your account password at specific times (every 90 days, for example). If you don't know this and fail to update your settings to match the new password, your card payments might not reach you, and the winner might actually keep trying to pay, and then think she has paid multiple times even though the card has never been charged.

The scary thing about this scenario is that, although the cardholder's money is not taken each of the multiple times she tries to pay, her credit limit is decremented in anticipation of those multiple charges. So, for example, if someone owes you $100 and tries unsuccessfully to pay you three times, her credit card's available balance will be decreased by $300 even though she hasn't really sent a dime to you.

Worse yet, these anticipatory charges often look like actual charges in online card account sites, which causes the cardholder to freak and to call both you and the card company. The card service rep will explain the situation to the cardholder, blame you, and send the cardholder back to you to reverse the charges, which can be difficult or impossible to do because you haven't really charged her or collected any money from her account. Eventually, usually 10–14 days later, the unclaimed charges will be released and the cardholder's available balance will increase, but you will have one unhappy buyer, and possibly some negative feedback. So keep an eye on the flow of your credit card payments. Talk to your merchant banker about how to do this and where the landmines lie.

There are some potential PayPal issues too. Sometimes, rather than using whatever checkout tool you have provided for your auctions, semi-savvy winners will go directly to their PayPal account and attempt to pay you directly from there. If your PayPal account isn't set up to automatically redirect the winner to your checkout system it is possible to get paid and not know it. So keep an eye on that PayPal account, and if payments show up there but not in your auction management software, find out why and plug the hole.

Check's in the Mail

Sometimes people really do put checks and money orders in the mail. Occasionally they will forget to tell you. If they time things just right it might take a week to 10 days for payments to reach you. For example, dropping a check in the mail after 5 p.m. on a Friday means it might not get moving until Monday under some circumstances. Around the holidays it could easily be the following Monday (10 days) before you get it. Before labeling folks as nonpaying bidders ask if they have mailed a payment and when.

Waiting for My Invoice

Some eBayers, especially new ones, expect an invoice even when it's obvious how much is owed. Consider sending invoices to everyone, or at least after you have not been paid in a day or two.

Spam Blocker Ate My Homework

Sometimes folks set their email account security and spam settings so tight that nearly nothing gets through. In theory, if you communicate with them through eBay's My Messages system they should be able to read your communications that way. But then if my grandmother had...well, you know. Some people need a phone call if you have the time and patience.

Hardship

People have some amazing hardship stories to tell when they can't pay or choose not to pay, or pay slowly. Many of the stories are truly convincing and sad. A few of them are true. It's up to you to decide what to do with these folks. If they eventually pay, I usually leave a positive feedback that says "Paid but slowly" or something equally lukewarm. Then I put them on my blocked bidders list.

Nonpayers are just that, and I suggest you treat them accordingly.

Buyers' Remorse

"Sorry, I accidentally won two of these and I don't need yours." Or "Oops, terribly sorry. My kid bid on this stuff when I wasn't looking."

If you have the time, explain the eBay policy: "Your winning bid was a commitment to buy." Threaten to file a nonpaying bidder claim. Send an invoice and reminder. Wait the allotted time and pull the trigger. Don't forget to add the "winner" to your blocked bidder's list.

REMINDING AND FILING

Begin by sending an invoice if you have not already. After a reasonable time, if you have not been paid, or at least heard from the winner, use the eBay reminder system. This begins the official process. If you use Selling Manager Pro, reminding is as easy as a few clicks. Selling Manager Pro even lists items that qualify for reminders, as you can see in Figure 30.1.

Before sending the reminder eBay asks you to state the reason for the reminder. That step is show in Figure 30.2.

At this point one of several things might happen. Hopefully, you will get paid. Or perhaps the winner will contact you and you will work something out (mutually agree to not complete the transaction, or whatever). If, instead, nothing new happens for seven days, you can start the process to recover your final value fees from eBay. Again, if you use Selling Manager Pro you will see a "filtered list" of items qualifying for fee recovery.

Tip

If you are not using Selling Manager Pro the same things can be done by going to the Dispute Console on eBay (reached via your "My eBay" page).

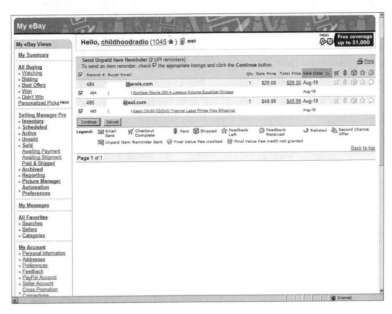

FIGURE 30.1

Selling Manager Pro reminds you to remind.

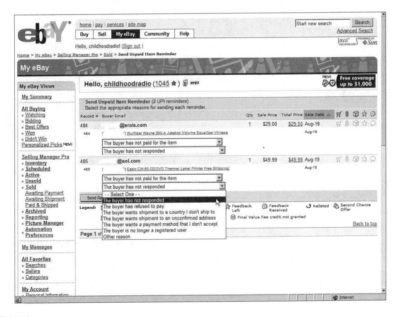

FIGURE 30.2

Specify the reason for the reminder.

SOMETIMES NPBS ARE A GOOD THING!

You can threaten and plead, and wait, and even tell eBay about a nonpaying bidder. Alternatively, you can mutually agree not to complete a transaction. This might be the best approach if you were disappointed in the auction results and want to try running it a second time. You are under no obligation to make second chance offers to the second highest bidder. I have tried this multiple times with next to no success. I simply relist, and often get a higher bid than the first time.

UNHAPPY WINNERS

Occasionally after paying for and receiving an item a buyer will be unhappy. Perhaps the winner thinks the item is not as you described it, or maybe it was damaged in shipping. Each unhappy buyer needs to be treated respectfully, but your response will probably need to differ from one incident to the next.

Hopefully you have stated your return policy clearly in all your auctions. But before agreeing to a knee-jerk return, it is a good idea to contact the seller directly (I like the phone for this), to see if something reasonable can be done to prevent the return. Returns are very costly and inefficient, especially if you are a Trading Assistant selling someone else's stuff. So a discount or free shipping might be a better remedy than completely unwinding the whole deal.

Occasionally you will need to take an item back, however. It's part of the business, and you should do this as cheerfully as possible. Be careful about return shipping costs, however. If you do agree to pay, be sure that you specify the permitted carrier and class. You don't want returns overnighted, but some winners will do this at your expense to speed up their refund. To avoid the problem some PowerSellers issue pickup tickets using their carrier of choice when they pay for return shipping costs.

Caution

There are some uncommon but important return-related scams to watch for, also. Particularly in the collectibles and jewelry categories winners have been known to win the real thing and return a fake.

It's a good idea to put a normally invisible security mark on valuable items. One common trick is to use a pen containing ink that only shows up under ultraviolet light. You can purchase these items on eBay from UVTOOLS and other PowerSellers.

When selling diamonds, watches, and other items containing serial numbers, make certain that you record the serial number of the item you have shipped. Then, when agreeing to take back an item tell the winner you will refund only after you hold the undamaged item in your hand and confirm the security mark or serial number on it. Sometimes folks change their minds about returning things when they learn this.

LOST/DAMAGED GOODS

Lost items are a real disappointment for everyone involved. But because we have all become more security conscious I have seen many things that appear to have been lost simply take forever to show up. This is particularly true of international shipments, which are often difficult to track. I have seen one shipment get to the United Kingdom in a few days, and the next takes 15 to 20 days. Because this all seems so random, even experienced buyers get spooked.

Your best bet is to be in regular contact with fidgety buyers, and agree to a reasonable but distant future date when you will refund the money, or start the insurance claim, or whatever.

If you insure items, or intend to use PayPal's protection programs, be sure you understand the requirements. Most such protection plans require a recipient's signature, confirmed addresses, or other details.

SPOOF EMAILS

By now you would think everyone in the world would know about, and simply ignore, spoof emails. Sadly, folks still fall for them. If you have employees they must be trained and reminded to ignore spoofs, or at least bring questionable things to your attention before acting, even if they look really important and time-sensitive. Take a look at Figure 30.3.

Holy cow. They might shut down our PayPal account Mr. Mansfield! It's a pretty impressive-looking email, at least until you examine it closely. Well, maybe not even that closely. For example, it arrived in the summer of 2005 and the promotional box on the right is inviting us to an event that happened more than a year earlier.

But there is much more wrong with this than the obsolete ad. PayPal and eBay and your bank will never send emails like this to you. In fact, this mail isn't even addressed to you, it's addressed "Dear PayPal customer." Legitimate e-commerce business

> # Note
>
> A note about USPS Priority Mail "tracking:" It's not really tracking in the FedEx step-by-step sense. Think of it more as a "Yeah, we dropped it on someone's doorstep today," kinda notification. It also takes a while for items with tracking numbers to even show up in the USPS online tracking system. I have actually received one or two Priority Mail packages before they were in the online tracking system. Sometimes your winners will need to be reassured about this.

> # Caution
>
> Drill this into employees' heads: Never click on links in emails, even if they are official looking. If eBay or PayPal really are trying to get your attention, a copy of the message will appear in you're My eBay's "My Messages" area.

will never ask you to click on email links to confirm or change passwords. You should only makes such changes from within their secure web site pages.

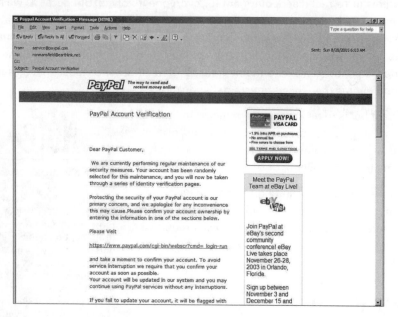

FIGURE 30.3

A spoof email.

Here are some other steps you can take to keep things secure:

★ Download and use the free eBay toolbar. Its Account Guard feature will often warn you if you have wandered into an unsafe site. It also provides links for reporting and researching fraud.

★ Purchase a community-driven spam filter such as Cloudmark's SafetyBar (www.cloudmark.com). Users click to report problem emails (both spam and fraud), and the SafetyBar automatically filters these out for you. It's an impressive tool.

★ Have a policy against indiscriminant browsing at work

★ Make sure your firewall settings are as tight as possible without causing operational problems.

★ Do not use a wireless adapter in your workspace.

★ Change passwords regularly, make them difficult to crack, and hand them out on a need-to-know basis. Always change them when an employee terminates. Never use the same password for your eBay and PayPal or other payment processing accounts.

ACCOUNT TAKEOVERS

Perhaps the mother of all nightmares is having your eBay and/or PayPal account taken over. This is as serious as it gets, and you need to act ASAP. Sometimes your first clue that something is wrong is that you can't log into eBay or PayPal. Confirm that none of your family members or associates have changed the passwords, and then go immediately to eBay's Help Search feature and search for "Account Theft." Fortunately, you will be able to do this even if you can't log in. The procedures, recommendations, and contact information provided by eBay and PayPal for account takeover change sometimes, so to get the latest, go to the web site immediately and follow the instructions you will find there.

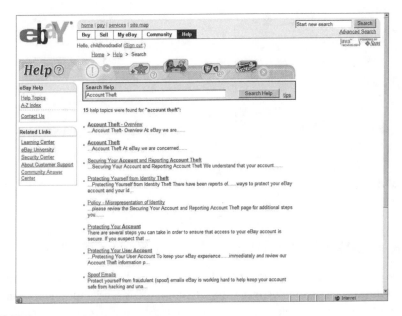

FIGURE 30.4
Begin the account takeover reporting process promptly.

If you have a PowerSeller rep, also contact him by phone, ASAP. If the problem involves PayPal call the company at 1-877-672-9725 or 1-800-836-1859. If you are a Premier PayPal account holder dial 1-888-221-1161 instead.

FRAUD INVESTIGATIONS TEAM (FIT)

Law enforcement and eBay are working closely now to beat back the bad guys. There is a link worth visiting for the Fraud Investigation Team (FIT) at http://pages.ebay.com/securitycenter/law_enforcement.html. There are some interesting things to learn at this site, and it can be a useful resource for your local authorities. You might want to send them the link if they have not heard of the site. Figure 30.5 shows a sample page.

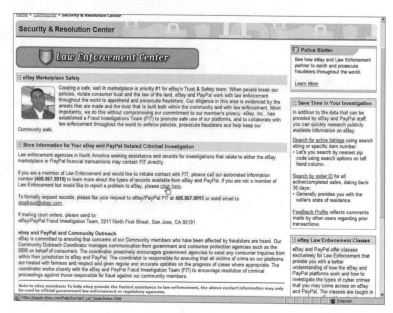

FIGURE 30.5
eBay and the Law working together.

BOOK DEALERS' ADVICE FOR EBAY USERS

Another site of interest is run on a donation basis by Tessa Hebert (http://www.mindspring.com/~bookdealers/ripoff.html). Although primarily for buyers, sellers can learn a lot here, and are also encouraged to contribute thoughts and recommendations. Tessa encourages sellers to include a link to this site in their "About Me" pages. It seems like a reasonable request to me. Figure 30.6 shows the top page of the site.

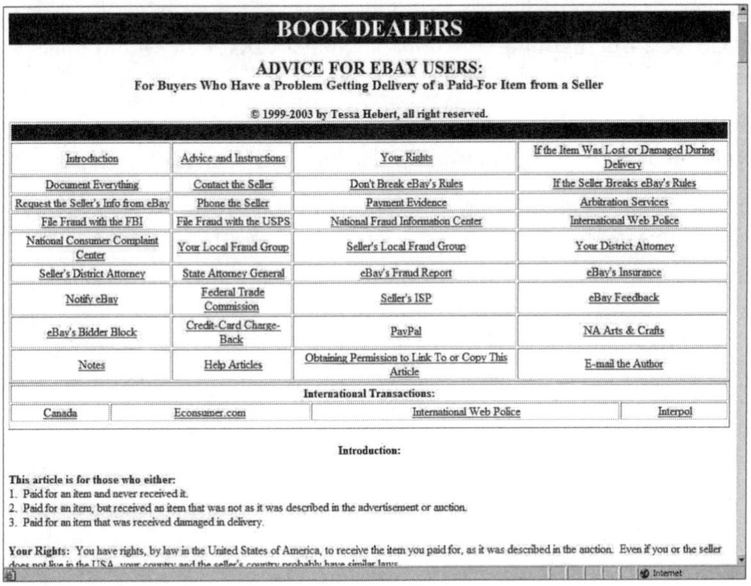
BOOK DEALERS

ADVICE FOR EBAY USERS:
For Buyers Who Have a Problem Getting Delivery of a Paid-For Item from a Seller

© 1999-2003 by Tessa Hebert, all right reserved.

Introduction	Advice and Instructions	Your Rights	If the Item Was Lost or Damaged During Delivery
Document Everything	Contact the Seller	Don't Break eBay's Rules	If the Seller Breaks eBay's Rules
Request the Seller's Info from eBay	Phone the Seller	Payment Evidence	Arbitration Services
File Fraud with the FBI	File Fraud with the USPS	National Fraud Information Center	International Web Police
National Consumer Complaint Center	Your Local Fraud Group	Seller's Local Fraud Group	Your District Attorney
Seller's District Attorney	State Attorney General	eBay's Fraud Report	eBay's Insurance
Notify eBay	Federal Trade Commission	Seller's ISP	eBay Feedback
eBay's Bidder Block	Credit-Card Charge-Back	PayPal	NA Arts & Crafts
Notes	Help Articles	Obtaining Permission to Link To or Copy This Article	E-mail the Author

International Transactions:

Canada	Econsumer.com	International Web Police	Interpol

Introduction:

This article is for those who either:
1. Paid for an item and never received it.
2. Paid for an item, but received an item that was not as it was described in the advertisement or auction.
3. Paid for an item that was received damaged in delivery.

Your Rights: You have rights, by law in the United States of America, to receive the item you paid for, as it was described in the auction. Even if you or the seller

FIGURE 30.6
A community effort to help buyers understand their rights.

PROBLEM RESOLUTIONS TIPS

Remember, most eBay problems won't go away by themselves. They tend to get bigger and uglier the longer you ignore them. Here are some more tips and reminders:

- ★ Make sure nonpaying bidders are not having checkout problems before yelling at or reporting them.
- ★ If you accept checks and money orders realize that these can take 10 days or more to arrive, especially around the Christmas holiday mail crunch.
- ★ Most eBayers are honest. Consider shipping before checks clear, particularly when buyers have great feedback.
- ★ Send invoices, especially to new eBay users who don't pay promptly, even when it's obvious what's owed. They might be confused.
- ★ Contact unhappy winners as soon as possible, by phone if possible. People are often nicer on the phone than in email, and will be impressed that you took the time to call.

★ Before offering to take an item back see if the buyer will accept a partial refund instead. Ask open-ended questions such as "What can I do to make you happy?"

★ Keep in touch with winners when items appear to be lost in transit. Sometimes they are just stuck, particularly if Customs gets involved.

★ Replying to spoof emails can cause huge problems. Make sure everyone in your organization knows how to spot and deal with them.

OPENING A TRADING POST

in this Part

In this Chapter

★ **Working in a Garage or Basement**

★ **Opening a Trading Post**

★ **Start Dreaming!**

"**You bet I use Listerine Antiseptic** and massage every time I wash my hair! I'm no dummy! I know how common and how catching infectious dandruff can be, and how hard it is to get rid of. And, in my book, Listerine Antiseptic is a jim-dandy precaution as well as a slick twice-a-day treatment. Nothing complicated about it at all . . . it's as easy as it is delightful.

"**It's really fun to use Listerine Antiseptic;** no greasy s —just good clean Listerine Antiseptic doused o away the old scalp gets a real antiseptic bath th great. And, get this: Listerine Antiseptic kills bacillus' by millions. That's the baby that a lot o is a causative agent of infectious dandruff.

"**Next comes vigorous fingertip massage.** That's to loosen those ugly flakes nd scales that embarrass a guy. I let Listerine Antiseptic stay on as long s I can. Boy, is my scalp clean! And does it feel wonderful! No wonder nen go for this routine! And don't think the little women

"**No kidding! It's a grand and glorious feeling** to reali hair look fresher and are fresher. It's satisfying taken a swell precaution against the infectious t

CHAPTER 31

LOCATION AND LAYOUT

Whether you are planning to work at home or sign your life away for a five-year retail lease you need to develop a workable floor plan. Every location and operation is different, so the suggestions in this chapter are just that, suggestions. You are going to need to mold your layout to fit your budget, neighborhood, and goals. Let's start at home.

WORKING IN A GARAGE OR BASEMENT

Many eBay sellers thrive in home-based businesses. Assuming you can find about 200 square feet or more, this might be the way for you to get rolling. Figure 31.1 shows a "space budget" and workflow pattern for a typical garage operation. It assumes only half of a typical two-car garage is used for the business. This is like living on a boat or in a motor home. It's doable, but challenging.

Notice that I have placed the shipping and shipping supply areas together, and in only about 60 square feet of space. This is a bit cramped, but so is the rest of the plan. If you are clever, when designing a garage space you'll keep enough of the garage door area clear so that you can open it, and then easily move parcels in and out when the delivery folks arrive.

Consider using tall shelves to scrounge as much vertical storage space as you can here and elsewhere in your garage or basement.

There's no need to spend $1,000 on a fancy shipping table. Build one out of two-by-fours and plywood or get a small workbench from Home Depot. The shipping table can be lower than a regular workbench or desk, and some shippers prefer this. Next time you visit a UPS facility notice the shipping table heights. They are pretty low.

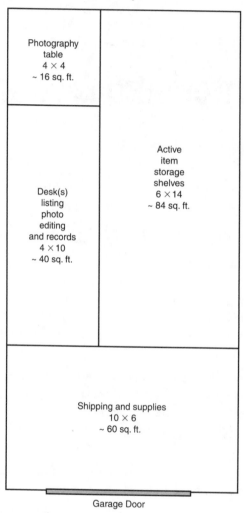

FIGURE 31.1

A space budget for a garage operation.

Moving on, the plan puts a desk or desks off to the left side of the garage space. This is where you will do the listings, edit the photos, do your bookkeeping, eat your lunch, and some days wonder what you have gotten yourself into. You will also need to keep at least your current paperwork in this space. It's possible for two people to work at once in such an environment, but you had better like each other a lot. Budget about 40 square feet for the "office" space.

Deeper in the garage is the photo area. You need a table that's at least four feet wide back there, and this is where you will want to hang your roll of backdrop paper and the lights. Because space is very tight in this scenario consider using small lights like the Cool-Lux Hollywood floods discussed in Chapter 8, "Computers, Office Equipment, and More"; otherwise, you will be constantly bumping into those umbrellas so many photographers use.

If possible, find a way to efficiently use the space under the photo table. Put in drawers to store your photo props, or make the table high enough to accommodate a mannequin stashed beneath it.

The rest of the space is for walking and for storing your inventory. You will need sturdy shelves and some empty floor space for oversized items that won't fit on the shelves. Plan on either numbering the shelves or buying numbered bins, or both.

Finish off your space by installing a smoke detector and fire extinguisher. If money is no object think about a carpet remnant and some nice overhead lighting, insulate the garage door, and perhaps add heating and air conditioning. Have an electrician upgrade the power if necessary. Park outside, and you will be in business.

OPENING A TRADING POST

A retail presence requires more space, money, and planning than a home-based business. We've already explored the task of picking the right location elsewhere in this book, so I'll just briefly review here. You want lots of the right kind of traffic, great parking, and a professional, safe-looking setting. If you purchase a franchise your franchisor will not only help you find the right location, but also they will most likely have the last say as to whether it's acceptable or not.

Plan for expansion. A bunch of the Trading Post owners I know wish they had bigger spaces. Don't be one of those. Hold out for enough of the right space at the right price.

Get Professional Help

Use a commercial realtor, not a residential realtor, even if he is your brother-in-law. Retail leases are tricky, and the negotiations are important. You want experienced help with this part!

The same goes for designing the store layout—especially if you will be building your own counters and other fixtures from scratch. Budget for some drafting and design time so that you can get things in writing. Then, check and double-check your measurements.

Know the Regulations

There will be federal, state, and local laws governing your store layout. Everything from how big your sign can be to whether you can have a neon "Open" sign in the window to how wide the aisles and bathroom doors need to be to accommodate wheelchairs will affect your store plan.

Make a Space Plan

After you have found the space of your dreams, you can create a layout, and then buy or build the items you need to make it all flow. Again, I think you should get professional help with this, particularly if it's your first retail endeavor. This is where a franchise operation can really help. They have seen a lot of raw spaces, and made them work. They can also tell you which ones won't work before you sign the lease.

Figure 31.2 shows a space and workflow plan for an average-sized Trading Post. It's about 1,500 square feet. It measures 25 feet wide and 60 feet deep, which is pretty typical but by no means standard. Retail spaces come in all sizes and shapes. Some have angled walls, windows on two adjoining walls, poles in the middle of the floor space, and so on. All of these quirks need to be factored into your design.

The Lobby

The front of the store needs counters where you will meet folks and check in their stuff. You will want two or possibly three computer workstations and printers in the front. Use a minimum of 200 square feet for the meet-and-greet or more if you can afford it.

Because customers sometimes come in pairs, particularly retired folks, it's nice to have a chair or bench for one visitor to sit on while the partner conducts business.

The front of the store can be a hospitality area if you like, with free coffee and a bulletin board, perhaps. The fancier you get, the bigger the lobby, and you don't want to waste too much space that you will later wish could be used for inventory storage. Make a nice lobby, but remember it ain't Trump Tower you are building here.

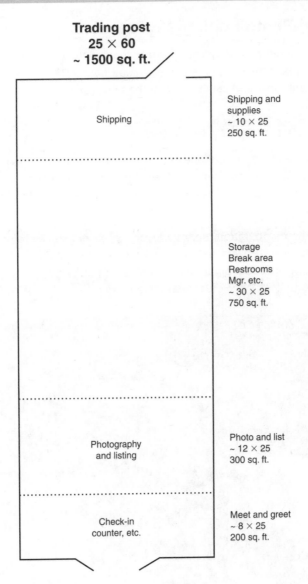

**Trading post
25 × 60
~ 1500 sq. ft.**

Shipping

Shipping and
supplies
~ 10 × 25
250 sq. ft.

Storage
Break area
Restrooms
Mgr. etc.
~ 30 × 25
750 sq. ft.

Photography
and listing

Photo and list
~ 12 × 25
300 sq. ft.

Check-in
counter, etc.

Meet and greet
~ 8 × 25
200 sq. ft.

FIGURE 31.2
A typical Trading Post space budget.

Photography

Behind the check-in area I would put a 300-plus square-foot photography and listing area, remembering my comments about shielding the photo table from as much extraneous light as possible. This might necessitate building a partial wall or adding curtains you can pull out when shooting on sunny days.

Listing and Photo Editing Workstations

The lister and photographer/photo editor both need their own computers. If you plan to use a computer to control the camera (see Chapter 23, "Photography") consider putting a laptop on an adjustable arm at the photo station.

Inventory and Employee Areas

Next comes the inventory storage area, along with any employee niceties—a break area; manager's desk, cubicle, or office; the safe; and a bathroom if required or desired. We have budgeted almost half of the available space for these things, about 750 square feet.

Just as in a home operation, here you want a mix of shelves for items in bins, and empty floor space for oversized things that won't fit on shelves—bikes, tires, and so on. Rolling carts can be a big help too. Just don't get so many that you start tripping over them. Figure 31.3 shows a great storage area.

FIGURE 31.3
A nice storage area complete with rolling carts.

When planning storage shelves, be sure you check with the fire department about maximum height rules, especially in areas with fire sprinklers in the ceiling. If you are in earthquake country, give that problem some thought too.

Shipping and Receiving

At the very end of this bowling alley is the shipping department. The plan in Figure 31.2 assumes that delivery folks can drive around to the back of your building and use the rear door for their visits.

Plan for a computer and some way to print labels back here. As I mentioned in Chapter 8, I think a laser printer is best back here because it can be used as a backup if the one in the lobby dies.

After you nail down the layout you will also need an electrical plan specifying outlets, computer network wiring, surveillance camera positions, and so on.

How Will It Look to Visitors?

Give some thought to what visitors will see when they walk in. You want them to be impressed by the equipment you have and the professional work you are doing, but not get the sense that they have just stepped into someone's cluttered garage.

Note

If there is no rear door, give serious consideration to how carts piled high with boxes will safely make their way through your store and out the front door, past customers checking things in. It's done all the time, sometimes more gracefully than others. Wide aisles and moving the (often noisy and unsightly) shipping area closer to the front door can help packages flow.

Figure 31.4 shows Richard and Helene Chemel's compact but efficient and comfortable space in Chatsworth, California. It doesn't exactly mirror the layout in Figure 31.2, but it works great, and they love it.

FIGURE 31.4
Richard & Helene's Chatsworth, CA iSold It store.

START DREAMING!

Get out the newspaper or hit the Internet. Give a commercial broker a call, and check out some 1500+ square foot, high-visibility retail spaces to see if the rents make sense in your area. Stand in the doorway of one or two of the most promising spaces. Think of a store as a big billboard for your services with a door in the middle of it.

When standing in your door can you see a Starbucks or other big draw? Can their customers see your space? Sit in your car during several times of day and on different days of the week. Talk with your potential neighbors. What's the traffic and parking like? Are there big trees and other obstacles that will hide your sign or store?

Take along a pad of graph paper (the paper with those little squares on it) and make floor plan sketches. Include the doors, windows, pillars, bathroom locations, and other features that could affect your layout. Write down the dimensions. Take some photos while you are there.

Imagine yourself in a space or two, and then recheck your spreadsheet to see if you can make it fly financially before spending money on real architectural drawings, fixture plans, and so on. This could be enjoyable if you like real estate shopping and are not in a terrible hurry.

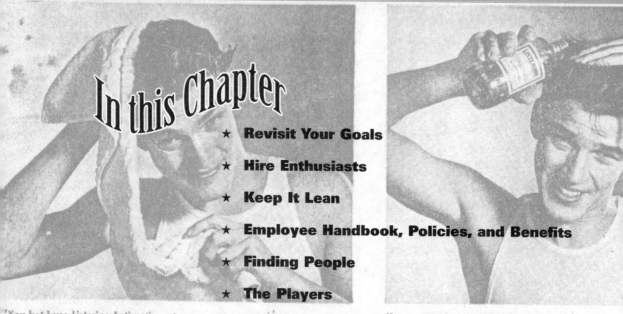

In this Chapter

★ **Revisit Your Goals**

★ **Hire Enthusiasts**

★ **Keep It Lean**

★ **Employee Handbook, Policies, and Benefits**

★ **Finding People**

★ **The Players**

★ **Sample Want Ads**

★ **Help Them Grow, Make Them Want to Stay**

CHAPTER 32

FINDING AND KEEPING GREAT HELP

Even solo PowerSellers need help growing their businesses. At some point you will want to carve out time to find new items to sell, network with local businesses, and so on. Because there are only 24 hours in a day, and only 7 days in a week, and you are already working most of that time, you need help.

Trading Posts, of course, must employ enough people to keep the doors open six or seven days a week, seven to nine hours each day. This means the equivalent of at least three full-time employees plus the owner—although in reality you might want to hire five or six part-timers instead. Having part-time employees, in the beginning especially, gives you more scheduling flexibility and can keep your employee benefits costs low. After the business gets established you will want to convert the most valuable of your folks to full-time employees with the best benefits you can manage.

REVISIT YOUR GOALS

And so, we are back to that goal setting you did in Chapter 3, "PowerSellers, Trading Assistants, and Trading Posts." Are you always going to work in the garage? Do you plan to open a chain of stores around the community? The answers to these questions should change the way you approach hiring. If you want to open multiple locations be sure you hire a few managers-in-training.

HIRE ENTHUSIASTS

Lots of the eBay-related help wanted ads that I read say "No experience necessary, we will train you." Some PowerSellers tell me they don't like to hire current eBayers because they are afraid these employees will not be "loyal" and become competitors. I disagree. You can't train people to be loyal. Employees are loyal to you because they believe in your dream, and because you are helping them reach theirs.

Especially in the beginning, I think you should hire experienced folks, particularly if you are not an experienced PowerSeller yourself, and have just opened a franchised Trading Post, for example. After you get rolling you will occasionally bump into inexperienced potential employees that you "just must have" because of their enthusiasm or particular skills you need; and at that point it starts to make sense to hire and train non-eBayers. But start with the strongest, most knowledgeable team you can muster.

Note

If you are considering opening a Trading Post or a franchise store and have not sold on eBay, please work part-time or even intern in someone else's Trading Post before you write that big check. Not everyone is cut out for retail eBay work. What if you hate it?

KEEP IT LEAN

I had been visiting with a struggling Trading Post. (Remember the one I mentioned in the introduction of this book?) The owner was kind enough to bring the whole staff in to meet me, and I offered to take a group photo in front of the store. They all lined up as I looked through the viewfinder and stepped back farther and farther and farther and...Cripes how many people is that? I was taking a picture of 11 people, mostly friends and relatives of the owner, many of whom had quit perfectly good jobs to share his dream.

This was a case of tragic overkill. If anything, in the beginning you want to be slightly understaffed.

EMPLOYEE HANDBOOK, POLICIES, AND BENEFITS

If you plan to hire a "real" staff for a Trading Post or other large PowerSeller operation, before you place your first help wanted ad, before you interview your first candidate, take a few hours to write an employee handbook. Get some help from an attorney or other guru (SCORE or your local small business incubator can help).

Note

Be very careful about encouraging friends and loved ones to quit their jobs to join you unless you can ensure their employment for a reasonable time. Letting people go is very traumatic for everyone, including the employees who get to keep their jobs. Laying off friends and relatives can be devastating.

To save some time and money consider Googling "employee handbook" and purchasing a sample handbook template, and then personalize it. Your manual should include at least the following topics along with any others suggested by your local advisors:

★ Employment policy boilerplate (at-will employment, EEO, and so on)

★ Probationary periods, if any

★ Hours of operation, weekend work expectations, and so on

★ When and how folks get paid (weekly checks, bi-weekly direct deposits, and so on)

★ Overtime policies

★ Holiday schedules (Trading Posts might be open some holidays)

★ Vacation accrual and use

★ Health, dental, and vision coverage, if any (and who pays what)

★ Drug and alcohol policy (mention testing if any)

★ Safety issues (reporting hazards, injuries, and so on)

★ Company info confidentiality policy

★ Use of technology policy (no personal surfing, selling, and so on)

★ Your "no shill bidding" policy

★ How disputes will be handled (arbitration and so on)

★ Leave policies (military, family, and so on)

Obviously, this all needs to be written in your local context. Different states have different family leave and overtime regulations, for example. And you should offer to provide only the benefits you can afford and write only policies you feel comfortable consistently enforcing.

FINDING PEOPLE

This can be the fun part. It could start with simply placing a "Now Hiring" sign in the window of your store before it opens. The next morning you will find résumés slipped under the door. Your cell phone will ring. "Cool," you'll think.

Being no fool, you tell your friends that you are looking for eBay-savvy employees. Word of mouth spreads. More emails arrive. Your cell phone voicemail box is full.

You place some free or reasonably priced ads on local classified web sites—CraigsList.org, for example, and even more candidates surface. You are beginning to regret that Monster.com ad. It's pulling in candidates, but cripes! When will you get to see them all?

You love the smile and helpfulness of the Starbucks cash register guy and ask if he's an eBayer. He is. This is almost too easy!

It can be painless to find qualified candidates; I know PowerSellers who have had experiences like the ones I just described. But like everything else, job markets differ. You might need to work a little harder to find a great team.

Not Getting Enough Candidates?

College placement offices can be a source of part-timers, and even fulltime employees around graduation time. Ask about all the school's recruiting resources. Does the school run a jobs web site? Can you advertise in the school paper? Will there be a career day? Is it possible to post help wanted fliers on bulletin boards?

Find out if your local chamber of commerce runs business expos. How much does it cost to set up a booth? What about local festivals—Strawberry Weekend, the Antique Car Parade, Big Hat Days? These can be great places to both promote your business and troll for new hires.

Deciding

Are you old enough to remember the song "Did You Ever Have to Make Up Your Mind?" It's that time. Sort the résumés in front of you. Weed out the obvious rejects. If you have asked candidates to tell you their eBay IDs look at their auctions and feedback. Which of the candidates are people you would be proud to have representing you?

Make a Yes and Maybe pile. Start with phone interviews. Be certain they understand the job, the hours, the pay, and career potential, if any. How are they on the phone? Does your gut tell you they will be able to handle the customer service tasks?

Meet the best candidates, ideally in a place with a working computer. Watch them use it. Have them show you their eBay auctions, web sites they have worked on, and so on. Are they enthusiastic? Upbeat? Do they, or could they, share your dream?

Imagine the whole team, especially when starting up. Do the candidates you like the best collectively have all the skills you need to keep the place running all the hours it will be open? Do you think they will work well together?

Always check references, and for key positions consider running background checks. I am not a big fan of drug testing, but if you are, go for it. Just be consistent and test everybody, or at least set up a random program with everybody's name in the hat. Before you do testing, get competent legal advice.

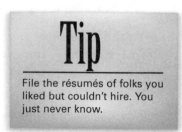

Tip

File the résumés of folks you liked but couldn't hire. You just never know.

THE PLAYERS

Let's look at the various jobs you will need to fill, first assuming you are a solo PowerSeller, and then we will look at the more specialized jobs offered by Trading Post Owners.

eBay Seller's Assistant

This is the garage seller's salvation. It's a part-time employee who can do enough things to free you up. Start by thinking about your least favorite PowerSelling tasks. Hate shipping? Would you rather write descriptions than take photos? Is bookkeeping your Achilles heel? Find a match.

If you are working at home, this needs to be someone you will be comfortable having there with you and around your family. You might want to interview away from home and check references before showing off your home-based operation. When advertising for an assistant, mix and match paragraphs from the want ads discussed a little later in this chapter, to attract the person you need to make your life easier and more productive.

Now let's turn to Trading Posts. It's time to specialize.

Manager

Many times the manager is also the owner. Sometimes a husband and wife team or financial partners own and manage Trading Posts.

It is very difficult to have one store with two managers. Instead, you need a manager and an assistant manager, or an operations manager and a financial manager. You see what I am getting at. If you are going to split this role, make it official, and make it easy for everyone to understand who does what. You don't want employees asking you for a decision, and then going to your spouse or partner with the same question because they did not like your answer. You don't want to argue among yourselves about who does what, either.

The manager's slot is the crucial position. This person will be trusted with keys, know the safe combination, hire, supervise, train, and fire employees and much more.

Managers need to work weekends. Even if it's not all weekend, or every weekend, managing means weekend work. Be up front about that when interviewing.

Note

A sense of urgency and attention to detail are key ingredients of a good Trading Post manager. If a candidate's résumé is a mess, and riddled with misspellings, what makes you think your store and listings are going to look any better?

Not all eBayers have great people skills. It's why some of them like computers so much. They help keep face-to-face human interaction to a minimum. These folks make super eBay listers but awful managers. If your candidate has trouble making eye contact and wrings her hands through the whole interview, or needs to be coaxed into conversation, put the résumé in the lister pile. Managers need to love socializing, or at least interact well with people.

Photographer

Because fantastic photos add value to your listings you want to find a great product photographer. You can train them, but why? There are usually plenty of willing applicants. It's another "attention to detail" job, but it's pretty easy to see if candidates have that trait by just looking at samples of their work. Always ask photography applicants to show you samples, and if your photo area is set up, ask them to take a series of shots in your store while you watch.

They need to understand it is product photography, not art, and that they need to be careful not to break things or misplace stuff. "Quick, creative, and careful" are the key ingredients.

Computer skills and experience with digital cameras are required because you will want this employee to move photos onto your computer, and probably edit them with Photoshop or PhotoLightning or some other editing tool (see Chapter 9, "Software," and Chapter 23, "Photography").

It's nice if photographers can be customer-friendly too because you will probably want yours to help on the counter when it gets busy. Some stores hire lister/photographers or even photographers who are willing to help with packing and shipping because this can work out nicely for scheduling and workflow reasons.

Lister

Listing is another key position. The work done here will affect selling prices. Attention to detail is required here as well. Can they spell? Write? Inspire? Hopefully listing candidates are eBayers, or at least have written catalog copy, marketing materials, or have other clips that demonstrate their ability to tell succinct interesting stories.

Listers should probably not be counter helpers. You want listers cloistered away writing, launching, and perhaps watching the progress of your auctions. Counter work can be very counterproductive here. (Apologies for the pun.)

Note

As I mentioned earlier in this chapter, some stores hire combination lister/photographers. Consider it, especially when your store is new.

Packer/Shipper

Here's a great entry position for someone willing and able to do a very physical job. There will be lifting and bending, stooping, and overhead reaching, and all of those things that make us ache at night. The hours can be a little more flexible than those of some other store positions, making this a great student job. Ideally, your packer/shipper will be presentable at the counter when things heat up.

SAMPLE WANT ADS

Here are some sample help wanted ads in a variety of styles designed to get your creative juices flowing. Above all, make sure that the flavor and tone of your operation shows in your ads. You want to attract compatible people. If it's a fun place to work, convince us. If you are "all business" skew the copy in a more serious direction.

I've assumed these will be online ads, and not be billed by the word. Obviously traditional classified ads should be shorter.

eBay Seller's Assistant

Help! I am an eBay PowerSeller, looking for someone to help me take my business to the next level. I need a part-time, eBay-savvy enthusiast to help me photograph, list, pack, and ship what will soon be hundreds of items each month. The hours are flexible, but predictable.

The pay will start at [pay], with potential increases as we grow the business together. You will be working at my home in [town].

You need to have current eBay selling experience to apply for this job. If you don't have items listed for sale on eBay right now, please list something before applying.

Please email your résumé and the names and phone numbers of at least three references to the address below. Include your eBay ID in your email so that I can look at your listings and feedback.

eBay Drop Store Manager Wanted

Here's a chance to work in a challenging, fun environment in what Entrepreneur Magazine calls "one of the hottest business categories ever."

We are opening a new eBay Trading Post at [address].

Our ideal Store Manager will have both eBay selling and retail management experience. This is a "take charge" job requiring great people skills, a love of details, and a "roll up the sleeves" attitude.

You will help us hire, train, schedule, and supervise a world class store staff. You will be responsible for the quality, timeliness, and success of hundreds of eBay sales each month. No two days will be the same.

This is a fulltime, salaried position with competitive insurance and other benefits. Your salary will be commensurate with your experience. Some weekend work is required.

If you think this sounds like you, please email your résumé along with the names and phone numbers of at least three references to the address below. Include your eBay ID in your email so that we can look at your listings and feedback.

eBay Photographer Wanted

Here's a chance to work in the best eBay Trading Post in the valley. Located at [address] we have quickly become the "go-to" place for people wanting to sell their items on eBay without the hassle. Check out our auctions at [eBay ID]

We have immediate need for your creative digital product photography skills. This is currently a part-time job that could develop into a rewarding career track for the right person.

We will provide the camera, lights and computer. You bring a sharp eye and your attention to detail. It's a fast-paced, fun place to work, and no two days are the same. You might even be asked to greet customers at the check-in counter when things get busy.

If you think you qualify, please email your résumé and the names and phone numbers of at least three references to the address below. We will want to see samples of your work, so please include a web site link, or attach no more than two (2) representative product photos to your email.

If you are currently selling on eBay that's a definite plus, so include your eBay ID in your email we'll take a look at your listings and feedback.

Experienced eBay Writer Wanted

COMPANY INFORMATION

[Company name] is creating the country's largest chain of eBay drop stores. Our goal is to be the brand that everyone thinks of when they think of eBay selling. With more than 100 stores open already we are well on the way.

JOB DESCRIPTION

Our [town name] store has an immediate opening for a professional writer capable of creating crisp professional eBay auction description copy. You need to be quick, careful, and thorough.

MINIMUM QUALIFICATIONS

At least one-year of eBay selling experience with exemplary feedback

Able to pass a typing test

Extensive computer skills

A four year college degree, ideally in English or journalism, or equivalent experience.

Packing and shipping experience a definite plus

SALARY AND BENEFITS

This is a salaried, fulltime position with excellent benefits, and advancement opportunities.

TO APPLY

Send your résumé in the body of an email (no attachments please). Include your eBay ID and the contact information for at least three references. No phone calls or faxes, please.

eBay Store Packer/Shipper/Greeter

Do you like it when every day is different? Does the thought of flipping burgers make you cringe? Are you looking for a chance to grow with a like-minded crew?

[Store name] is looking for a part-time person to help pack and ship the items we sell in our eBay auctions. You will also help greet customers at the counter, explain our services, and get to see a truly amazing variety of collectibles, gadgets, and "stuff."

This could grow into a permanent position, so please bring a smile, be willing to work hard, and be drug free. It's pretty physical work, so the successful applicant will need to routinely lift, bend, stoop and reach overhead.

Email your résumé today since we need somebody great, like yesterday!

HELP THEM GROW, MAKE THEM WANT TO STAY

Once you have that crew, do your best to keep them. Don't mess with their hours any more than you must. Part-time doesn't mean "whenever." College students have car payments and housing costs, just like everybody else. They deserve something approaching a predictable paycheck, even if they must work flexible hours to achieve it.

In the beginning your balance sheet will probably not have enough fat for a profit sharing plan, but you can do little things to create a similar effect. If you have a particularly good month, hand out a small "Thank you all" bonus, or throw a barbeque.

Put in some free snacks and drinking water. Consider providing logo wear—T-shirts, aprons, and so on. Let them pick the music, but within guidelines, and at sound levels that won't drive customers out of the store.

Cross-train and promote from within. Employees notice these things, and your interest in them will be repaid many times over.

Be respectful. Ask for and consider their suggestions. Treat them the way you like to be treated and it should be "all good," and a lot of fun!

HAVE FUN!

And remember, whatever you do, have some fun. Good luck with your new venture, and let me know how it turns out!

Index

A

E

H

I

U – V